SR Supplements / 18

SR SUPPLEMENTS

Volume 18

Young Man Shinran
A Reappraisal of Shinran's Life

Takamichi Takahatake

Published for the Canadian Corporation for Studies in
Religion/Corporation Canadienne des Sciences Religieuses
by Wilfrid Laurier University Press

1987

This book has been published with the help of a grant from the Canadian Federation for the Humanities, using funds provided by the Social Sciences and Humanities Research Council of Canada.

Canadian Cataloguing in Publication Data

Takahatake, Takamichi
  Young man Shinran

(SR supplements ; 18)
Bibliography: p.
Includes index.
ISBN 0-88920-169-2

1. Shinran, 1173-1263.   2. Priests, Shin – Japan –
Biography.   3. Shin (Sect) – History.   I. Title.
II. Series.

BQ8749.S557T34 1987   294.3'61   C87-094544-8

© 1987 Canadian Corporation for Studies in Religion/
    Corporation Canadienne des Sciences Religieuses

87 88 89 90 4 3 2 1

Cover design by Michael Baldwin, MSIAD

Order from:
Wilfrid Laurier University Press
Wilfrid Laurier University
Waterloo, Ontario, Canada   N2L 3C5

Printed in Canada

To my parents

and

Masako, Takashi, Naoko

Contents

List of Tables

Preface

The Japanese Pure Land master Shinran (1173-1262) was a product of his age. His angst in the period of the decay of the Dharma, his subsequent search for spiritual liberation, and his ultimate discovery of the path of the nembutsu could not have occurred isolated from the social temper of his time, any more than his religious thought could have developed beyond the fabric of traditional Japanese Buddhist teachings and practices.

Much has been written about Shinran and his religious tradition, particularly by Japanese scholars who have been members of this tradition (Jōdo shin-shū kyōdan). Yet little study has been devoted to Shinran's early life as the formative years in the history of a religious leader. While he saw himself simply as the disciple of his master Hōnen, his teaching and practice would soon become a vigorous movement of its own. Thus an issue of the greatest significance is identifying the factors in Shinran's life and thought that would provide the momentum to enable a new tradition to develop and endure.

This study proposes to examine the issue by concentrating upon the relationship between Shinran's experiences in the first half of his life and their historical and social environment. Both the boldness and the subtlety of his ideas begin to emerge in such examination, moving beyond the hagiographical limitations often characteristic of Shin tradition research. Numerous Shinran studies have been bound by the strengths and limitations of either purely historical or religious-philosophical analysis. But these two approaches have rarely been combined, and since Shinran's early life and his cultural environment together constitute not only the basis but also the matrix of his mature thought and practice, such a combination could well reveal both the power of his ideas and the cultural factors that stimulated their development.

While Shinran wrote twenty-nine book-length treatises (excluding letters) during his ninety years of life and all of these are extant today, primary documentation relating to the first half of his life barely exists. This phenomenon is not mere historical accident, but is instead indicative of the institutional demands and restraints that have acted upon most scholars of the Shin tradition. For more than 750 years this tradition has concentrated its efforts on the study and transmission of Shinran's mature thought. Because Shin members perceived his mature thought to be a self-contained system and the natural end point of his religious development, it appeared to them unnecessary to preserve materials relating to his formative years and to the teleological process of his intellectual development. Any progress in this Shin tradition research has largely consisted of synchronic studies of Shinran's mature teachings about the path to salvation, almost completely ignoring the diachronic process through which he reached such conclusions.

Again, much of the material on Shinran's life available today is strongly hagiographical, written to hail or beatify an exemplary Shinran to the adherents of his tradition. Historians, on the other hand, in lacking autobiographical material, have had to further their research through contemporary historical sources. At present such scholars continue to attempt an objective restructuring of how Shinran's thought did develop, in order to obtain a historical and human image of Shinran beyond the Shin tradition's religious vision. Although the objective evaluation of Shinran made by historians outside the tradition has permitted a greater understanding of the Shinran portrayed by the resources within the tradition, there has been little formal meeting or exchange of research results between them.

Therefore, one of the most urgent and exciting requirements for the future study of Shinran is a synthesis of the Shinran exemplified in the biography and religious-philosophical analysis of the Shin tradition with the Shinran of recent cultural history research outside the tradition. The conclusions derived would furnish a remarkably sound foundation for re-evaluating his thought and practice as seen in his own writings.

This study is an initial effort to examine the Pure Land master Shinran using such combined approaches and results of research. As an exploratory study encompassing various kinds of research, it concentrates upon his early life and concludes when Shinran became forty-two years of age. Any examination of his later life is an undertaking significantly greater in scope and materials, possibly a life-long effort, and one beyond the introductory nature of the present work.

My acknowledgements are due, first of all, to my two teachers, Professor Nobuya Bamba, presently with Osaka University, Japan, by whom I was taught historical methodology and study in the form of a combination of a theoretical approach derived from sociology and the methods of historical research developed by the humanistic discipline. His inspiring, kind and painstaking guidance throughout my studies is greatly appreciated. To Professor Sokusui Murakami of Ryukoku University, Japan, I owe my acknowledgement not only for the introduction to the study of Shinran and his tradition, but also a deep respect for learning.

I would also like to express my sincere appreciation to Professor Masatoshi Nagatomi of Harvard University for having read the entire manuscript and given invaluable suggestions while assisting me in my work at the Yenching Library of Harvard University, where all materials used in this study were obtained.

My thanks also go to Donald Haslam, Mark Sedgwick, and Carol Hyland, who gave me generous and great assistance in the preparation of this manuscript.

I must express my gratitude to my respected friend, Dr. Dennis Lishka, for his extremely kind and helpful suggestions—he read my manuscript carefully, page by page, chapter by chapter; his patient work greatly improved my manuscript. Without his efforts, this book would never have materialized. I would further like to express my appreciation to Proword and its staff for their solicitous and patient technical preparation of the manuscript for publication. For any errors or misinterpretations, however, I alone am responsible.

Also, I would like to express my deep gratitude to Professor Harold Coward of the University of Calgary and to Professor Maurice Boutin and Professor Jacques Langlais, both of l'Universite de Montreal, for their encouragement in preparing this work for publication as a book.

Finally, I want to express my thanks to the professors in the History Department of McGill University, especially Professor Ella Laffey and Professor Pei-chih Hsieh, presently with the University of Regina, for giving me helpful guidance in their respective fields of research to help me complete my graduate studies in my years at McGill.

T. Takahatake

Introduction

One of the major currents of the Chinese civilization imported by the Japanese from the sixth century onward was the Buddhist tradition. Monk after monk undertook the long and dangerous journeys from China and Korea to introduce the various schools of Buddhist teaching and practice that would be founded in great monastic centres under imperial and aristocratic sponsorship. Soon enthusiastic Japanese disciples of these early foreign masters would perform Buddhist ritual and propagate their teachings, eventually travelling themselves to seek scripture, practice and iconography on the Chinese mainland.

Yet modern historians speak of the growth of a native tradition, a truly Japanese Buddhism. It is seen as a long process that began with a Japanese understanding of Buddhism within the structure of imported teachings and practices. This process would culminate in a native interpretation of the Buddhist experience based on Japanese ways of thought and expression and in response to native religious needs. The turning point would occur at the end of the twelfth century, as the political and social life of Japan would undergo the swift and dramatic changes of the Kamakura period (1185-1333), and a remarkably creative era in the history of Japanese Buddhism would emerge. The earliest innovators of this new age were the Pure Land master Hōnen (1133-1212) and the Zen master Eisai (1141-1215). Several masters would soon follow them—either disciples who inherited their teaching and practice to interpret, reorganize or clarify it, or monks who would inherit their strong sense of an overwhelming need for change and would develop new and different forms. All of these masters extracted teachings and practice of minor status from the older Buddhism and conducted intense searches for continuity with major Buddhist values. When seen in terms of the earlier sixth-century court-dominated Buddhism, six great masters would come to be known as reformers because each absorbed and reacted to what he saw as tremendous degeneration in the older Buddhism, and began the movements or schools of Kamakura Buddhism that would propose a new central religious experience to all levels of Japanese society. The six and their movements were Hōnen and the Jōdo school, Eisai and the Rinzai Zen school, Shinran (1173-1262) and the Jōdo Shin school,[1] Dōgen (1200-1253) and the Sōtō Zen school, Nichiren (1222-1282) and the Nichiren school and Ippen (1239-1289) and the Ji school.

Their reforms began during the transition between the Heian and Kamakura periods, when Japanese society experienced such rapid change that fear and uncertainty became the basis for the daily life of an entire nation. Before this time, at the upper levels of society, an imperial family and aristocracy enjoyed a leisurely life of ceremony, poetry, and romance, observing a subtle social calendar and striving to secure promotion at court. Their common religious goal was an affirmation that the pleasures, status, and material wealth of this life could continue for eternity, and to this end the early Buddhist schools conducted ritual and prayer (for them and for their patronage). In essence the early Japanese Buddhist experience became another extension of the aristocratic aesthetic that dominated all aspects of a court-centred society, as it basically consisted of witness to the splendour of future rebirth in a Buddhist paradise (a future courtly existence) by means of ritual presentation in the present and by patronage to secure such rebirth. Wealthier members of the upper class even attempted to fuse their present existence to a splendid future by extravagantly constructing lavish artistic and architectural copies of paradise, but the social unrest at the decline of the Heian period clearly eroded both the actual wealth and the pampered naivete of the court and aristocracy. Yet change and disruption in an older order of living in the present life only intensified spiritual yearning for a better existence in the future. While the lower classes of peasants, merchants and soldiers had always exhausted themselves merely struggling for survival, the chaotic and crumbling social and political structure now claimed the upper class as its victims, and the entire society soon came to strongly feel a spiritual poverty from the established schools of early Japanese Buddhism. The eclectic classification of teachings and extensive and esoteric ordering of practice by the prevalent Tendai and Shingon schools of the Heian period offered much to the monastic but little to the layperson. The role of simple witness and donor to the elaborate rituals and monasteries of these schools led from the position of bystander in practice to bystander in belief. Thus the decline in political order, the critical social conditions, and a perception by the majority of the irrelevance of early Buddhist experience in the changing present, furnished the setting for the emergence of the new Kamakura-period Buddhist reformers.

The sensual or emotional dimensions of human experience cannot alone produce a new ideology, for these sources of motivation find expression only within the language, values, and way of thinking of individuals and of eras. Once an individual's ideas and actions are expressed, and to some degree comprehended and accepted by a community, they become a vehicle for cultural expression. During the twelfth and thirteenth centuries of Kamakura Japan, the newer Buddhism would so accurately reflect and respond to the needs of Japanese society that its religious teachings and practices would make it the major stream of Japanese thinking, the form in which the Japanese developed solutions to individual and collective problems and issues. Thus the basic purpose of this work is to explore the relationship between Shinran's early life and teachings in the contexts of the Buddhist tradition and Japanese society, by concentrating upon his social experiences and intellectual development from childhood through the age of forty-two. But in a larger sense, by viewing a major Buddhist master and his experience, we should come to see not only growth in the Buddhist tradition but also a major form of

Japanese response to the anxiety and questioning of values during a period of great social upheaval and transition.

Introduction Notes

1. It should be noted that Shinran used several names during his lifetime, particularly after he began training as a Buddhist novice. His earliest name was Hannen, and he later called himself Shakkū, Zenshin, Fujii Yoshizane, and finally Gutoku Shinran. For the sake of clarity his final and best-known name, Shinran, has been used throughout this study. (He also received the posthumous religious title of Kenshin Daishi, the "Great Master Kenshin," by imperial decree in the Meiji era.)

As Shinran's teachings and activities attracted an ever-growing body of followers who would distinguish his doctrine and practice from other Pure Land movements, one can appropriately view his followers as a new movement in Kamakura-period Buddhism. This movement was first formally recognized as a distinct Japanese Buddhist tradition or school in 1872 and given the title Jōdo-shin-shū ("True Pure Land School"). Because the earlier tradition begun by Shinran's master Hōnen is both commonly and formally known as the Jōdo-shū ("Pure Land School"), the simple name "Shin" (school, movement, tradition) shall be used to identify Shinran's distinct teachings and practice, as well as the tradition that emerged from them.

The common difficulties with Japanese counting of age and names should also be considered at this point. Japanese ages are given in traditional manner in this study, reckoning by counting the length of time from day of birth to the end of the year of birth as the first complete year of age. Also the names of all Japanese personages prior to the twentieth century will appear in traditional surname-first order, while the names of modern personages will be rendered with personal name first.

Chapter 1

Shinran Wrapped in a Shroud of Mystery

A. His position in Buddhist biographical literature

Shinran's stature as a significant figure in the history of Japanese Buddhism has been affirmed in modern times, despite an earlier tradition of academic and religious commentary which either ignored him or attempted to question his existence.

In 1702 the Zen monk Shiban (1625-1710) edited the *Honchō-kōsō-den* ("Biographies of Eminent Japanese Monks") in 75 volumes. Although this massive work contains the biographies of 1,664 Japanese monks from the introduction of Buddhism to Japan in A.D. 552 until the eighteenth century, no mention of Shinran is in evidence. Yet by the year this biographical encyclopedia was compiled, 440 years had passed after Shinran's death. The Shin movement he founded had grown into a major school of Japanese Buddhism, and its name was quite familiar to a majority of the Japanese populace.

Evidence of the school's size and importance as a major social force could be found at least a century earlier. During the turbulence of warring political factions in early seventeenth century Japan, Tokugawa Ieyasu recognized the Shin school as a possible threat to his efforts to establish a unified nation under a totalitarian samurai government (bakufu). It was his central purpose to systematically overwhelm or affect compromise with all political and social opposition of any strength, and thus in July of 1651 the Shin membership as a group voluntarily presented an oath of allegiance to the bakufu and acknowledged the complete authority of Tokugawa Ieyasu as the shōgun or military dictator of Japan. Thirty-nine years later the school became the spiritual guardian of the Tokugawa family, as the funerary tablets of Ieyasu and the four Tokugawas who succeeded him as shogun were entrusted to memorial at the Shin headquarters, the Honganji in Kyoto.[1] It becomes inconceivable in light of such events only twenty years before 1702 that any omission of the school's existence or of its founder could merely be due to simple ignorance on Shiban's part.

In recent times, two centuries after Shiban, controversy concerning Shinran and his efforts has appeared. In this case, however, the phenomenon occurred in two separate works by twentieth-century monk-historians who used modern methods of historical research—both coming virtually to question the fact of Shinran's existence. In an article *"Shinran-shōnin-ron"* ("A Study of Shinran") by Kenkai Naganuma published in 1910[2] and in the book *Shijō no Shinran* ("Shinran in History") by Kenmyō Nakazawa in 1920, both authors attempted to prove that Shinran had never existed, by using diaries and records of parties contemporary with Shinran and only those that met with strict historical verification.

Credible explanations do exist for Shiban's omission and Naganuma's and Nakazawa's challenges about Shinran. Shinran's position as a monk who deliberately married in an effort to dissolve traditional Buddhist monastic-lay distinctions and organize a community of common believers in practice could have been seen as radical apostasy by Shiban and led him to exclude Shinran from any consideration as a legitimate Buddhist figure. It is my opinion that both Naganuma and Nakazawa questioned Shinran's existence as scholarly but iconoclastic challenges against the mist of fiction that surrounded Shinran's life (and that is still maintained as completely factual by present day Honganji religious authority).

In contrast to questioning by Naganuma and Nakazawa, two other modern historical scholars have affirmed Shinran's existence beyond reasonable doubt. Bunshō Yamada discovered important biographical materials in his monograph *Shinran to sono kyōdan* ("Shinran and His Followers")[3] and Zennosuke Tsuji made a study of Shinran's handwriting which formed the basis of Tsuji's brilliant and renowned work, *Shinran-shōnin hisseki no kenkyū* ("A Study of Shinran's Penmanship").[4] The earliest extant records about Shinran were written by his great grandson Kakunyo (1270-1351). These obviously supported Shinran's existence, although Kakunyo's four separate biographies were couched in language that tended to glorify Shinran as a great religious hero. In spite of various historically weak claims and statements, Kakunyo's biographies have certainly furnished valuable supportive data which have been carefully studied and confirmed as accurate in recent years. It is because of solid scholarship by people such as Yamada and Tsuji, substantiated by the verified materials found in Kakunyo's early biographies, that Shinran's existence can no longer be readily dismissed or even strongly questioned by the modern historian.

B.   Shinran described in the biographical literature

The first issue in attempting to dispel the myths surrounding Shinran's career should consist of a critical examination of his life. The four major biographies of Shinran were written by Kakunyo, and there are also five supplementary works by Kakunyo, his son Zonkaku, and by Rennyo, the great Shin chief abbot of a century later.[5]

Kakunyo's major biographies are *Zenshin-shōnin dene* ("Illustrated Life of the Revered Master Zenshin [Shinran]") written in October 1295;[6] *Zenshin-shōnin shinran dene* ("Illustrated Life of the Revered Master Zenshin, Shinran") written in December 1295; *Honganji-shōnin dene* ("Illustrated Life of the Revered Master of Honganji") written in 1343, and *Honganji shinran-shōnin dene* ("Illustrated Life of Shinran, the Revered Master of Honganji") written in 1344. These biographies appear to have been composed with the broad purpose of collecting extant information about

Shinran's life and teachings and simply organizing it within the chronological format of a biography. The works actually contain a great deal that is exegetical as well as occasional polemical modification of Shinran's ideas. Kakunyo's efforts are those of an orthodox but ambitious Shin leader and close relative rather than a brief compilation or unbiased account of the events in Shinran's life. In Nakazawa's words, "these works are not to be considered very useful [as biography] but they are excellent in explaining Shinran's teachings."[7] A biography of Kakunyo, entitled *Boki-eshi* ("Memories Return in Sketches and Words"),[8] covers the period during which Kakunyo's four Shinran biographies were written and circulated. It records that these were widely read and even revered by Shin followers. As illustrated biographies common to the large and extremely popular picture-tale or illustrated narrative genre (i.e., emakimono) that arose during the Kamakura period, such text and brush-drawn illustration combinations had great communicative appeal to literate and illiterate alike. Often such illustrations were removed from the text and displayed, sometimes assuming near iconographic status. Yet it should not be concluded that Kakunyo's biographies were worthless in regard to credible biographical information, because the two *Zenshin-shōnin dene* were written at a time when Kakunyo could still have received accurate dates for events from the immediate disciples of Shinran yet alive in eastern Japan.

The five supplemental biographies are *Tandoku-mon* ("Sentences in Praise of [Shinran's] Virtue") by Zonkaku in 1366; *Hōon-kōshiki* ("Observances in Gratitude [to Shinran]") by Kakunyo (date of composition unknown but copies were made by Rennyo in 1468); *Tandoku-mon* ("Sentences in Praise of [Shinran's] Virtue") by Rennyo (the undated "popular" version, *Hōon-kōshiki* ("Observances in Gratitude [to Shinran]") by Rennyo (the "popularized" version written in 1461); and *Gozoku-shō* ("Record of a Dignified Worldliness") by Rennyo in 1477.[9]

The two *Hōon-kōshiki* are largely description and instruction for the observance of the anniversary of Shinran's death. Believed to have been initiated by Kakunyo, the annual memorial is held to confirm the Shin movement's gratitude to its founder and emphasize Shinran as the true recipient of his master Hōnen's Pure Land tradition. The two *Tandoku-mon* are brief writings that celebrate Shinran's religious accomplishments from the perspective of the Shin tradition. The *Gozoku-shō* also records his achievements and utilizes these as a model for the development of faith by the Shin adherent. Definite factual information about Shinran's life is present in the somewhat overly laudatory content of each of these five biographical pieces. It is my impression that the five were composed by their authors as propagative pieces to introduce Shin teachings and its central practice of faith, with emphasis upon the difficulties and successes of Shinran's exemplary career, rather than as any factual account of his life's events.

A comparison of important common points in the four major biographies will produce a common framework of events in Shinran's life. According to Tatsurō Fujishima, the Senjuji biography most accurately records Shinran's activities in chronological order and is closest to the author's original draft form among the four major biographies.[10] A comparative table (Table 1) of these four major biographies can thus be developed through the use of the Senjuji biography as basis of comparison.

This type of comparative table raises the issue of why the Nishi honganji (1295), Shōganji (1344), and Higashi honganji (1346) biographies contain an extra chapter or chapters in contrast to the Senjuji biography (1295). One key to this question is that these extra chapter(s) all appear as the final chapters in respective volume(s) and each concerns an identification during a dream of Shinran with a Buddha or bodhisattva figure. Thus, in each case, Shin followers always heard the story of a glorified Shinran, even though they would hear the biography read to them only a volume at a time.

The next step, outlined in Table 2, involves a simple comparison of the contents of these four biographies at their points of major contrast.

It is apparent from these two comparative tables that the Nishi honganji, Shōganji, and Higashi honganji biographies all seem to have "grown out" of the Senjuji original. The extra chapters were inserted without any regard for chronological accuracy, and as previously mentioned, the biographies were primarily meant for reading aloud to Pure Land adherents. In this manner various conventions glorifying Shinran's spiritual prowess could have easily been appended.

The Shōganji biography contains two such extra chapters which both concern the extraordinary spiritual abilities of Shinran and which both appear as the final chapters in each volume (not fitted into the chronological sequence of the body of each text). This discrepancy will probably remain open to discussion and criticism by modern scholars. But rather than attributing such errors to Kakunyo as the compiler of the original biography (which itself has yet to be definitively established), such chronological mistakes must have happened much later than previously thought and were caused by someone who handled the biographies in the volumes as presently organized. The changes may have occurred during a restoration or rebinding of the original biography or during divisions of the volumes to suit various groups of Shin followers. Modern historians have made numerous discoveries of new material about Shinran as well as the existence of writings by critics that involve questions about the oldest biographies. Yet no matter what has been or may be written about their accuracy, these biographies qualify such criticism due to their great value as primary sources of information on Shinran's life and times.

Therefore, a simple but reliable chronology of the major events in Shinran's life has had to involve a brief review of the occasional conflicting data in the four major biographical sources as well as the analysis of modern scholars of these discrepancies, but a basic chronology of Shinran's life is presented for the convenience of the reader in Table 3 (based on the Senjuji biography with contrasting points in the other biographies noted).

Table 1

Comparison of Shinran's Major Biographies

Biography & Collection	Total Volumes	Total Chapters	Major Differences	Clerical Errors
Zenshir-shōnin shinran dene; Senjuji collection (1295)	5	13	—	Volume 1, Chapter 3: error in Japanese year
Zenshir-shōnin dene; Nishi honganji collection (1295)	2	14	Final chapter (Chapter 7) in Volume 1: a dream by Jōzen that Shinran is an incarnation of the Buddha Amida. (This is an extra chapter in comparison with the Senjuji biography.)	Volume 1, Chapter 3: error in the sexagenary cycle
Honganji shinran-shōnin dene; Shōganji collection (1344)	4	15	Final chapter (Chapter 4) in Volume 1: a dream by Shinran's disciple Renni that Shinran is an incarnation of a bodhisattva. Final chapter (Chapter 4) in Volume 2: dream by Jōzen (identical to the Nishi honganji biography.) (Therefore, a total of two extra chapters in contrast to the Senjuji biography.)	Volume 1, Chapter 3: identical error in Japanese year to Senjuji biography
Honganji-shōnin shinran dene; Higashi honganji collection (1346)	4	15	Additional materials identical to the Shōganji biography.	Identical to the Shōganji biography

Table 2

Points of Contrast with the Senjuji Biography
(Zenshin-shōnin dene, 1295)

Senjuji Biography Volume & Chapter	Event in Shinran's Life	Shinran's Age	Other Biography Additions
Volume I			
Chapter 3	A bodhisattva appears to Shinran during a dream. (*Shinran's disciple Renni has a dream about Shinran as an incarnation of the Buddha Amida.)	29	(*In Nishi honganji, Shōganji and Higashi honganji biographies)
Volume II			
Chapter 6	Discussion while with Hōnen's group that true faith does not depend on a person's intellect or knowledge, and Shinran's response as identical to Hōnen's on this issue. (*The artist Jōzen has a dream of Shinran as an incarnation of a bodhisattva.)	33 to 35	(*In Shōganji and Higashi honganji biographies)

Note: An asterisk denotes a contrast of additional material in the other three major biographies.

Table 3

Basic Chronology of Shinran's Life

Senjuji Biography Volume & Chapter	Events in Shinran's Life	Shinran's Age
Volume I		
Chapter 1	Genealogical accounts of Shinran's family; Shinran enters Mt. Hiei to begin study and practice there.	9
Chapter 2	Shinran joins Hōnen.	29
Chapter 3	A bodhisattva appears to Shinran during a dream. (*Shinran's disciple Renni has a dream about Shinran as an incarnation of the Buddha Amida—In the Nishi honganji, Shōganji and Higashi honganji biographies.)	29

Note: An asterisk denotes a contrast of additional material in the other three
      major biographies.

C. Historical context of Shinran's times

As the five-century-long development of imperial and aristocratic clan rule began to wane in the eleventh century, great turbulence surrounded a growing vacuum of political power, which contending warrior families eagerly attempted to fill. For some twenty years preceding Shinran's birth, political instability had prevailed when pure aristocratic political control finally disappeared with the civil warfare of the Hōgen and Heiji rebellions in 1156 and 1159. The head of the dominant warrior clan, Taira no Kiyomori (1118-1181) became prime minister in 1167, and members of the Taira clan (also known as the Heike) joined the aristocracy and later monopolized key positions in the court bureaucracy. Kiyomori became the true power in Japan at this time because he commanded far greater resources of wealth and military strength than any member of the imperial family, the aristocracy, or rival bushi (warrior) clans. He possessed a strong base in the enormous wealth built through China trade by his father Tadamori (1095-1153) and himself, with numerous dominant positions in relationships with his own clan and with other warrior families.[11] Kiyomori had skilfully taken advantage of the strain common to competing imperial rivals, in this case the power struggle between Emperor Nijō (1143-1165) and ex-Emperor Goshirakawa (1127-1192). He exploited the situation by marrying his daughter Tokuko into the imperial family, as she became the wife of Emperor Takakura (1166-1181) in 1172. It took Kiyomori only ten short years to reach the position of actual ruling power in Japan, and the rapid rise of the Heike family led to gossip that anyone not of the Heike could only be considered as less than human in terms of influence.[12]

As the fortunes of the Heike clan increasingly flourished, those of the former aristocratic family of power, the Fujiwara, came to decline.   The future for any branch of the Fujiwara, including Shinran's family in the Hino branch of the clan, became just as dismal.

Heike power was seized with their victory during the Hōgen and Heiji rebellions, which on the surface had been a struggle between rival factions of the imperial family and their respective warrior armies. Though the Heike assumed actual power, they exercised it within the traditional superstructure of court government.   Heike clansmen simply stepped into key positions within the existing ritsuryō-kokka (the Sui and T'ang dynastic legal codes adopted in Japan during the Nara period).   After great influence in the Nara period the ritsuryō-kokka declined, subject to the strong machinations of court rivalries, but the Heike appropriated this political framework as their own, overwhelming aristocratic officeholders in head-on confrontation.   Away from the capital, however, strong movements arose among the rising warrior class to free itself from any form of the entire ritsuryō-kokka system. The people of rural areas and distant provinces thus became as antagonistic toward the new warrior ruling power as they had been toward the former aristocratic rule, strongly opposing any retention of the ritsuryō-kokka structure.

The fact that Taira no Kiyomori failed to realize the widespread opposition of the warrior class he had led from the countryside to seize national power in the capital was the beginning of his tragic downfall. Soon Kiyomori and the Heike clan would stand alone against growing hostility and resistance by the former ruling aristocratic factions and the warrior class itself. In 1177, when Shinran was five years old, the frustration and anger of contending forces were provoked by the discovery of a secret anti-Heike plot in Shishigatani, Kyoto. After the leader of the intrigue, a Tendai school monk named Shunkan (1142-1178), and several followers were executed, Kiyomori stationed spies throughout the precincts of Kyoto in an effort to infiltrate and expose anti-Heike sentiment and rebellion.[13] These actions simply bred fear in the populace and further exaggerated feelings against him, strengthening isolated pockets of resistance. The more Kiyomori grew aware of anti-Heike activities, the more repressive his political measures became.

When Shinran was seven, in 1179, several thousand Heike soldiers raided Kyoto. Ex-Emperor Goshirakawa was imprisoned, and Fujiwara no Motomichi (1160-1233) assumed Fujiwara no Motofusa's (1144-1230) position as chief advisor to the emperor. Intrigue ran rampant as a three-year-old emperor, Antoku (1178-1185) ascended the throne. The young emperor was Kiyomori's grandson, a fact which enabled Kiyomori to exercise even tighter control over the centre of the imperial institution. The fortunes of the Heike appeared to increase in successful consolidation of power, but strong opposition remained, waiting for appropriate opportunities to act effectively. Just when all apparent anti-Heike forces seemed to have been checked and brought under control, several great Nara and Kyoto Buddhist monastic centres organized armies and became an immediate threat. Originally formed for self-defense during the instability at the end of the Heian period, novice monks from the warrior clans gravitated in large numbers to Kōfukuji, the Hossō school headquarters in Nara, and to Mt. Hiei, the Tendai school headquarters in Kyoto. As monastics who wore military garb over their robes, these characteristically rough bands (known as sōhei or "monastic soldiers") continually descended to Kyoto carrying the sacred Shintō regalia affiliated with their Buddhist monasteries to provoke imperial and warrior authority, often engaging in large skirmishes and retreating to the extraterritorial safety of their Buddhist institutions. Kōfukuji at this time was able to muster sixty thousand men to oppose the Heike.[14] The Heike finally reacted against the constant sōhei threat, burning Onjōji, a major Tendai school centre near Kyoto, in November 1180, and Tōdaiji, the Kegon school headquarters and most influential Nara-period monastery, in December of the same year.

Such destructive anti-Buddhist raids stilled immediate military opposition, but stimulated the growth of intense antagonism toward the Heike at all levels of society in the capital and in the provinces. The Heike reached the zenith of their influence and prosperity at the time of Emperor Antoku's enthronement, but by 1180 once again insurrection enveloped their rule and their fortunes began to fall. In

April 1181, Minamoto no Yorimasa (1104-1180) led against the Heike a combined army of Minamoto warriors and the sōhei of major Kyoto and Nara establishments, under the titular command of Mochihitoō (1151-1180), the second son of ex-Emperor Goshirakawa. After a solid month of constant battle, this attack on the Heike was frustrated with Yorimasa's defeat and Mochihitoō's death. In August of the same year, Minamoto no Yoritomo (1147-1199) raised another attack in the Izu area, and in September Kiso no Yoshinaka (1154-1184) led a third army in revolt in Shinshū, the provinces of central Japan. Taira no Kiyomori died in 1181, during warfare and social turmoil that brought his fourteen year political dominance to an end.

In addition to catastrophic political and military events, there were numerous natural disasters during this time. In November and December of 1173, the great Kyoto Buddhist temples Kiyomizudera and Rokuharamitsuji were burned to the ground. Great earthquakes followed in April 1176, and in April of the following year over one-third of the city of Kyoto disappeared in a major fire. June of 1181 brought drought, followed by severe wind storms and flooding in the autumn, resulting in poor harvests that lasted well into 1182.

It was at this time that Shinran made his decision to enter a monastic career.

D.   Circumstances leading to Shinran's monastic career

Referring to the day that Shinran committed himself to become a monk, Kakunyo wrote at the beginning of the *Honganji-shōnin shinran dene:*

> The family of the revered master [Shinran] was of the Fujiwara clan . . . there was Arinori, a court official in the service of the dowager empress, and the revered master [Shinran] was his child. He was a person who could have grown in glory with purity in heart and mind, reaching the inner chambers [of the court] with great responsibility in the palace. Instead, when he was nine years old, because the major reason of spreading the Dharma was growing within him together with the attendant cause of wanting to benefit all sentient life, he went to visit the great monk Jien, with his uncle Noritsuna who was a court official of the third rank-lower grade. He was given tonsure [as a novice] and received the name Hanen.[15]

From the outset of this first section of Kakunyo's biography, it appears that neither of Shinran's parents was present at their nine-year-old son's novitiate ordination. He was instead accompanied only by an uncle (the reasons for this absence will be subsequently examined).

According to this account, the major reason for his entering a new life was "spreading the Dharma." Thus he renounced any attempt at a promising future in society and instead decided to embrace the Dharma (the spiritual reality of the teachings) of the Buddha. A Buddhist calling is certainly an appropriate response by any person whose early childhood consisted of exposure to the social and historical conditions so briefly outlined above. Yet if the chaos and destruction of a society in transition were the simple and sole motivation for renouncing the world and entering religious life, then far more of his contemporaries could have been expected to choose the same course. The tradition's standard explanation emphasizes that Shinran's strong emotional realization that all facets of existence are characterized by the major Buddhist doctrine of impermanence (Sanskrit: 'anitya'; Japanese: 'mujō') convinced him to seek meaning in monastic life, but this alone may not be a suitable explanation. It is more probable that this critical decision was made for the nine-year-old (seven years of age by Western counting) boy by his guardians. To clearly understand the situation, one must investigate Shinran's family background.

There is another biography written much later, by Ryōkū (1669–1733), called the *Shinran-shōnin seitō-den* ("Biography of the True Lineage of the Revered Master Shinran").[16] In it Ryōkū relates that Shinran's father Arinori died when Shinran was four years old and that his mother Kikkōnyo died when he was eight. If this is true it would explain his parents' absence at his ordination as a novice. Shinran was ordained within the following year at the age of nine. However, the accuracy of Ryōkū's dating is questionable, especially the precise year of Shinran's father's death. A reliable source, the postscript written by Zonkaku to the copy made of the Pure Land sūtra, the *Daimuryōjukyō (Wu-liang-shou-ching)*, states:

> On December 15, 1351, the Japanese grammatical notations here written in red ink [inserted in the Chinese text of the sūtra] have been completed. This sūtra copy was prepared in observance of the forty-ninth day after the death of Mimurodo no Daishinnyūdō Arinori, the father of Shinran. This was written by Kenyū and copied by me. The calligraphy of the title of this copy was written by Shinran.[17]

Kenyū (b. 1179) was Shinran's younger brother (Arinori's third son), and this record suggests that their father died only after Kenyū had studied for a period of time sufficient to reach a literacy capable of understanding and creating the rather difficult Japanese grammatical notations (the verb endings and nominative marker particles known as kunten) for the original Chinese text of the *Wu-liang-shou-ching* sūtra. Thus Kenyū was at least in adolescence before his father's death, as this would be the minimum time required for such mastery of written Japanese and difficult Buddhist Chinese. Kenyū was Shinran's younger brother, so Arinori must have been alive until Shinran did reach adulthood.

A plausible explanation for how the date of Arinori's death became falsified and popularly accepted could be the following—in

1176 when Shinran was four years old, something disastrous occurred to his father while he was in the service of the emperor's mother (or possibly in service to the emperor's wife). Around the year 1176 there was a succession of four emperors, an indication of unusually swift events and changes in official court life. The imperial mothers, grandmothers and wives of the four emperors are:

1. Fujiwara no Tokuko (1117-1160)—mother of emperor Konoe (1138-1155)

2. Fujiwara no Teishi (1133-1176)—empress to Konoe

3. Fujiwara no Tashi (1140-1201)—second wife to Konoe

4. Taira no Shigeko (1142-1176)—mother of emperor Takakura (1161-1181).

By tracing the genealogy of the Hino family (Shinran's family branch of the Fujiwara clan), one can safely conclude that Arinori was in the service of the emperor Goshirakawa and his family, as his forefathers had served successive emperors for many generations. (Goshirakawa succeeded Konoe as emperor in 1155 but would reign only three years in total.) Further investigation shows that Arinori also served Taira no Shigeko, the mother of Emperor Takakura (and Takakura was the seventh son of ex-Emperor Goshirakawa). Taira no Shigeko died in 1176 (the second year of the reign era Angen), and this coincides with the commonly accepted year of Shinran's father's death. Thus it is most probable that Arinori did not die in 1176 but simply lost his position at court and retired, a common occurrence in times of great intrigue and rapid change in leadership and influence at court.

According to Hino family genealogy, Arinori held an extremely low position at court. His rank was fifth-rank senior grade and by the customs of the times, only third-rank or higher was held to be of any importance in society.[18] Sei Shōnagon (exact dates unknown), the noted courtier and authoress of the famed literary diary of the times, the *Makura no sōshi* ("The Pillow Book [of Sei Shōnagon]") wrote that both people of the country and officials of the fifth rank were unseemly.[19]

Lack of social esteem in light of the demands of such positions was another common reason for retirement from active court administration during this time. In addition to any prevalent social attitudes, Arinori's status should also be seen in comparison with that of his brothers, Noritsuna (dates unknown) and Munenari (dates unknown). In the traditional Japanese family structure Arinori was the youngest child and so was considered the son of least importance. His brother Munenari was a highly educated and ambitious person who held the position of fifth-rank third grade. Yet until the age of sixty-one Munenari continued to struggle against great odds for promotion within the court hierarchy, finally succeeding despite jealousy and opposition by influential members of the court. As would be seen in Shinran's lifetime, Munenari was a man of strong character whose self-confidence and ability steadfastly met with the rigours of the social system in refusing to be deterred by its barriers. Noritsuna, Arinori's other brother, was a poet as well as a political advisor to Emperor Goshirakawa. His position was important enough to have a direct and identifiable influence on the course of Japanese history at this time. Noritsuna's fourth rank was lower than Munenari's but higher than Arinori's fifth, and he commanded influence because he was an astute court army officer. Despite the success of his brothers, Arinori never moved beyond fifth rank (which was the lowest position within the palace).[20] It would still seem highly unlikely, however, for Arinori to retire while the major responsibilities of supporting a young family existed.

E. Conflicting genealogical accounts of Shinran's grandfather

The following is the entire beginning statement (the first four complete sentences) of the first section of the *Honganji-shōnin shinran dene* (previously omitted for purposes of brevity and clarity):

> The family of the revered master [Shinran] was of the Fujiwara clan. The twenty-first descendant of prince Amatsu Koyane was the grand minister Kamatari, and five generations after him there was lord Uchimaro of the first-rank junior grade who was general of the imperial guards and a state minister. Then six generations after Uchimaro there was lord Saishō Arikuni, general of police. After five more generations passed, there was Arinori, a court official in the service of the dowager empress, and the revered master [Shinran] was his child.[21]

Shinran's genealogy can also be traced in four other sources which offer additional information. These are:

> 1. A section called *Hinoke honganji keizu fujiwara hokke* ("Honganji Lineage of the Hino Branch of the Fujiwaras") of the major Japanese genealogical compendium, the *Sonpi-bunmyaku* ("Veins of Nobility and Ignobility") edited by Tōin Kimisada (1340-1399).[22]

> 2. Another *Sonpi-bunmyaku* section, entitled *Teiji-ryū fujiwara nanke* ("The Teiji Line of the Southern Fujiwara Family").

> 3. *Hino-uji keizu* ("Genealogy of the Hino Branch [of the Fujiwara Family]").[23]

> 4. *Ōtani-ichiryū keizu* ("Genealogy of the Singular Ōtani Lineage").[24]

A comparison of these four sources will produce the composite genealogical outline illustrated in figure 1.
According to the sources contained within the enormous

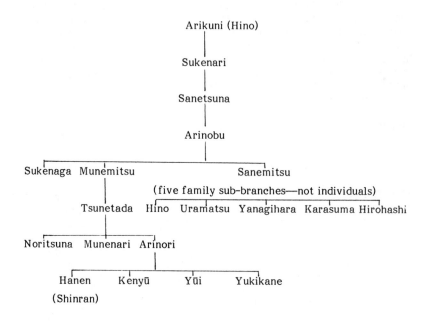

Figure 1

compendium of Japanese historical records, the *Gunsho-ruijū*
("Nation's Writings Ordered by Kind"), Arikuni held the position of
state councillor (sangi) during the time of the great mid-Heian-period
statesman Fujiwara no Michinaga (966-1027).[25] Arinobu (d. 1099) was
the great-grandson of Arikuni and a very successful official in his
own right, for the clan prospered to the extent that this Fujiwara
branch did itself become a "main house" with five family sub-
branches at the time of Arinobu's oldest son Sanemitsu (d. 1147). The
surnames of these sub-branches were Hino, Uramatsu, Yanagihara,
Karasuma and Hirohashi. (It should be noted that the genealogy
credits each generation with several literary figures within its ranks.)
Until recent times, the consensus was that Shinran's family line was
Arinobu——Arinori——Hanen (Shinran). In other words, Arinobu was
long taken to be Shinran's grandfather when Arinobu was actually
Shinran's great-great grandfather. Arinobu died in 1099 and Shinran
was born in 1173. If Arinobu is seen as Shinran's grandfather and if
Shinran's father Arinori was born even as late as the year of Arinobu's
death (1099), Arinori would have been seventy-five years of age when
Shinran was born in 1173. It is most unlikely that Arinori's first son
could have been born when Arinori was at the advanced age of

seventy-five (particularly for those times) and that he would go on to father three other children after reaching seventy-five. It is based on this discrepancy that Shinran's genealogy was held in doubt until the recent discovery of the *Teiji-ryū fujiwara nanke* by Yamada Bunshō.[26]

According to this discovery, Shinran's grandfather was Tsunetada, an infamous courtier who was censored for licentious behaviour. All of Shinran's ancestors except Tsunetada were men of some distinction (as can be seen in the Hino genealogy), while Tsunetada was the sole black sheep whose behaviour was sufficiently embarrassing to hold the clan back from achieving greater success. The diary of Hōnen's disciple, Kujō Kanezane (1149-1207) is known as the *Gyokuyō* ("Precious Leaves [of the Imperial Family]") and it illustrates this point quite clearly. In 1182 Tsunetada's second son, Munenari, took the traditional hōryaku ("devising the proper course") examination for promotion within the court bureaucracy (which suggests that Munenari was a very capable person by the mere fact of his attempt).[27] The diary reads: "Munenari's family is extremely coarse and thus such ambition on his part is rather unbecoming."[28] Munenari passed the examination four months later and the noted chronicler of his age, Fujiwara no Teika (1162-1241), wrote the following in his diary, the *Meigetsu-ki*("Record of a Moon's Clarity"): "Munenari has an extraordinary literary ability. Yet it is astonishing that any person from such a disreputable family could ever pass the examination."[29] It was probably because of this common opinion of his family's background that Munenari's promotion was delayed until he was sixty-one (which was a very late age for such honour).

In light of the weight of opinion in the tiny and closed society of Heian court and bureaucratic life, a notorious family member made life very difficult, furnishing ammunition for intrigue and the frustration of a family's status by its rivals. It was common practice in Japanese genealogies of this era simply to neglect or erase the names of persons whose notoriety could so strongly affect the family's present status and future reputation. Thus Tsunetada (exact dates unknown) was omitted from the Hino genealogy in various records. If Munenari, who was a man of strong accomplishments, had such major difficulties in his own promotion, it must have been even harder for his brother Arinori, whose rank was not only lower than Munenari's but who appeared frozen at that lowest level of court bureaucracy and whose status most chose to ridicule. Arinori then lost even this position when Lady Taira no Shigeko died. The conclusion, formed by consideration of the various genealogical material as well as court customs and values and how these affected individuals and families at the time, would be that Arinori was forced to retire at a relatively early age, essentially because the combination of his family's reputation, his own frustration at low court status, and the untimely death of his only patron meant that there was little or no hope for a stable future in court life. Hino genealogy also suggests that none of Shinran's relatives were in a sufficiently high social position to ensure Shinran any possibility of a decent future at court. Although both uncles succeeded in achieving

middle-level positions at court, this was only when they reached
retirement age—so that neither had a position consolidated or broad
enough to support the social progress of their young nephew.
Shinran's only hope lay in some form of education. The major avenue
toward literacy and any active role in society outside of court life
would be some form of monastic career. It was to this end that his
uncle (and probable stepfather) Noritsuna and his other uncle
Munenari focused their efforts and applied what limited influence
they possessed. Consequently, Shinran was given a rigorous education
in a stern family environment, which was his family's best means to
prepare him for a future in difficult times.

Nine years of age is extremely early for even a precocious child
to commit himself to such a major path in life. However, many noted
Japanese monks of that particular period did enter monastic life at a
similarly early age—Hōnen (1133-1212) at nine, Eisai (1141-1215) at
eleven, Jien (1155-1225) at thirteen, Myōei (1173-1232) at nine,
Dōgen (1200-1253) at thirteen, Nichiren (1222-1282) at twelve, Eizon
(1201-1290) at eleven, Ninshō (1217-1303) at eleven, and Ippen (1239-
1289) at ten. Thus Shinran's case was typical, at least of the major
Buddhist figures just mentioned. The reader should not view this
situation where a young boy leaves his family to enter a Buddhist
career at an early age in terms of sacrifice or tragedy, but instead
should attempt to regard the situation within the historical context
of the values, goals and limited opportunities that the difficulties of
the age offered to the lad in his family's specific circumstances. It is
safe to say that the decision was made for the boy by adults with
great awareness of the vicissitudes of life at this time and who
proceeded to act with love and concern for the child's best interest.

One other point to be noted is that the great Buddhist monastic
institutions at Mt. Hiei and Nara were not the only Buddhist
organizations to resist Taira no Kiyomori's efforts at control, to
retain their own independent positions of wealth and power. As the
power of the nobility in general was declining against the rising
influence of the warrior class, Shinran's family, with its difficult and
unstable status, was especially vulnerable, due to its strong ties of
service to Emperor Goshirakawa and due to the subsequent defeat
and death of Emperor Goshirakawa's second son Mochihitoō in leading
the first unsuccessful uprising against Taira no Kiyomori. At this
precise moment Mt. Hiei and Nara were seen by Shinran's family as
natural sanctuaries for its children as well as the only remaining
opportunity for its sons.

Many sons of the decaying nobility turned to Buddhist life both
for sources of opportunity and immediate refuge after the mid-Heian
period, as the military seized wealth and influence and its families
gradually replaced the nobility in high government positions.

A religious vocation was particularly attractive in terms of the
bleak future facing this aristocracy. There was not only a crisis of
political authority, but a much more profound questioning of the very
foundations and values of an aristocratic culture so strongly tied to a
five-century past of glory and influence, now proven decadent and
defeated on all fronts by a much newer and stronger warrior culture

in the present. The term *aristocracy* originally referred to government by the best of cultured citizenry, and *nobility* is derived from *naturi noscere*, "to know." Although these are European concepts, they well reflect the institutional values that an established ruling class may develop to justify its position in terms of some definition of power and superiority. At the end of the Heian period in Japan, court aristocracy was stripped of any pretence of exercising temporal power, so it sought psychological justification for its impoverished, uncertain, and frustrated existence in the worlds of religion and ideas. When physical power was lost and cultural values so fiercely questioned, many of the nobility came to respond to the temporal authority and actual physical control of Japan by the Heike and their successors, by looking for answers in a life with the possibilities of a superior spiritual authority and values. Because the aristocracy would easily be defeated in any military confrontation with the warrior class, they began to seek a protective cloak of spiritual authority and the potential of Buddhist- (and Shinto-) invoked divine retribution for any attack on their persons or their status.

The close cultural and political ties which had existed from the introduction of Buddhism to Japan some six centuries earlier between the nobility and the monastic institutions now readily enabled the nobility to move into religious life. The centuries of aristocratic patronage and leadership in Buddhist institutions and the temples' strong ties to court life had given the monasteries independent bases of wealth and extra-legal status (hence their resistance to warrior control). In their spiritual capacity as sources of power through ritual and prayer, the Buddhist monasteries could provide spiritual support and physical sanctuary for the increasingly disenfranchised aristocracy. New temples and monasteries were built with what aristocratic wealth remained, and the positions of authority in these new institutions were captured and held almost exclusively by descendants of the nobility.[30] In time most important posts of many of the newer Buddhist monasteries would be monopolized by the aristocracy.

There are several incidental factors arising from Shinran's family background which might also explain his taking up the Buddhist life precisely when he did. Mochihitoō, who had been of very high birth as an emperor's son, was seldom seen or met except by an exclusive few members of the inner court. When he died in battle in revolt against the Heike, there was no one available immediately who could identify him. Shinran's uncle Munenari had been Mochihitoō's tutor, and so Munenari was summoned by the Heike to identify Mochihitoō's body and authenticate his death.[31] Although Mochihitoō's death was confirmed by Munenari in an unpleasant and possibly dangerous duty, the capital was full of rumours for many months that Mochihitoō was still alive and planning new insurrection. (Such rumours were groundless.) Mochihitoō's death dimmed any immediate hopes of a future for the Hino family, and a credible case has been made that his death and its aftermath were the direct cause of Shinran's entering the monastic life.[32] Some scholars have also suggested that the major reason that Shinran's family was placed in an awkward and unfavourable position when Minamoto no Yorimasa rose up against the Heike was that Shinran's mother had probably been born in the opposing Minamoto (or Genji) family.[33] This assumption is based on the fact that Shinran's grandmother (Tsunetada's wife) was a Minamoto, but since very little is known of the social background of Shinran's mother, one can go no further and the question must remain unsettled at present.

Thus in this world of political chaos and declining fortunes and perhaps even some degree of immediate danger, the question loomed of what the present and future of the Hino family and its friends would be. Although the Hino were members of the nobility, they had not directly participated in the political intrigue or the violent warfare of the era. Therefore, while death by political vendetta was not probable for any sons of the Hino, Shinran's uncles undoubtedly felt that the young boy would simply have the most secure future within the monastic life and so concentrated their efforts upon securing such an opportunity for him.

Chapter 1 Notes

1. Toshihide Akamatsu and Kazuo Kasahara (eds.), Shinshūshi gaisetsu (Kyoto: Heirakuji Shoten, 1963), p. 332.

2. Kenkai Naganuma, "Shinran-shōnin-ron," Shigaku zasshi, vol. 21:5 (Tokyo: Tokyo University, 1910), pp. 72-106. Kenmyō Nakazawa, Shijō no Shinran (Kyoto: Bunken Shoin, 1920).

3. Bunshō Yamada, Shinran to sono kyōdan (Kyoto: Hōzōkan, 1948).

4. Zennosuke Tsuji, Shinran shōnin hisseki no kenkyū (Tokyo: Kinkōdo, 1920).

5. Kakunyo was the third hosshu (chief abbot) of the Shin tradition. When he was seventeen years old, he was ordained as a monk by Shinshō (dates unknown), a chief abbot of Ichijōin, Kōfukuji temple, and Hossō school monk of prominence in Nara. Kakunyo mastered the Mahāyāna Buddhist school of Yogācāra (the 'vijnapti-mātrāta' or "consciousness-only" system) under Gyōkan Hōin (dates unknown). Once he had thoroughly mastered major Buddhist systems of thought and practice, he was initiated into the Shin movement under the guidance of Nyoshin (1239-1300) who was Shinran's grandson, Kakunyo's own father, and the second patriarch of the school at Honganji headquarters.

Zonkaku (1290-1373) was Kakunyo's eldest son. At the age of fourteen he went to Nara and later to Mt. Hiei to undergo monastic training and study of the major Buddhist schools of the time. He spent much of his adult life helping his father in Shin propagation and leadership, following his father as chief abbot in 1322.

Rennyo (1415-1499) was the eighth chief abbot of the Shin tradition. At the age of seventeen, he began to study under Sonnō (d. 1514) at Shōren-in. In 1447 he began an organizational pilgrimage to sites significant to Shinran's career in the Kantō or eastern half of Japan. He became the chief abbot of Honganji headquarters at the age of forty-three. He is regarded as the restorer of the Shin tradition, largely because of his efforts to spread Shin by using a strong vernacular Japanese and by vigorously establishing Shin in Kantō urban areas and small rural centres.

6. Zenshin-shōnin dene, written on October 12, 1295, in Shinran-shōnin zenshū, vol. 4 (Kyoto: Hōzōkan, 1969), pp. 101-140; manuscript in the Nishi honganji collection in Kyoto.

Zenshin-shōnin shinran dene, written on December 13, 1295, in Shinran-shōnin zenshū, vol. 4, pp. 52-98; manuscript in Senjuji collection, Mie prefecture.

Honganji-shōnin shinran dene, written on November 2, 1343, in Shinran-shōnin zenshū, vol. 4, pp. 3-50; manuscript in the Higashi honganji collection in Kyoto.

Honganji shinran-shōnin dene, written on November 1, 1344,
Enjun Miyazaki, ed. (Tokyo: Daihōrinkaku, 1979), 3 volumes, 1
introductory volume; manuscript in the Shōganji collection, Chiba
prefecture.

7. Kenmyō Nakazawa, Shinshū genryūshiron (Kyoto: Hōzōkan, 1951),
p. 162.

8. Boki-eshi written by Jūkaku (1295-1360) in 1351. Found in Shinshū
shiryō shūsei, vol. 1 (Kyoto Dōhōsha, 1974), pp. 907-929.

9. Tandoku-mon by Zonkaku, written on November 16, 1359. Found
in Shinran-shōnin zenshū, vol. 4, pp. 175-181; manuscript in the Nishi
honganji collection, Kyoto.
Hōon-kōshiki by Kakunyo (1270-1351). Found in Shinran-shōnin
zenshū, vol. 4, pp. 143-155; manuscript in the Higashi honganji
collection, Kyoto.
Tandoku-mon copied by Rennyo on December 8, 1461. Found in
Shinran-shōnin zenshū vol. 4, pp. 185-191; manuscript in the Nishi
honganji collection, Kyoto.
Hōon-kōshiki copied by Rennyo in middle of December, 1468.
Found in Shinran-shōnin zenshū, vol. 4, pp. 159-181; manuscript in
Nishi honganji, Kyoto.
Gozokushō by Rennyo in early November 1477. Found in
Shinran-shōnin zenshū, vol. 4, pp. 195-198; manuscript in the Hōunji
collection, Mie prefecture.

10. Tatsurō Fujishima, "Kaisetsu, Shinran-shōnin dene" in Shinran-
shōnin zenshū, vol. 4, pp. 203-234.

11. Shō Ishimoda and Eiichi Matsushima, Nihonshi gaisetsu, vol. 1
(Tokyo: Iwanami Shoten, 1955), p. 173.

12. Genpei seisui-ki ("Record of the Rise and Fall of the Taira and
Minamoto") by author unknown, cited in Ishimoda and Matsushima,
op. cit., p. 173.

13. Ibid., p. 175.

14. Ibid., p. 176.

15. Honganji-shōnin shinran dene, op. cit., p. 3.

16. Shinran-shōnin seitō-den, found in Shinshū shiryō shūsei, vol. 7
(Kyoto: Dōhōsha, 1975), pp. 310-370. Ryōkū wrote this biography in
1717 (489 years after Shinran's death), using material from the
Shimotsuke-engi ("Origins of Shimotsuke") written by Shinran's
disciple Junshin (d. 1597). The Shimotsuke-engi is no longer extant,
so its authenticity and Ryōkū's use of it are open to question.

17. "Jōrakudai sambukyō okugaki," found in Honganjishi, vol. 1
(Kyoto: Nishihonganji, 1961), p. 227.

18. Haruki Kageyama, Hieizan (Tokyo: Kadokawa shoten, 1960),
p. 104. Ivan Morris, The world of the Shining prince—court life in
ancient Japan (London: Oxford University Press, 1964), pp. 63-69.

19. Makura no sōshi in Nihon koten bungaku taikei (Tokyo: Iwanami shoten, 1967), vol. 19, pp. 222-223.

20. Junkō Matsuno, Shinran—sono kōdō to shisō (Tokyo: Hyōronsha, 1971), p. 26.

21. Honganji-shōnin shinran dene, op. cit., p. 3.

22. Sompi-bunmyaku is a classical historical compendium and exists only in hand-copied versions, never completely published in modern times, although various summary studies and scholarship about specific sections do exist, e.g., Akira Tada, "Keizu to keifu" in Iwanami kōza nihon rekishi, vol. 3 (Tokyo: Iwanami shoten, 1934).

23. Hinouji-keizu, found in Shinshū shiryō shūsei, vol. 7 (Kyoto: Dōhōsha, 1975), pp. 502-503.

24. Ōtani-ichiryū keizu, p. 504.

25. The Gunsho-ruijū was compiled from 1779 and completed and published in 1819, while its continuation (Zoku or "Further" Gunsho-ruijū) was begun in 1822 and completed and published in 1912. To my knowledge a modern version has not been published.

26. Bunshō Yamada, Shinran to sono kyōdan (Kyoto: Hōzōkan, 1948), pp. 29-40.

27. Gyokuyō entry of September 7-18, 1182, quoted by Akamatsu, op. cit., pp. 22-23.

28. Gyokuyō entry of August 3, 1212, quoted by Matsuno, op. cit., p. 24.

29. Meigetsuki entry for December 26, 1212, Meigetsuki, vol. 2 (Tokyo: Kokusho Kankōkai, 1911-1912), p. 227.

30. Tsuneyuki Kawasaki and Kazuo Kasahara, eds., Shūkyōshi in Taikei Nihonshi sōsho, vol. 18 (Tokyo: Yamakawa Shuppan, 1964), p. 136.

31. Toshihide Akamatsu, Shinran (Tokyo: Yoshikawa Kōbunkan, 1961), pp. 21-22.

32. Ibid., pp. 21-22.

33. Yūsetsu Fujiwara, Shinshūshi kenkyū (Tokyo: Daitō shuppansha, 1939), pp. 47, 111-113.

Chapter 2

Shinran and Tendai Thought and Practice on Mt. Hiei

A. Saichō, the founder of the Japanese Tendai School

Shinran began his monastic career at the age of nine and would come to spend a quarter of his lifetime at the monastic centre on Mt. Hiei. It was during these formative years that his character developed and the foundation was laid upon which his future *Weltanschauung* would rest.

Saichō, the founder of the Japanese Tendai school on Mt. Hiei, began his own monastic life roughly three centuries earlier under the guidance of the Sanron school national master (kokushi) Gyōhyō (722-797). In his childhood Saichō was known as Hirono, but he adopted the monastic name Saichō ("Ultimate Ascent") after ordination at the age of fourteen in A.D. 780.[1]

He received the precepts in full ordination at Tōdaiji in Nara on April 6, 785, when he was nineteen.[2] This occurred only five months after the nation's capital was transferred from Nara to Nagaoka in November 784. Saichō was impressed by the significance of Buddhist impermanence as he considered the difficult life of the populace in a capital which had been the nation's grand political and social centre for nearly a century, but now had begun a startlingly rapid deterioration in the course of only a few months.

At the time Gyōhyō was affiliated with the national temple (kokubunji) system, so Saichō studied the teachings of the government-sponsored Japanese Kegon school (originally the Chinese Hua-yen school) of Nara-period Buddhism. He was particularly interested in the ideas found in the *Ta-ch'eng ch'i-hsin-lun-i-chi* ("Record of the Essentials of the *Awakening of Faith in the Mahāyāna")* where Fa-ts'ang (643-712), its author and the third patriarch of the Hua-yen (Japanese: Kegon) school, expressed admiration for the teachings of the Chinese T'ien-t'ai school (which Saichō would ultimately establish using the Japanese rendering of its Chinese name, as the Tendai school).[3]

T'ien-t'ai teachings differed in design from those of the Hua-yen because the former emphasized the systematic development of the human character rather than the ever-expanding awareness of the interrelationship among ideas, phenomena, and living things. The Japanese Kegon school tended toward abstraction in doctrine and increasingly distanced itself from the ordinary person by its emphasis on formal ritual and prayer in practice. Kegon study was characterized by broad exposure to both abstract discussion and intellectual interpretation of an entire philosophical evolution of Buddhist thought.

Saichō was attracted to T'ien-t'ai teachings and laboured to master its central scripture, the *Lotus sūtra*. There were few texts in Japan to aid him in this task except for those which had been introduced to the country by the Chinese monk Chien-chên (686-763) in 754.[4] Saichō's exploration of T'ien-t'ai teachings led him to see Buddhism as a truly religious tradition for the first time, instead of the disparate academic discipline and ritual pageantry emphasized by the major Nara Buddhist schools during centuries of court and government support. A strong emphasis upon T'ien-t'ai teachings and practice as the answer to Japanese religious needs would become Saichō's lifelong goal and would eventually result in his founding the Tendai school in Japan.

B. Saichō and the direction of his thought

In January of 803 at the request of Wake no Hiroyo (dates unknown), Saichō delivered a lecture on T'ien-t'ai doctrine at Takaozan in Kyoto. He received a very favourable response from an audience which included Emperor Kanmu. As a result of this exposure, Kanmu (737-806) received Saichō at court and Saichō later presented him with a statement of personal belief. It stated in part, "the Sanron and the Hossō schools are schools of discourse (ron-shū) but the T'ien-t'ai is the school of the teachings (kyō-shū)."[5]

According to this distinction, a Buddhist school of discourse based its doctrine on interpretations of the Buddha's original teachings, whereas a school of the teaching was founded directly upon the sūtras (as the Buddha's actual statements) without the mediation of interpretation. Saichō spoke of the Buddhism practised by the prominent Nara-period Sanron and Hossō schools as a Buddhism of scholarly pursuit, while maintaining that his new Tendai teaching and practice was based on the *Lotus sūtra*—the words, teachings, and experience of the Buddha.[6]

This lecture at Takaozan and the subsequent interest of the emperor opened the door for Saichō to go abroad and pursue the study of Buddhism in China, which he did in September of the same year.[7]

Saichō not only professed great interest in T'ien-t'ai teachings but also held great regard for the brilliant founder of the Chinese school, Chih-i (538-597). Of course, by the time Saichō went abroad in 803, Chih-i had already been dead for more than two hundred years. (The school itself was named T'ien-t'ai after Mt. T'ien-t'ai in Chekiang province where Chih-i underwent religious training and formulated his sophisticated overview of Buddhism based on the *Lotus sūtra*.)

Saichō studied T'ien-t'ai doctrine and practice with Tao-sui (dates unknown) and Hsing-man (d. 824).[8] In June 805, he was ordained as a T'ien-t'ai monk by Tao-sui after a brief stay of less than two years.[9] As did most Japanese monks of the day who journeyed to China, Saichō returned to Japan bearing a large collection of Buddhist scriptures and commentary literature, said to have totalled 230 texts in 460 volumes.

It was about this time that Saichō's religious thought began to mature. The concept he termed 'convergence of time and opportunity' (jiki sōō) formed the basis of his thought. His development of this principle reflects his deep awareness of history and the maturation of his own beliefs. Saichō's religious thought was to exercise a strong influence on subsequent Japanese Buddhism, particularly as the vehicle of the new Kamakura schools during the religious reformation that would sweep Japan some two hundred and fifty years after his death. We will now turn to examine briefly this 'convergence of time and opportunity' as Saichō worked with it at Mt. Hiei after his return to Japan.

C. Saichō's 'convergence of time and opportunity' as historical consciousness

Upon his return to Japan, Saichō introduced the highly eclectic T'ien-t'ai system of doctrine and practice, and following the custom of government-sponsored monks who had traveled to China, he presented the emperor with several copies of the newly imported scriptures as a result of his study abroad. As a forward to this presentation, Saichō wrote an inscription on the sūtras: "In this degenerate world, it is difficult for any person to exist in a truly religious manner, and in times of great calamity, both heaven and earth will come to mourn together."[10]

This feeling was first expressed when Saichō had been studying at Nara at the age of nineteen, and as he grew older he never altered his sense of hopelessness toward older forms of Japanese Buddhism. This outlook was precisely his understanding of the ramifications of Buddhist impermanence on all phases of political, social, and most significantly, religious life in Japan. His awareness became the ideological impetus of the Dharma (mappō) ideology he would repeatedly emphasize in his writings of later years.[11]

> The ages of the True and Complete Dharma (shōhō) and of the Artificial Dharma (zōhō) have passed—we are now already in the age of the decay of the Dharma (mappō). Thus, those days when one could actively practise [traditional] Buddhism [and achieve enlightenment] have already long disappeared.[12]

From the beginning of his religious training and throughout his life, Saichō constantly believed that the time in which he lived was near the age of the decay of the Dharma. It was for this reason that his 'convergence of time and opportunity' formed the definitive part of his Buddhist development. The decay of the Dharma concept strongly emphasized that the Buddhist teachings, practices, institutions, and values of extant Japanese Buddhist schools (referring to the established and prominent Nara-period Kegon, Sanron, Jōjitsu, Kusha, Hossō, and Ritsu schools) were incapable of responding in any significant way to the desperate religious needs of the Japanese people. In its simplest and strongest sense, the decay of the Dharma in Saichō's eyes meant that people could no longer achieve enlightenment through the teachings and practices of the Nara Buddhist schools, so alternate or new methods were of urgent necessity. 'Convergence of time and opportunity' in conjunction with the decay of the Dharma then justified Saichō's new Tendai Buddhism as the only possible Buddhist path where time (the era of the decay of the Dharma) and opportunity (the chance to practise effective Buddhism under a skilled Tendai master) came together.

His 'convergence of time and opportunity' combined with the decay of the Dharma ideology greatly contributed to the introduction and development of Pure Land teaching and practice in Japan, which itself had been developed in China as a great soteriological response to the original Chinese Buddhist acceptance of decay of the Dharma thought and its spiritual ramifications.

The Tendai school as Saichō and his successors would develop it was a veritable encyclopedia or academy of prevalent Buddhist teachings and practices, and it was within this vast and eclectic structure that the earliest Pure Land texts, ideas, and meditations would be found. One of the first such efforts was Saichō's disciple and the early Tendai master Ennin (794-864), who brought back from China the sophisticated Pure Land meditation known as the 'Dharma of the samādhi on the nembutsu' (nembutsu zanmai no hō). He also introduced the 'Dharma of the samādhi of constant practice' (jōgyō-zanmai no hō) and built the Jōgyō-zanmai-dō meditation pavilion on Mt. Hiei for its practice. In his work, the *Jakkōdo-ki* ("Records of the [Tendai School] Buddha-lands of Irrevocability, Peace, and Brilliant Wisdom"), Ennin expresses the view that in a degenerate age where the decay of the Dharma is rampant, all people are drawn away from traditional paths to enlightenment and toward the Pure Land.[13] Indeed, he emphasizes that many Mahāyāna sūtras indicate a single path to humanity's rebirth in the Pure Land, and this way is by means of the teachings of the Buddha Amida (Sanskrit: Amitābha/Amitāyus).

Such Pure Land teachings were studied by the Tendai monk Ryōgen (912-985) and compiled in his writing, the *Kubon ōjō-gi* ("Essence of the Nine Levels of Quality in Pure Land Rebirth").[14] According to the *Jiei-daishi-den* ("Biography of the Great Master Jiei [Ryōgen]"), Ryōgen regarded Amida as his own teacher and master during the era of the decay of the Dharma, and it is said that he died uttering this master's name.[15] The Pure Land thought begun by Ryōgen in his *Kubon ōjō-gi* is more thoroughly developed by an even greater Tendai Pure Land advocate, Genshin (942-1017), in his *Kanjin ryakuyō-shū* ("Collection of the Essentials of [the Tendai school's] Meditation on One's Heart").[16]

During his study on Mt. Hiei, Shinran was exposed to the Tendai system with such major doctrines as the decay of the Dharma, Saichō's basic 'convergence of time and opportunity', and the pioneer Pure Land thought of Tendai masters such as Ennin, Ryōgen, and Genshin. These would profoundly affect the development of his own thought, but one further element would also play a large role in

Shinran's maturing awareness, and this was a prevalent religious consciousness in society known as the "veneration of Shōtoku-taishi" (taishi shinkō). What influence this religious attitude of general society beyond the monastic precincts would have on the closed religious environment of Mt. Hiei and on Shinran himself will now be considered.

D. Veneration of Shōtoku-taishi, the "father of Japanese Buddhism"

When Shinran entered Mt. Hiei, both decay of the Dharma thought and Shōtoku-taishi worship were prevalent in Japan. Shōtoku (574-622) was traditionally credited with the formal adoption of Buddhism in Japan. As an imperial prince, he found Buddhist teachings (in combination with Confucianism and Taoism) to be a solid moral rationale for the unification of clan-dominated lands and individual clan (Shintō) deities into a nation under the Yamato imperial clan. He utilized Buddhist teachings as a common bond between disparate elements of archaic Japanese society, incorporating this ideology against strong opposition into his noted *Jūshichi-jō kempō* ("Seventeen-article Constitution"). He existed as a political figure whose personal life was that of a serious Buddhist and thus became the Japanese ideal of the devout Buddhist layman dedicated to the welfare of his people.

By the end of the Heian period, one form of social anxiety was a growing desire by clergy and laity alike to push back beyond institutionalized Japanese Buddhism in an effort to find the original teachings and practices of the Buddha. While reformist monks were beginning to explore new forms and discover vitality in discarded forms, popular cults of devotion to specific bodhisattvas and great historical Buddhists were also on the rise among the laity. Buddhist anguish at this time involved frustration at Japan's enormous distance in time and space from the India of the Buddha and early Buddhism.[17] This notion of Japan's great isolation from India combined with yearnings for a national role in Buddhist history and led to an intense devotion to Shōtoku-taishi as the Japanese Vimalakīrti (the ideal Indian Mahāyāna lay bodhisattva), as the "father" of Japanese Buddhism, and as a manifestation of the greatest bodhisattva, Avalokiteśvara (Chinese: Kuan-yin; Japanese: Kannon), the bodhisattva of compassion. Kannon veneration as cult practice reached such prominence that special Kannon-dō (halls of Kannon veneration) were constructed. Shinran was at Mt. Hiei when the Shōtoku-taishi cult reached its peak, and it is known that he practised sanrō (worship involving a set period of days and nights dedicated to a specific veneration and often a distinct vow) at temples and Kannon-dō associated with Shōtoku-taishi.

> In the middle of the Heian period it became popular for people to shut themselves for days in a chamber where a statue of a Buddhist figure was enshrined . . . for the purpose of praying for guidance and inspiration.[18]

Early Kamakura-period Buddhists believed that Shōtoku-taishi was the first Japanese to fully experience the essence of Buddhism in Japan, and the tendency arose to associate him with the glories of earlier Indian and Chinese Buddhism as well as the recent classical Japanese past.

This was the religious environment when Shinran arrived on Mt. Hiei: Mt. Hiei as the centre of Saichō's Tendai school and its encyclopedic gathering of Buddhist teaching and practice; his legacy of the 'convergence of time and opportunity' and the decay of the Dharma; Pure Land meditation; and popular lay cults devoted to deities and exemplary Buddhist figures. Here the young Shinran, in coming to understand and utilize the environment and its elements in his future, would develop in character and in thought based on his own experience as a human being and his creativity as a Buddhist master.

E.   Shinran's life on Mt. Hiei

No autobiographical reference can be found in Shinran's own writings that directly relates to any period of his twenty years on Mt. Hiei, nor is there any mention of this experience in any of the writings of his contemporaries. The single statement pertinent to this period is contained in the brief twenty-four character letter of Shinran's wife to her daughter, where it states that he lived as an ordinary temple monk (dōsō) on Mt. Hiei.[19]

Two things must be borne in mind in examining the probable course of Shinran's Mt. Hiei period. One can locate the sources of his thought by studying the original documents which he cited in a lifetime of writing. At the same time his attitudes toward his exposure to influences he received while on Mt. Hiei will thus become clear, and his overall ideology can be better understood. The second step involves searching for the reasons why he eventually left Mt. Hiei and returned to society. By looking through his writings that discuss the reasons for his leaving, we can piece together some aspects of the life that he led during his training in this monastic environment.

As attention is to be particularly directed at Shinran's activities in the process of forming his ideology, this second step concerning his ultimate descent will be used to clarify his religious life while on Mt. Hiei. His position as an ordinary temple monk (dōsō) in terms of his attitudes toward Shōtoku-taishi will be discussed in detail because the concrete evidence of the letter written by his wife concerns his decision to abandon his position of monastic practice on Mt. Hiei.

> Shinran left Mt. Hiei, remained in retreat for a hundred days at the Rokkakudō, and prayed for the salvation of all beings.   Then, on the dawn of the ninety-fifth day, Shōtoku-taishi appeared in a dream, indicating the path to enlightenment by revealing a verse. . . .   He [Shinran] called on the master Hōnen to be shown the way to salvation.[20]

It is this letter of Shinran's wife, which was only recently discovered by Washio Kyōdō in 1921, that indicates Shinran's monastic status on Mt. Hiei.[21] Thus a brief view of the ranks and responsibilities of a temple monk on Mt. Hiei will be the starting point for examining his life at this time.

F. Tendai practice on Mt. Hiei

Based on the diaries of court nobles contemporary with Shinran, standard monastic custom on Mt. Hiei divided monks into three basic classes—student monks (gakushō), attendant monks (dōshū), and ordinary temple monks (dōsō). The student-monk position was filled by those of aristocratic blood, while attendant monks were the former retainers of court nobility (now to serve their former-masters-turned-student-monks and also act as monastery caretakers).[21] Ordinary temple monks were the lowest of these three classes of monastics, and their primary duty consisted of devotional practice informally known as the unceasing nembutsu (fudan nembutsu).[22]

As a typical temple monk, Shinran's daily activities would follow the standard monastic career on Mt. Hiei in those times. One began by entering the Buddhist path about the age of ten (Shinran was nine), becoming partially ordained after five years, and taking formal and full ordination of the Buddhist precepts after an additional five years of study. During the remaining period of his twenty-year residence, he would progress along a course of study and meditation that dealt with the Tendai school's two kinds of practice—the practice of cessation and realization (shikan-gyō) and the practice of meditation on the Buddha Mahāvairocana (shana-gō).[23]

Saichō developed the practice of cessation and realization as study and meditative practice of such Mahāyāna scriptures as the *Lotus sūtra*, the *Suvarṇaprabhāsa sūtra* ("Sūtra of the Golden Radiance"), the *Sūtra of the Benevolent Emperor* (Sanskrit original unknown), etc.[24] He also developed the Tendai bodhisattva morality (ekayāna śīla) and Chih-i's fundamental 'cessation [of delusion] and realization [enlightenment]' (shikan-gyō) as found in his exhaustive and systematic treatise on Buddhist meditative practice and its importance, the *Mo-ho shih-kuan* ("Mahāyāna Cessation and Realization").[25] It is within Chih-i's systematization that the four kinds of Tendai samādhi or meditative ecstasies (shishu-zanmai) are found: i) 'constant sitting samādhi' for ninety days, singularly meditating on the name of the Buddha to the exclusion of all other activity, as explained in the *Saptsatikā-prajñāpāramitā sūtra*; ii) 'constant moving samādhi', which involves ninety days of circumambulation around the central Buddha figure of the Buddha hall in chanting meditation on the name of the Buddha Amida, as described in the *Pratyutpanna-samādhi sūtra*; iii) 'half-sitting, half-moving samādhi', which consists of several samādhi of seven, twenty-one, or thirty-seven days, length of sitting and circumambulatory meditation around the central Buddha figure, as suggested in the

Lotus sūtra and the *Mahā-dhāraṇī sūtra;* iv) 'neither sitting nor moving samādhi', which encompasses all other kinds of meditation, based on the *Pañcaviṃśatisāhasrikā-prajñāpāramitā sūtra.* The practice of meditation on the Buddha Mahāvairocana (shana-gō) is the second category of meditative practices, basically several levels of esoteric Buddhist awareness and action based upon the *Mahāvairocana sūtra.*[26]

A more common name for the second of the four kinds of Tendai samādhi, the 'constantly moving samādhi', was 'unceasing nembutsu' (fudan nembutsu). As suggested, it consisted of non-stop chanting of the sacred name of the Buddha Amida while circling the dais on which rested the major Buddha figure of the monastery. It was generic of the esoteric Buddhist mantra, a type of continuous meditation through the use of sacred sound. By such total immersion within the regularity of the meditative experience generated by uninterrupted chanting and motion, the practitioner was gradually to develop both detachment from other sense stimuli and abilities of concentration toward the goal of Buddhist realization. The process shares with numerous forms of Buddhist meditation an attempt to create an environment conducive to terminating ordinary sense response to the external world. Traditional Far Eastern Buddhist theories of consciousness have always suggested that sense perception is necessarily accompanied by intellectual conceptualization, emotional evaluation, and the assertion of an individual ego that values and reacts to such conceptions, to create karma in acting thought. An elaboration of common points between these two men can lead to an understanding of Shinran's conception and veneration of the greatest figure in early Japanese Buddhism.

G. Shinran's debt to Shōtoku-taishi

The circumstances underlying Shinran's sanrō practice and his spiritual experience concerning Shōtoku-taishi are set forth in Eshinni's letter:

> This letter attests to the fact that your father [Shinran] was an ordinary temple monk (dōsō) on Mt. Hiei, that he left the mountains and secluded himself in the Rokkakudō for one hundred days, and that while praying for the salvation of all sentient beings, Shōtoku-taishi appeared and showed him the way, at the dawn of the ninety-fifth day. I have written this and sent it to you so that you can read this for your own understanding. ... Shinran left Mt. Hiei, remained in retreat for a hundred days at the Rokkakudō, and prayed for the salvation of all beings. Then, on the dawn of the ninety-fifth day, Shōtoku-taishi appeared in a dream, indicating the path to enlightenment by revealing a verse.[27]

Further evidence of the depth of his experiencing contact with Shōtoku-taishi is found in his Mukoku:

> When due to the retribution of previous karma the practitioner is involved in sexual experience, I will incarnate myself as a striking woman and become the recipient of the act. Helping to bring some beauty to his present life, at the precise moment of his death I will guide him to the Land of Ultimate Happiness.[28]

A profound spiritual relationship between Shinran and Shōtoku-taishi would be established by this experience, and it would be concretely reflected in Shinran's thought and writings, as for example in his later 190 wasan or hymns in praise to Shōtoku.[29]

However, no evidence exists which specifically identifies Shinran's dedication to the Buddha Amida (so central to his Pure Land thought) with any such belief by Shōtoku-taishi, so it is highly unlikely that Shōtoku's beliefs and writings would have been the source of Shinran's Pure Land foundations.[30]

Early Japanese Buddhism, with its strong government patronage, enabled many native monks to travel to China to pursue advanced study of Chinese Buddhism. This sponsorship usually resulted in fresh directions in Buddhist thought and practice coming directly to Japan with their return. The person who had inaugurated this religious study abroad at the end of the sixth century and established it as a basic characteristic of Japanese Buddhism was Shōtoku-taishi.[31] There are several texts purportedly written by him but whose authorship is the subject of much modern scholarly debate, yet regardless of authorship, these do prove that he did study Buddhist scriptures and teachings with Korean monks such as Eji (d. 623) and Ekan (dates unknown) on his own initiative. Shōtoku certainly did open the door that enabled Buddhism to enter Japan and become permanently established. The outstanding characteristic of this patronage and study abroad effort was that he encouraged it not only as a major aspect of the Chinese civilization the Japanese desired to adopt but as a primary religious system as well.

The results of his efforts can be traced today in two documents traditionally attributed to Shōtoku-taishi. The first is the oldest sūtra commentary written by a Japanese, which is known as the *Sangyō-gisho* ("Commentaries on the Essentials of the Three Sūtras").[32] These commentaries are on the *Lotus*, *Vimalakīrti*, and *Śrīmālā-devi sūtras*. In the *Vimalakīrti sūtra* commentary a text is cited which was published in China after Shōtoku's death, and this had led to extensive speculation that he did not write the *Sangyō-gisho*.[33] But the *Sangyō-gisho* is stylistically consistent in syntax and diction, so one common view is that it was a joint effort by Shōtoku and his study group but that the work was completed only after his death.

As a compilation of commentaries on three major Mahāyāna sūtras, the *Sangyō-gisho* evidences an excellent understanding of Mahāyāna Buddhist doctrine. Even a simple glance at the basic ideas shared by these three sūtras as well as their respective emphases will indicate their attraction to Shōtoku in terms of his religious ideals and national goals. From his role as a formulator of a national ideology to be culled from all aspects of Chinese civilization, Shōtoku selected the *Lotus sūtra* because it taught that social philosophy and law were not contradictory with Mahāyāna Buddhist thought and practice. The *Vimalakīrti sūtra* complemented this rationale with its emphasis on the positive use of wealth in the life of a lay Buddhist, while the *Śrīmālā-devī sūtra* featured the role of the lay female practitioner and the role of the ruling and cultured class in the promotion and practice of the Buddhist life on an individual and national level.

The underlying spiritual theme of these three sūtras is the Mahāyāna concept of the universality of the Buddha nature and the shared or collective practice to develop this common potential for Buddhahood into a progressive enlightenment for all (known as the ekayāna or "singular vehicle" doctrine)—a theme also present in such noted Mahāyāna sūtras as the Prajñāpāramitā literature, the *Avataṃsaka sūtra*, the *Aparimitāyus* ("Larger Sukhāvatī-vyūha") *sūtra* and the *Mahāparinirvāṇa sūtra*. This singular-vehicle doctrine (Japanese: ichijō shisō) stressed the universality of the Buddha nature, which is to say that all sentient beings can achieve enlightenment, not by mere practice for each individual's own progress, but by practice as dedication of merit and action for mutual benefit of the collective sentient effort and interrelated karmic ties that are the environment for an entire society's potential Buddhist destiny. Shōtoku's concentration on such teachings in his commentaries of these three sūtras indicates the political ideology of his developing nation and a fundamental religious hypothesis for the spiritual life of its people.

The second indication of the sophistication that characterized Shōtoku's understanding and practice of Buddhism as a religion (over his political application of it as a unifying national ideology) is found in his will. "Everything that happens in this world is impermanent—the Buddha alone is eternally real."[34] Ienaga Saburō states that this will is an authentic basis for understanding Shōtoku-taishi's beliefs, unlike the controversial *Sangyō-gisho*. Ienaga strongly values Shōtoku's will as a revolutionary testament which uprooted and replaced the commonly held archaic Japanese outlook on the world. The will's potential as a religious proposition remained unrealized fully until the beginning of the thirteenth century and some five hundred years after Shōtoku's death, when Kamakura Buddhist leaders such as Hōnen and Shinran emerged to begin movements of a strong universalist tendency that reached beyond the aristocracy. Ienaga referred to Shōtoku as the first true native philosopher.[35]

The power of this logic was not apparent in social attitudes until the decline of the nobility at the end of the Heian period. Then an overwhelming sense of frustration turned to ennui, and the nobility became conscious of the transitoriness of its values and institutions, as shown by the disharmony, decay, and chaos in the nation's political and social order. Had the environment been a settled and harmonious one, this collective *weltschmerz* would not have appeared. The rising warrior class itself concentrated solely on the consolidation of power in a struggle so intense that both the vistors and the survivors soon became painfully aware of the transitory nature of their own recent hard-won goals. The constant tension from renewed chaos and the ever-present threat of future warfare over control of the nation qualified their newly established values and institutions and led them to realize the terrible fear, suffering, and bloodshed upon which their accomplishments were based. This warrior concern was clearly a questioning of their own immediate past actions rather than any sense of criticism of the earlier aristocratic order.

The taking of life was a major precept in the Buddhists' way of life, greatly contributing to a spiritual tension in any society that adopted Buddhism and attempted to integrate it within established social institutions of warfare, capital punishment, hunting, fishing, etc. Whether the struggle for survival was at the warrior class level of rebellion, warfare, and assassination or at the lower class level of hunting, petty thievery, and murder, the society shared a bewildered dissatisfaction and fear of life at the end of the Heian period. How each person comprehended and related individual responsibility to efforts toward permanent security and success at the individual level and at the collective level of social institutions and values was the point of Shōtoku's concern about the long-range impermanence of everything except the realization of Buddhist reality.

The foundation of Shōtoku's sense of impermanence as a logic of negation is thoroughly based upon the major values of the Buddhist tradition:

> What is material is perishable and cannot be preserved; however, the Three Treasures [the Buddha, the Dharma, the Buddhist community or Saṃgha] are permanent and can forever be accomplished.[36]

> People rush for desire and greed, and it is extraordinary for any person to pursue the path to truth. Moreover, people do not separate themselves from life and death [saṃsāra], and thus cannot reach nirvāṇa.[37]

> Most who crave for knowledge are trapped by their six senses [touch, sight, hearing, taste, smell and thought] and their delusion blinds them from reality.[38]

> Cease negative and evil actions.[39]

Shinran's views are often quite parallel to Shōtoku's:

> Truly I do realize—it is tragic that I, Gutoku [the "foolish and fuzzy-headed"] Shinran, am overwhelmed in vast oceans of lust and bewildered among the enormous mountains of fame and profit, never rejoicing to belong to the multitudes who will strive to be reborn in the Pure Land nor enjoying any approach to the realization of true enlightenment. What a shame, what a terrible sorrow![40]

The primary differences between these two men were their actual social positions, their status as Buddhist (Shōtoku as a great layman, Shinran as a monastic), and their respective eras. Shōtoku-taishi was the regent during one of the most chaotic periods in early Japanese history. Although he lived in the very worldly and turbulent environment of political and national development, he nevertheless successfully practised Buddhist teachings without the benefit of a monastic career. Shinran's admiration of Shōtoku was based in a recognition that the latter had interpreted Buddhist doctrine in terms of a human salvation which was accessible to all levels of Japanese society, including the common people.

Shōtoku in the seventh century and Shinran in the thirteenth century are distant in time but share the strong continuity of seeking a Buddhism highly relevant and readily available to the religious needs of the entire Japanese nation. It was Shinran's discovery of the possibility of a universalist and Japanese-directed emphasis to Buddhism in Shōtoku's writings and thought that motivated him to identify closely with Shōtoku's religious goals and to seek new solutions to these goals at the beginning of the Kamakura period. This is obvious from any serious consideration of the great many hymns he dedicated to Shōtoku's memory and Buddhist objectives.[41] As Shinran was engaged in the typical sanrō practice of a temple monk (dōsō) on Mt. Hiei, he reflected Japanese Buddhist aspirations and turned to the leading Buddhist figure in Japanese history for direction. The combination of Shōtoku as the central object of devotional practice and as a serious consideration of his writings and thought led Shinran to identify strongly with Shōtoku's purposes and accomplishments. These Shinran interpreted to discover a Buddhist path that would respond to the most profound suffering and religious needs of all Japanese in his time. Thus Shinran's discovery of Shōtoku-taishi became the prime model in his search for and his ultimate discovery of Pure Land thought and practice as the answer. This discovery, as well as his actual meeting and relationship with the Pure Land master Hōnen, will now furnish the next subject for examination.

H.   Material related to Shinran's meeting with Hōnen

Five sources deal with the period immediately preceding Shinran's joining Hōnen's followers and the time during which he practised with Hōnen.

1) *Shinran muki* ("Record of Shinran's Dream"). There are two copies of this account of Shinran's dream or vision, one written by Shinran himself and the other by a disciple (dates of these texts unknown).[42]

2) *Kangyō-amidakyō-shūchū* ("Annotated *Amitāyur-dhyāna sūtra* and *Sukhāvati-vyūha sūtra"*). The earliest of these two commentaries by Shinran appears to have been written before he was forty-five.[43]

3) Shinran's own recollections of his relationship with Hōnen, found in a statement in his *Kyōgyōshinshō*.[44]

4) The letter of Shinran's wife, Eshinni, addressed to their daughter.

5) The account of the dream/vision recorded in Kakunyo's *Honganji-shōnin shinran dene.*

A fruitful inquiry can be made by carefully examining the *Shinran muki*, the *Kangyō-amidakyō-shūchū*, the *Kyōgyōshishō.* statement, and the *Honganji-shōnin shinran dene.* accounts.

There is one copy of the *Shinran muki* by Shinran's disciple Shimbutsu (1209-1261), and another recently discovered by Hiramatsu Reizo which has been authenticated to be in Shinran's handwriting.[45] The *Shinran muki* text reads as follows:

> "When due to the retribution of previous karma the practitioner is involved in sexual experience, I will incarnate myself as a striking woman and become the recipient of the act. Helping to bring some beauty to his present life, at the precise moment of his death I will guide him to the Land of Ultimate Happiness." The Bodhisattva Avalokiteśvara [Kannon] offered this to Zenshin [Shinran]—"It is my vow. Zenshin, you shall proclaim the meaning of this vow everywhere, so that every sentient being hears of it." He [Shinran] addressed them as commanded by the Bodhisattva, and when he imagined that he had come to the end of his address, he awoke from his dream.[46]

The content clearly refers to a sexual union, possibly including the institution of marriage. The immediate questions are: when and where did Shinran experience this vision or dream? Both the Shimbutsu copy and the one which Hiramatsu discovered are undated. However, it is recorded in the *Honganji-shōnin shinran dene* as having occurred early in the morning of April 5, 1203.

> On the fifth day of the fourth month in the third year of the era Kennin (1203), when the revered master was twenty-nine years old, he received a vision in the evening ... The record states that the Bodhisattva Avaloki-tesvara of the Rokkakudō ...[47]

The *Honganji-shōnin shinran dene* is apparently in error in stating Shinran's age as twenty-nine in the third year of Kennin (1203) because by Japanese reckoning he would then have been thirty-one years old. If, on the other hand, Shinran did have this vision when he was twenty-nine, it should have been recorded as the first year of Kennin (1201), which is the year that Shinran joined Hōnen's followers.[48] If Shinran had the experience in 1203, it would have been after he became Hōnen's disciple, for 1203 was the year before Hōnen obtained the signatures of his closest disciples on the Seven Article Pledge (shichikajō no kishōmon) which he presented to Mt. Hiei monastic authorities to protest moves to curtail increasingly popular Pure Land practices there. These dating contradictions can be viewed as simple copy errors or perhaps as accurate indications of two separate dream experiences generally alike in structure, principal elements, and events but with subtle differences in content.

I. The two versions of the dream

Among the five sources listed in the previous section, those which most directly concern Shinran's turning his attention to the master Hōnen are the recollections of the two dreams, those in the *Honganji-shōnin shinran dene* and in Eshinni's letter. As explained in chapter 1, the contents of the *Honganji-shōnin shinran dene*, which discusses Shinran's experiences and travels, are believed to be accurate, for only a few of the recorded dates and years have failed tests of authenticity and consistency.

Unfortunately, there is questionable accuracy with its dating of Shinran's dream. Occasionally a few of the dates in the several extant copies of the *Honganji-shōnin shinran dene*, contradict one another. Three existing copies of the text are the concern of present scholarly debate: the texts in the Nishi honganji collection, the Senjuji collection, and the Higashi honganji collection.[49] The dates of these three copies relating to the occurrence of Shinran's dream, his age at the time of the dream, and the time when he began to practise with Hōnen may be compared in the following table.

Table 4
Comparison of Dates in Dream Accounts

Temple Collection copy	Year Shinran joined Hōnen	Year of the Mukoku (Sexagenary cycle)	Remarks
Nishi honganji copy	1201: Shinran is 29	Kigai: 1203	Year copy made is unknown (probably the same period as the Senjuji copy)
Senjuji copy	1203: Shinran is 29	Shinyū: 1203	Copied December 13, 1295
Higashi honganji copy	1203: Shinran is 29	Shinyū: 1203	Copies by the author Kakunyo in 1343

As noted in the above table, the Higashi honganji and Senjuji copies do correspond in dating. However, each has a double error, since the dates given by Shinran of the time he joined Hōnen are 1203 at age twenty-nine, and the year 1203 was Kigai and not Shinyū in the sexagenary cycle. If the calculations were accurately based on the Shinyū period of this cycle, then the year would be 1201.[50] The Nishi honganji copy contains no contradictions in this matter in contrast to the other two copies, but it is not without some questionable points. The Nishi honganji copy states that Shinran's dream occurred after he joined Hōnen's group. This directly contradicts Eshinni's letter, the one other major source pertaining to the dream. Eshinni wrote to her daughter that Shinran joined Hōnen only after one hundred days had passed from the experience of the dream.[51]

If copy dating is seen as accurate, then two different versions of the dream experience are possible, and it may well be that each version records a separate dream. The *Honganji-shōnin shinran dene* version says:

> The record states that the Bodhisattva Avalokiteśvara of the Rokkakudō appeared in the form of a monk whose face was radiant with the beauty of enlightenment and who wore the white cassock of an accomplished and celebrated practitioner. He was seated with a great white lotus at each side, and addressed Zenshin [Shinran] in an authoritative manner. "When due to the retribution of previous karma the practitioner is involved in sexual experience, I will incarnate myself as a striking woman and become the recipient of the act. Helping to bring some beauty to his present life, at the precise moment of his death I will guide him to the Land of Ultimate Happiness." The Bodhisattva Avalokiteśvara [Kannon] offered this to Zenshin [Shinran] — "It is my vow. Zenshin, you shall proclaim the meaning of this vow everywhere, so that every sentient being hears of it."[52]

Eshinni's version is:

> Shinran left Mt. Hiei, remained in retreat for a hundred days at the Rokkakudō, and prayed for the salvation of all beings. Then, on the dawn of the ninety-fifth day, Shōtoku-taishi appeared in a dream, indicating the path to enlightenment by revealing a verse. He immediately left the Rokkakudō in the morning and found the revered master Hōnen to be instructed in the way to salvation. And just as he had confined himself for a hundred days at the Rokkakudō, he visited Hōnen every day for a hundred days, rain or shine and regardless of the obstacles. He heard the master teach that the way to break the bonds of eternal rebirth in one's future lives, regardless of whether a person was good or evil, was simply a single speaking of the nembutsu. The teaching he received penetrated

deeply in his heart, and when others asked about this he would reply that wherever the revered master [Hōnen] would go, regardless of what others might say and even if he would have to cross into ways of evil [i.e. paths to the Buddhist hells] he would follow, because he had already wandered through countless rebirths and that now he had only his delusion to lose.[53]

After a careful comparison of these two passages, the following should be noted. The dream in the *Honganji-shōnin shinran dene* is referred to as the dream *"of* the Rokkakudō" while Eshinni describes it as the dream *"at* the Rokkakudō." It is quite possible that these two accounts may not refer to the same experience, based on a comparative difference in expression and content.   The question arises — how would two distinct dreams be significant to Shinran's life at this time?

The dream described by Eshinni contains Shinran's motivation to begin study and practice under Hōnen for a one-hundred-day period. Eshinni states that the dream's precise content is described in a separate enclosure with her letter, but no such enclosure has ever been discovered. Tatsurō Fujishima suggests the probable content of this nonextant separate enclosure, taking care to avoid unjustified conclusions.   There is a significant verse often found in Shinran's writings about Shōtoku which is given near-iconographic status by Shinran and his early followers.   The verse is usually entitled "Taishi byōkutsu-ge" ("Verse [the Buddhist Chinese version of the Sanskrit gathā form] of the Site of the Prince's Veneration"), and it is found at the end of the *Jōgu-taishi gyoki* ("The Record Honouring the Prince of the Higher Palace [Shōtoku-taishi]").[54] This 'Taishi-byōkutsu-ge' could be what Shōtoku said to Shinran in his dream. It exists today in Shinran's handwriting, and these same words appear as well in slightly varied form in the *Kōtaishi shōtoku hōsan* ("Hymns of Respect to Imperial Prince Shōtoku") which Shinran composed.[55]   Even after Shinran's death this collection of hymns was treasured by early Shin followers. There is also evidence that the Chinese characters of this title expressed special devotion to Shōtoku and were thus often written on his portrait as a devotional practice.

The 'Taishi byōkutsu-ge' is associated by Shinran in various contexts in his writings, such as the following:

> I am the reincarnation of the Bodhisattva Avalokiteśvara in this world, as my wife is the reincarnation of the Bodhisattva Mahāsthāmaprāpta (Japanese: Dai-seishi). The mother who carried and raised me is a reincarnation of the Buddha Amida, the great bearer of compassion. These reincarnations exist to save people in the age of the decay of the Dharma and occur in this place and at this time once again.[56]

The major symbol in this hymn is the Pure Land triad of the Buddha Amida with his two attendant bodhisattvas Avalokiteśvara and

Mahāsthāmaprāpta identified as a family—mother, husband, and wife respectively. Also present is a prevalent theme from Shinran's interpretation of Shōtoku-taishi's ideals, the compassionate response (of the Amida triad) to save all sentiency during the era of the decay of the Dharma.

Up to the time of his Rokkakudō seclusion, Shinran performed dōsō practice and probably reached some degree of scholarly accomplishment in his twenty years of monastic life at Mt. Hiei, but he had not yet experienced the climax of his search as a profound awakening of faith. The type of training he underwent would offer scattered occasions of Pure Land teaching and practice, while any further possibilities for exposure would result from an individual's initiative and cannot readily be surmised. However, Shinran's life and developments of Pure Land thought centre upon the crucial issue of faith over all other Buddhist values and practices, so a 'conversion' to a central belief in the Pure Land would have had to occur at some point. If scant Pure Land resources were available to a Mt. Hiei temple monk, it is not difficult to realize that Shinran was motivated to seek Hōnen's instruction, based on his identification and interpretation of Shōtoku's goals and by his growing interest in the Buddha Amida and the Pure Land. This fundamental conversion experience to Pure Land faith occurred either before he joined Hōnen or as a result of such intense practice under Hōnen. It is in this context that such evidence as the Rokkakudō dream or dreams assumes such importance in the course of Shinran's spiritual development. The dream experience related in Eshinni's letter suggests his motivation to find Hōnen, for it had to be more than a young monk's curiosity that would motivate him to begin such intense study under Hōnen, particularly after a strong philosophical identification with the Buddhist values of Shōtoku-taishi and a great spiritual identification and new-found goals evidenced by the dream.

J. The *Shinran muki* and Shinran's marriage

Did the content of the *Shinran muki* pertain to Shinran's later marriage to Eshinni, an act of great moral and spiritual significance in the history of Japanese Buddhism? It is my opinion that it did, tying in this second momentous step in Shinran's career with the first major step of his converting to Pure Land faith and seeking out Hōnen, as described in the *Shinran muki*. The *Shinran muki* dream resembles what is described in Eshinni's letter about Shinran's turning to Hōnen, but also includes this significant passage:

> When due to the retribution of previous karma the practitioner is involved in sexual experience, I will incarnate myself as a striking woman and become the recipient of the act . . . .

Miyazaki Enjun argues that, because this statement is put in the future tense, Shinran must have not yet married Eshinni.[57] The other point is that, after joining Hōnen's group, Shinran came to realize that Hōnen believed in a universal Buddhism accessible to all laity to the degree of transcending many monastic-lay distinctions, whereas up to this time Shinran himself continued to observe strictly the traditional Tendai monastic practice (including celibacy).

After the one hundred days with Hōnen, Shinran became totally convinced of the immense value of Hōnen's teachings about the Pure Land, that faith in it must take complete priority over all traditional practices for a viable Buddhism to exist in the new era of the decay of the Dharma. Witnessing his master Hōnen's extremely timely interpretation of Buddhist thought and practice amidst the turbulence of Japanese life at the time, Shinran would strenuously question what faith and practice actually meant. It is my opinion that it was this intense questioning of his Buddhist experience in light of newly realized Pure Land teachings that provoked Shinran's dream experience and his fundamental conversion.

K. Hōnen as a Pure Land master

Eshinni's letter describes Shinran's response to Hōnen and his teachings with the following:

> And just as he had confined himself for a hundred days at the Rokkakudō, he visited Hōnen every day for a hundred days, rain or shine and regardless of the obstacles. He heard the master teach that the way to break the bonds of eternal rebirth in one's future lives, regardless of whether a person was good or evil, was simply a single speaking of the nembutsu. The teaching he received penetrated deeply in his heart, and when others asked about this he would reply that wherever the revered master [Hōnen] would go, regardless of what others might say and even if he would have to cross into ways of evil [i.e. the paths of the Buddhist hells] he would follow, because he had already wandered through countless rebirths and that now he had only his ignorance to lose.[58]

Shinran was profoundly inspired by Shōtoku-taishi while practising sanrō as a temple monk and decided to go to Hōnen in the year 1201, for he was already familiar with Hōnen's reputation. At this time Hōnen was sixty-nine, and twenty-six years had passed since Hōnen had begun practising 'senju-nembutsu' ("dedication and invocation of Amida Buddha's name as the sole practice") after his study of Shan-tao's *Kuan-wu-liang-shou-ching-shu* ("Commentary on the *Amitāyur-dhyāna sūtra")*. In the ten years before Shinran joined him in 1201, Hōnen had rapidly established his position as the leading Pure Land advocate by debating Pure Land teachings with the scholar-monks on Mt. Hiei and in Nara. In 1189, Kujō Kanezane (who held the office of kanpaku or the emperor's chief minister in the Kamakura government) was converted to Pure Land Buddhism by Hōnen. In 1190 Hōnen lectured on the three Pure Land sūtras at

Tōdaiji in Nara. In 1191 Kujō Kanezane's daughter, Gishūmonin Tōko, also converted to Pure Land Buddhism and Hōnen wrote a declaration on the founding of a new Japanese Buddhist school, the Jōdo or Pure Land school, then known as the 'Senjaku-hongan nembutsu-shū' ("the School of the Fundamental Vows Chosen [by the Buddha Amida] on the Nembutsu"). Shinran thus joined the group three years after it was founded as a new movement.

What kind of ideological environment existed on Mt. Hiei when he made his decision to follow Hōnen? How did Shinran come to understand Pure Land doctrine and how did he recognize Hōnen's reputation and then decide to study with him? These are questions that must presently be addressed.

It has already been mentioned that Shinran was an ordinary temple monk (dōsō) at the Jōgyō-zanmai-dō when he left Mt. Hiei to find Hōnen. At the time three different Jōgyō-zanmai-dō existed. According to Yūsetsu Fujiwara, these were individually known as Jōgyō-zanmai-in ("Hall of the Dharma of the samādhi of constant practice"), Nishi jōgyō dō ("Western Pavilion of Constant Practice"), and Ryōgon-zanmai-dō ("Pavilion of the Sūraṃgama-samādhi").[59] Shinran had been ordained as a Tendai monk by the Tendai master Jien (1155-1225), and as Yūsetsu Fujiwara has suggested in his conjectures about which specific jōgyō-zanmai-dō Shinran did practise at, Shinran probably kept close contact with Jien when he reached Mt. Hiei.[60] He could well have been a temple monk at Ryōgon-in, where Jien was the kengyō (chief "administrator") and the jōgyōdō attached to it was the Ryōgon-zanmai-dō, where Ryōnin (1073-1132), an early Pure Land pioneer and the founder of the Japanese Yūzū-nembutsu ("All-permeating nembutsu") school, had once lived.[61]

L. Pure Land teachings on Mt. Hiei

The Ryōgon-zanmai-dō may well have been the place where Shinran first heard of Hōnen. Hōnen had studied for six years under the Tendai master Eikū (?-1179), and Eikū had been a major disciple of Ryōnin.[62] This Genshin-Ryōnin-Eikū-Hōnen-Shinran lineage was carried on at the Ryōgon-zanmai-dō (located northeast of Yokawa).[63]

Genshin (942-1017), who himself had lived at Kurodani in Yokawa, was one of the earliest major Japanese Pure Land advocates; he authored the *Ōjō-yō-shū* ("Collection of Essentials for Rebirth [in the Pure Land]"). Shinran regarded Genshin as the true founder of the Japanese Pure Land movement, as can be seen in this *Kyōgyōshinshō* passage:

> Genshin extensively revealed the teachings of the [Buddha's] single lifetime,
> But he preferred to take refuge exclusively in the [Pure Land of] Serene sustenance, recommending this to all.
> His mind firmly grasped the singularity [of the nembutsu]

and the profusion [of the other practices] to
distinguish between the profound and the shallow,
To truly establish through discourse the true Pure Land
and any provisional Buddha-lands.
Those whose evil is the most serious need only call upon
the Buddha [Amida] — I as well exist within his
power,
Even though I cannot see, for my eyes are veiled by
frustration [Sanskrit: kleśa],
The great compassion untiringly shines upon me without
end.[64]

Shinran also wrote in the *Kyōgyōshinshō:*

In terms of all the types of practices toward rebirth in the
Pure Land, the monk Tao-ch'o spoke of them as the
"myriad practices," the monk Shan-tao called them the
"many different acts," and the meditation master Huai-
kan referred to them as the "various practices." The
monk Genshin followed Huai-kan and Genkū [Hōnen]
depended upon Shan-tao.[65]

The preface to the *Kyōgyōshinshō* states:

Thus, I, Gutoku Shinran, a follower of Śākyamuni, indeed
am fortunate to have so luxuriantly received the revered
scriptures from the 'Western lands' [India, as the 'land of
the western barbarians' to the Chinese and Japanese] and
central Asia and all the commentaries of Buddhist
masters from the 'Eastern splendour' [China] and the
'Realm of the sun' [Japan] and to have been able to hear
what is so difficult to know.[66]

Shinran emphasized his study of the writings of the great Indian
Mahāyāna and Chinese Pure Land masters such as Nāgārjuna and
Vasubandhu, T'an-luan, Tao-ch'o, Shan-tao, etc. while he had been a
temple monk on Mt. Hiei. He certainly recognized their essential
contributions to the development of Pure Land thought within the
entire Buddhist tradition and also his debt to their ideas in the
evolution of his own Pure Land thought.
Shinran recognized not only an intellectual debt to the Buddhist
tradition but also a striking emotional obligation which both placed
him solidly within the tradition and hinted at his growing emphasis
upon faith as his central attitude as a Buddhist:

Thus, I, Gutoku Shinran, a follower of Śākyamuni, in
inheriting the śāstra masters' [Nāgārjuna and Vasubandhu]
explanations of meaning and the inspiration of the [Pure
Land] masters [T'an-luan, Tao-ch'o and Shan-tao] have
left forever any provisional approach based on the myriad

practices and the various positive actions, and have been separated eternally from any rebirth under the twin sala trees [from any rebirth in a Buddha-land through self-effort and positive or merit-producing actions], and have been converted to the true approach of roots in goodness and virtue, preferring to give rise to the inconceivable heart of [true] rebirth. Yet having now separated myself in particular from any temporarily manifested attraction to the true approach [due to the creative response of upāya], I have turned to the vast waters of the chosen vows [of Amida]. Having far separated myself from an inconceivable heart of rebirth that in any way could desire to [intellectually] follow the inconceivable or could deliberate about this rebirth, the result that will follow my dedication has its source in goodness.[67]

Hōnen left Mt. Hiei at the age of forty-three, began his movement of monks in the Higashiyama area of Kyoto in 1175, and started preaching about the nembutsu. Hōnen had left Mt. Hiei before Shinran joined his movement, but it does appear likely that Shinran was aware of Hōnen's Senju-nembutsu group before he himself left Mt. Hiei.

Hōnen's major disciples, who inherited his teachings and further developed his Pure Land movement, were Shinkū (1146-1228), the leader of the Shirakawa monto; Genchi (1183-1238), the leader of the Murasakino monto; Shōkō (1162-1238), the founder of the Chinzei-ha; Shōkū (1177-1247), the founder of the Seizan-ha; Chōsai (1184-1261), the leader of the Shogyō Hongangi; Kōsai (1163-1247), the leader of the Ichinengi; Ryūkan (1148-1227), the leader of the Tanengi, and Shinran (who would found the 'Jōdo Shin' or "True Pure Land" school). They all became Hōnen's disciples after 1190, when Hōnen was fifty-eight years old, and they had all followed the course of his ideas for the fifteen years after he had left Mt. Hiei to live at Yoshimizu, east of Kyoto. Shinran must have had an early exposure to Hōnen's teaching and joined him upon leaving Mt. Hiei, because he knew Hōnen's *Senju-nembutsu* so thoroughly that he could copy his master's work from memory only four years after he had joined the movement.

Shinran's gradual awareness of Hōnen and his teachings during his residence at Mt. Hiei has been suggested. Part of such awareness was a major phase of Shinran's own spiritual development—an intense frustration at his mastery of Tendai teachings and several kinds of practice while feeling devoid of any meaningful spiritual experience from his Tendai life. Hōnen's teachings, as we shall see, would appear exceedingly attractive to one who lived within this type of contradiction. Moreover, Shinran's ideal of Shōtoku-taishi inspired him to extricate himself from this contradiction because he saw Shōtoku as a great Japanese Buddhist whose sincere Buddhist faith in response to the Japanese people paralleled Shinran's own sensitivity and which would eventually lead him to the very heart of Pure Land thought and practice. In many ways Shōtoku influenced Shinran's decision to leave Mt. Hiei and follow Hōnen.

Saichō's 'convergence of time and opportunity' (jiki sōō) had strongly influenced the thinking of many who sensed the decay of the Dharma on Mt. Hiei, and it would soon form the nexus of Japanese Pure Land teaching as well. When Shinran lived on Mt. Hiei, he was both immersed in Saichō's teachings and intensely practised the Dharma of the samādhi on the nembutsu (nembutsu-zanmai no hō) already established there.

The Pure Land Buddhist doctrine and practice present on Mt. Hiei would be combined with the Tendai 'convergence of time and opportunity' doctrine by Shinran, toward his own major Pure Land doctrine of the pre-eminence of faith in the Buddha Amida over any and all other kinds of action in a viable Buddhist life.

Chapter 2 Notes

1. Tatsunosuke Ōno, <u>Nihon bukkyō shisōshi</u> (Tokyo: Yoshikawa Kōbunkan, 1961), p. 90.

2. Taishun Mibu, <u>Eizan no shimpū</u>, volume 3 of <u>Nihon no bukkyō</u> (Tokyo: Chikuma Shobō, 1967), p. 30.

3. <u>Dengyō-daishi zenshū</u>, vol. 1 (Tokyo: Tendai-shū shūten kankōkai, 1912), p. 41. For Fa-tsang's <u>Ta-ch'eng ch'i-hsin-lun-i-chi</u>, see <u>Taishō</u> 44:1846, pp. 240-286.

4. Tsuneyuki Kawasaki and Kazuo Kasahara, <u>Shūkyōshi</u> (Tokyo: Yamakawa Shuppan, 1964), p. 52.

5. Ibid., p. 54.

6. See <u>Taishō</u> 9:262, pp. 1-62; and for an English translation, see Leon Hurvitz, trans., <u>Scripture of the Lotus Blossom of the Fine Dharma</u> (New York: Columbia University Press, 1976).

7. Mibu, op. cit., p. 89.

8. The eight noted monks sent to China by the court government in the early Heian period were Saichō, Kūkai, Engyō, Jōgyō, Ennin, Eun, Enchin, and Shūei. None of them had found any facilities for studying the spoken Chinese language before their departure, and their terms of study in China were generally too short for them to learn to speak Chinese competently. They communicated with Chinese monks primarily by using the written language. Consequently their main concern involved collecting Buddhist scripture and ritual implements instead of conversing or being instructed in Buddhist doctrine. Saichō was the only one to take an interpreter with him, although Kūkai possessed a remarkable brilliance in (written) classical Chinese. The eight monks did admit their shortcomings at oral communication, for one of them stated: "I could write Chinese but was unable to speak it. Thus when I had a question to ask I would write it down." Another said, "I could not speak the Chinese language but could write it. I had paper brought to me (whenever I wanted to ask a question) and would write it out." See Hajime Nakamura, <u>Tōyōjin no shii-hōhō</u>, vol. 3 (Tokyo: Shunjūsha, 1960), p. 6.

9. Tadashi Hashikawa, <u>Nihon bukkyōshi</u> (Tokyo: Kokushi kōza kankōkai, 1933), p. 67.

10. Mibu, op. cit., p. 91.

11. The decay of the Dharma doctrine (mappō) was the third phase of the Three Periods of the Dharma theory, which first appeared in the writings of such Chinese Buddhist monks as Pei-ch'i Hui-szu's (515-577) <u>Nan-yüeh-szu chan-shih li-shih yüan-wen</u> and Hsin-hsing's (540-

594) School of the Three Stages (san-chieh-tsung). This Three-Periods theory consisted of three distinct periods in the evolution of Buddhism, characterized by the religious effectiveness of Buddhist teachings and practices and by the possibility of achieving enlightenment. The effectiveness of these three criteria was combined with estimates of duration to produce the three periods:

1) the Period of the Complete and True Dharma (beginning with the career of the Buddha) where the teachings, practices, and possibility of enlightenment existed in full;

2) the subsequent Period of the Artificial Dharma, where teachings and practice existed as before but the possibility of enlightenment was absent;

3) the subsequent Period of the Decay of the Dharma, where only teachings still exist but practice and enlightenment have disappeared. Based on whatever scriptural sources extant gave as the dates of the Buddha's life (usually historically inaccurate), the length of these three periods would then be calculated. There were four simple theories on their length.

Period	Complete and True Dharma	Artificial Dharma	Decay of the Dharma
Theory 1	500 years (from the Buddha's parinirvāna)	next 1000 years	next 10,000 years
Theory 2	1000 years (from the Buddha's parinirvāna)	next 500 years	next 10,000 years
Theory 3	500 years (from the Buddha's parinirvāna)	next 500 years	next 10,000 years
Theory 4	1000 years (from the Buddha's parinirvāna)	next 1000 years	next 10,000 years

Based on the traditional Chinese reckoning of the parinirvāna as having occurred around 950 B.C., the most popular theory (number 4) led reformist Kamakura Buddhist masters to calculate the decay of the Dharma to have begun from roughly 1050 A.D.

12. Shugo kokkai-shō ("Chapter on Protecting the Nation"), in Dengyō-daishi zenshū, ibid., vol. 2, p. 342.

13. See Jiei-daishi-den in Zoku-gunsho-ruijū, vol. 8, part 2 (Tokyo: Zoku-gunsho-ruijū kanseikai, 1904), pp. 683-699.

14. See Kubon-ōjō-gi in Dai-nihon bukkyō zensho, vol. 24 (Kyoto:

Dainihon bukkyō zensho kankōkai, 1910-1922).

15. Jiei-daishi-den, op. cit., pp. 741-742.

16. See Kanjin ryakuyō-shū in Dai-nihon bukkyō zensho, op. cit., vol. 31.

17. In a verse praising his master Hōnen for his efforts in spreading Pure Land Buddhism throughout Japan, Shinran characterized Japan as the "distant islands":
Genkū [Hōnen], the master of the [Jōdo] school—well-versed in the teachings of the Buddha
Pitying the ordinary person—whether good or bad,
He spread the teachings of the true [Pure Land] school throughout the distant islands.
He propagated the Fundamental Vows Chosen [by the Buddha Amida] in this world of evil.
Shōshin nembutsu ge, Shinran-shōnin zenshū, vol. 1, p. 90.

18. Toshihide Akamatsu, Zoku-kamakura bukkyō no kenkyu (Kyoto: Heirakuji Shoten, 1966), p. 32.

19. This letter was discovered by Kyōdō Washio only in 1921. The Shin school has known little of the first twenty-nine years of life of its founder until the recent age of modern historical scholarship. And after seven and a half centuries since Shinran, it is nearly impossible to develop a solid and complete factual account. See Eshinni monjo, no. 3, Shinran-shōnin zenshū, vol. 3, p. 186.

20. Ibid., p. 187.

21. Sokusui Murakami, Shinran dokuhon (Kyoto: Hyakkaen, 1968), p. 16.

22. See 'Hyōhan-ki' entry for September 24, 1167, in Shiryō-taisei, vol. 20 (Kyoto: Rinsen Shoten, 1965), p. 265; and 'Shōu-ki' entry for October 29, 988, in Shiryō-taisei, vol. S-1, pp. 80-81.

23. Haruki Kageyama, Hieizan (Tokyo: Kadokawa Shoten, 1960), p. 104.

24. Paul Groner, Saichō—The establishment of the Japanese Tendai school (Berkeley: Berkeley Buddhist studies series, 1984), pp. 65-76.

25. Tetsuei Satō, Tendai-daishi no kenkyū (Kyoto: Hyakkaen, 1961), pp. 364-401.

26. Shindai Sekiguchi, Tendai shikan no kenkyū (Tokyo: Iwanami Shoten, 1969), pp. 143-158.

27. Eshinni monjo, no. 3, Shinran-shōnin zenshū, vol. 3, pp. 186-187.

28. Shinran muki, Shinran-shōnin zenshū, vol. 4, p. 201.

29. Shinran's wasan concerning Shōtoku-taishi are gathered in the following collections:
    a) 11 wasan subtitled 'Kō-taishi shōtoku hōsan' ("Hymns of Respect to Imperial Prince Shōtoku") in his wasan collection entitled

Shōzōmatsu-wasan ("Hymns on the Complete and True Dharma,
Artificial Dharma and the Decay of the Dharma"), Shinran-shōnin
zenshū, vol. 2, pp. 157-225;
       b) 75 wasan entitled Kō-taishi shōtoku hōsan ("Hymns of
Respect to Imperial Prince Shōtoku"), Shinran-shōnin zenshū, vol. 2,
pp. 229-248;
       c) 104 wasan entitled Dai-nipponkoku zoku-san-o shōtoku-taishi
hōsan ("Hymns of Respect to Prince Shōtoku, Ruler of the Great
Japanese Nation as the Land of Scattered Grain [the small size of
Japan in contrast to the large areas of India and China]"), Shinran-
shōnin zenshū, vol. 2, pp. 251-284.

30. Mizumaro Ishida contends that Shōtoku possessed little
knowledge of Pure Land teachings: "It is not possible to find a faith
in the Buddha Amida in the Prince's beliefs. It is true that some
mention of the Buddha Amida is present in the Lotus sūtra and
Shōtoku did write a commentary on this scripture, but there is no
comment whatsoever in the "Yakuō bosatsu honji-bon" ("The Former
Affairs of the Bodhisattva 'Medicine King'"—Chapter 23) regarding
this sutra which teaches that a female could be born to paradise. It
can be said that the prince lacked sufficient knowledge of Pure Land
teachings rather than to conclude that he possessed no belief in
them." Mizumaro Ishida, Jōdokyō no tenkai (Tokyo: Shunjūsha,
1965), p. 51.

31. When Empress Suiko acceded to the throne in 593, Shōtoku-taishi
co-operated with the chief court administrative officer, the grand
minister Soga no Umako to order the nation more securely by
adopting Chinese political and cultural ideology, including the use of
general Mahāyāna Buddhist doctrine. In order to bring Chinese Sui
dynasty Buddhist culture into Japan, they began the dispatch of a
Japanese emissary to the Sui court (kenzui-shi). This act was the
first diplomatic effort since that of Emperor Yūryaku a century
before, and it signalled the re-establishment of direct Japanese-
Chinese foreign relations. See Kōjirō Naoki, "Kodai kokka no
seiritsu" in Nihon rekishi, vol. 2 (Tokyo: Chūōkōronsha, 1962), p. 92.
       It was soon after Shōtoku's death in the year 623 that the monk
Esai and four others returned from China; in 632 the monastic
Nichimon came back, and the lay student Takamaku no Ayahito
Kuromaro returned to Japan in 640. Thus the fruit of Shōtoku's
endeavours began to appear, but only after his death. See Saburō
Ienaga, "Asuka-hakuhō bunka" in Nihon rekishi (Tokyo: Iwanami
Shoten, 1962), pp. 321-327.

32. Shōmangyō gisho ("Commentary on the Srīmāladevi sūtra"),
Taishō 56:2185, pp. 1-19; Yuimakyō gisho ("Commentary on the
Vimalakīrti sūtra"), Taishō 56:2186, pp. 20-63; Hokke gisho
("Commentary on the Lotus sūtra"), Taishō 56: 2187, pp. 64-129.

33. Kōjun Fukui, "Sangyōgisho no seiriesu-o utagau," Indo-gaku
bukkyō-gaku kenkyū 4:2 (1961), pp. 1-13.

34. Quoted in Saburō Ienaga, Nihon shisōshi ni okeru hitei no ronri no

hattatsu (Tokyo: Shinsensha, 1969), p. 41.

35. Ibid.

36. Daianji-garan engi, quoted in Tatsurō Fujishima and Shunsei Nogami, eds., Dentō no seija (Kyoto: Hyakkaen, 1961), p. 277.

37. Ibid., p. 278.

38. Ibid.

39. Nihon-shoki, quoted in Hashikawa, op. cit., p. 18.

40. Kyōgyōshinshō, Shinran-shōnin zenshū, vol. 1, p. 153.

41. Shinran wrote over 500 hymns (wasan) during his lifetime, 307 of which are dedicated to eight specific individuals. As already mentioned, 190 are about Shōtoku-taishi, whereas the other 120 or so are dedicated to the seven patriarchs of the Pure Land movement: Nāgārjuna (10 wasan), Vasubandhu (10), T'an-luan (34), Tao-ch'o (7), Shan-tao (26), Genshin (10), and Hōnen (20).

42. Found in the Senjuji collection, Mie prefecture, and in Shinran-shōnin zenshū, vol. 4, pp. 201-202. The title "Shinran muki" was given to the piece by later historians, not by Shinran.

43. Akamatsu, op. cit., pp. 78-85. Most of Shinran's writing was done between the ages of fifty-two and eighty-eight.

44. Shinran's statement is: ". . . Shinran, abandoned the sundry acts and took refuge in the Original vow in the Kanoto no tori year of Kennin [A.D. 1201]. In the Kinoto no ushi year of Genkyū [A.D. 1205], I copied his Senjaku shū . . ." Kyōgyōshinshō, Shinran-shōnin zenshū, vol. 1, pp. 381-382.

45. Since Shimbutsu died when Shinran was eighty-six years old, it is very likely that the copy Shimbutsu made of Shinran's account is accurate. See Reizō Hiramatsu, "Takada hōko shin-hakken shiryō ni yoru shiron," Takada gakuhō, no. 46 (1959), pp. 14-24.

46. Shinran-shōnin zenshū, vol. 4, p. 201.

47. Honganji-shōnin shinran dene, chapter 3 entitled "Rokkaku musō" ("Rokkakudō Dream"), in Shinran-shōnin zenshū, vol. 4, p. 201.

48. Kyōgyōshinshō in Shinran-shōnin zenshū, vol. 1, p. 381.

49. Matsuno, op. cit., p. 72. Note that each of these three copies has points of authenticity and inaccuracy. Although the Nishi-honganji and Senjuji copies were made at a very early date, they are still copies and not Kakunyo's original. If these copies were made in the same period, it is probable that they are true to the original and no serious problems should exist. It appears that the two copies were made in the same year as the original was written, but there are indications that some additions and corrections were inserted in the years that followed. The Higashi-honganji copy is supposed to be a copy made by Kakunyo himself from his original but approximately fifty years after the original was written. Kakunyo's copy is in his

own handwriting, but contradictions are found in content here as well. Kyōgyōshinshō, Shinran-shōnin zenshū. vol. 1, p. 811.

50. The sexagenary cycle which is used in the Chinese calendar is a combination of ten celestial stem signs and twelve horary signs and gives a name to each year. According to this method, the year with the same name recurs every sixty years. The year A.D. 1203, thus calculated, is the year of Kigai and not Shinyū, invariably an error made by Kakunyo in his Honganji-shōnin shinran dene.

51. Eshinni monjo, no. 3, Shinran-shōnin zenshū, vol. 3, p. 187.

52. Honganji-shōnin shinran dene, Shinran-shōnin zenshū, vol. 4, p. 187.

53. Eshinni monjo, no. 8, Shinran-shōnin zenshū, vol. 3, p. 201.

54. Tatsurō Fujishima, "Shōtoku-taishi to shinran-shōnin," Nihon bukkyō gakkai nempō, no. 29 (1963), pp. 265-282.

55. Kō-taishi-shōtoku hōsan, Shinran-shōnin zenshū, vol. 2, p. 229.

56. Taishi-byōkutsu-ge, Shinran-shōnin zenshū, vol. 6, p. 213.

57. Enjun Miyazaki, Shinran to sono montei (Kyoto: Nagata Bunshōdō, 1951), p. 26.

58. Eshinni monjo, no. 3, Shinran-shōnin zenshū, vol. 3, p. 187.

59. Yūsetsu Fujiwara, Shinshūshi kenkyū (Tokyo: Daitō Shuppan, 1939), p. 14.

60. Fujiwara, op. cit., p. 95.

61. Junkō Matsuno, Shinran (Tokyo: Sanseidō, 1959), p. 2.

62. Zennosuke Tsuji, Nihon bukkyō-shi 2:1 (Tokyo: Iwanami Shoten, 1960), p. 29.

63. Matsuno, op. cit., p. 3.

64. Kyōgyōshinshō, Shinran-shōnin zenshū, vol. 1, p. 90.

65. Ibid., p. 291.

66. Ibid., p. 7.

67. Ibid., p. 309.   Shinran completed his review of both the true approach and "any temporarily-manifested" (provisional) approaches to the Pure Land in the first five chapters and the preceding sections of this chapter in the Kyōgyōshinshō. At this point he is looking back at the process that he had undergone to reach the Other-power teaching of the Buddha Amida's eighteenth vow (from his earlier self-effort practice as a Tendai temple monk).   The process consists of three stages culled from the three Pure Land sūtras, as follows:
    a) the Essential approach of the nineteenth vow of the Buddha Amida toward rebirth under the twin sala trees (i.e., the explicit teachings of the Amitāyur-dhyāna sūtra);
    b) the true approach of the twentieth vow of the Buddha Amida

toward incomprehensible rebirth (i.e., the explicit teachings of the Smaller Sukhāvatī-vyūha sūtra);

c) the approach of the universal or eighteenth vow of the Buddha Amida (i.e., the teachings of the Larger Sukhāvatī-vyūha sūtra).

These three vows are together called the sangan-tennyū or "turning to the three vows," denoting a progressive conversion from nineteenth to twentieth to eighteenth vows as the fundamental process in leaving any reliance on or faith in self-effort and truly, thoroughly accomplishing complete faith in Other-power (the power of the Buddha Amida as the sole source of salvation).

Chapter 3

Shinran as Honen's Disciple

A. Hōnen and his teachings

Hōnen was one of the first Japanese Buddhist masters to attempt to secure an independent status for the Pure Land movement in Japan, and he himself named this new movement the Pure Land school (Jōdo-shū).[1] He realized that any effort to establish a new school within the environment of conservative, institutionalized Japanese Buddhism would require a sophisticated rationale of justification. He went back to Chinese Buddhist history to develop and apply the chiao-p'an (Japanese: kyō-han) concept of doctrinal evaluation and classification. This ahistorical-critical-doctrinal apparatus had been developed by the founders of Chinese Buddhist schools to justify their teachings and practices, and it came to be the major tool applied when a new school was founded.[2] Doctrinal evaluation and classification involved the founder of a new school carefully placing his ideas within the history of Buddhist thought and practice and establishing their relation to the scriptural sources of the Buddha's teachings. It consisted of establishing new teachings within the context of the Buddhist tradition and its major values, indicating not only that a new system was a logical emergence from prevalent doctrine but also that the religious tone or atmosphere of the new was consistent with and respectable to all major movements of the tradition. A founder either ranked prominent doctrine in an evolutionary categorization tied to specific types of scripture or categorized and structured kinds of doctrine and practice in a manner that indicated the need for the new teachings.

This was not the first time that a Japanese Buddhist had applied the kyō-han concept, for Kūkai (774-835), the founder of the Japanese Shingon ("True Word") school, had used it skilfully during the Heian period to introduce tantric Buddhist thought and practice to Japan. However, Hōnen's application of doctrinal evaluation and classification took place during the transition from the classical court society of the Nara and Heian periods to the new mediaeval warrior society of the Kamakura period, when a changing social environment had drastically affected religious needs and the existential significance of the decay of the Dharma thought was strongly realized in the hearts of many Japanese Buddhists.

Hōnen's basic teachings are described in his major work, the *Senjaku-hongan nembutsu-shū* ("Collection of the Fundamental Vows Chosen [by the Buddha Amida] on the Nembutsu"). He began this text with the nembutsu itself ('namu amida-butsu'—"Praise and dedication to the Buddha Amida") to show its central position in his

movement.   Hōnen systematized Buddhist writings by dividing them
into three categories according to their function in the history of
Buddhist thought—a sūtra category (kyō), a sāstra category (ron), and
a commentary category (shaku).   With this categorical philosophical
structure, Hōnen systematically examined the doctrines of the texts
and schools he classified.   After subjecting them to doctrinal
analysis, he found them wanting as viable possibilities in the era of
the decay of the Dharma, proposing in their place the practice of the
nembutsu as the only Buddhist path.   He called his philosophical and
spiritual process of evaluation and qualification "discarding, closing
off, sealing up and abandoning" (sha-hei-kaku-hō), and its conclusion
was a total dedication to nembutsu practice toward Pure Land
rebirth, to the exclusion of all other teachings and practices.[3]   Hōnen
developed additional categorical structures to make this process
more apparent.   He first divided all of Buddhism into two approaches,
the "Approach to the Revered Path" (shōdō-mon) and the "Approach
to the Pure Land" (jōdo-mon).   The former he characterized as
traditional Buddhism based upon self-effort (jiriki) which emphasized
the individual practice of good actions to develop positive karma and
better rebirths or systematic meditation toward enlightenment.   He
found self-effort to be futile in the era of the decay of the Dharma
and then concentrated on carefully defining the Approach to the Pure
Land.   This Approach to the Pure Land was viewed as two distinct
kinds of practice—True practice (shōgyō) and other practices.[4]   True
practice was divided into five kinds: sūtra recitation; meditation on
the Buddha Amida, his attendant bodhisattvas and the Pure Land;
worship of the Buddha Amida; chanting the nembutsu; making
offerings to the Buddha Amida.[5]   These five true practices were
selected as the most appropriate exercises because they could be
easily observed by all kinds of people during the era of the decay of
the Dharma.   Hōnen finally arranged these five true practices into
two groups, so that four of them were made supplementary to the
central act of chanting the nembutsu (shōmyō), which he saw as the
major way a practitioner could reach the power of Amida's
compassion and virtue (as found in Amida's forty-eight vows) to
attain Pure Land rebirth.[6]

   Such major doctrines are found in Hōnen's *Senjaku-hongan*
nembutsu-shū, but they are actually elaborations on teachings of two
great Chinese Pure Land masters, Tao-ch'o and his disciple Shan-tao.
Tao-ch'o's doctrine was termed the "Distinction of the Two
Approaches—the Revered and the Pure Land" (Shêng-ching erh-men-
p'an; Japanese: shōjō nimon-han).   These Chinese Pure Land masters
saw traditional Buddhism as the revered approach of gradual practice
through numerous rebirths of self-effort, while the Pure Land
approach was described as the "sudden teaching of the singular
vehicle" (tun-chiao i-ch'eng; Japanese: tongyō ichijō) by them.   It is
sudden because Pure Land rebirth is achieved instantaneously, and it
is of the singular vehicle (ekayāna) because it is accessible to all
sentient beings.   Hōnen followed Tao-ch'o and Shan-tao's teachings
but basically streamlined these by emphasizing both the ease and
paramount efficacy of nembutsu practice.   Nembutsu practice thus

became his own lifetime effort and his solution for all Japanese religious needs of the times. His spiritual stance led him to develop a vigorous critique of all the Buddhism he viewed as based on self-effort and which emphasized the cumulative attainment of Buddhist wisdom as the fundamental prerequisite for spiritual rebirth.

Hōnen explains in his work why the nembutsu is essential for salvation but includes little about nembutsu practice itself. He also neglected to explain the relation between action, good or harmful, and its effect on the desire to be reborn in the Pure Land through nembutsu practice. What he does state on this important issue is found in his *Kuroda no hijiri-ni nokosu-sho* ("Text Bequeathed by the Holy Man of Kuroda"):

> Whether you may be a habitual and serious wrongdoer or have an occasional light fault, and though you may already know you will be saved, remember not to commit even the most minor of misdeeds. Yet even wrongdoers, whether their offense be serious or not, can be reborn into the Pure Land.
> Chant the nembutsu as many times as possible, although you may become certain that a mere one time or ten times is sufficient. Even though the utterance of a simple one time or ten times is enough for salvation, there is no doubt about the salvation of a person who has uttered the nembutsu a great many times.[7]

From his words, it is not clear how frequent nembutsu chanting can influence salvation in light of human good and malevolence. Hōnen himself was very open-minded with regard to the frequency and quality of nembutsu practice. It was apparently beyond conventional morality:

> Do not be bothered by the standards of the world—live by chanting the nembutsu.
> If you are ordained as a monk and are unable to utter the nembutsu, take a wife and say the invocation. If you are married and unable to chant the nembutsu, join the monastic life and say the invocation.[8]

Hōnen remained a monk and recited the nembutsu seventy thousand times daily. Since there was no definitive regulation on the frequency of nembutsu chanting or moral discussion of the relationship between action and Pure Land salvation, some confusion did arise among those who had not carefully considered his teachings, often leading to a severe moral dilemma concerning an irreparable dichotomy (action versus nembutsu practice) in his teachings.

B. Hōnen's estimation of Shinran

The courage of Shinran's decision to turn to Hōnen has been suggested. He described this decision in his *Kyōgyōshinshō:*

> I, Gutoku Shinran, abandoned the [self-effort way of] myriad actions and took refuge in the Fundamental Vows [of the Buddha Amida] in the Kanoto no tori year of Kennin (1201).[9]

His disciples later wrote of this decision, quoting his words:

> To those who practise the nembutsu exclusively and wholeheartedly, the turning of the heart occurs only once. The turning of the heart takes place when one who has previously been of the Fundamental Vows now realizes, by being endowed with the wisdom of the Buddha Amida, that rebirth cannot be attained with his own mind and heart which he has always cherished so strongly. Thus he converts this normal heart to trust in the Fundamental Vows. This is really what the turning of the heart means.[10]

Shinran firmly believed that true spiritual conversion is a religious experience which can happen only once in a person's lifetime.

> As for me, Shinran, there is nothing left but to receive and believe the teachings of the revered master [Hōnen]—that we are saved by the Buddha Amida simply through the chanting of the nembutsu. . . . I will have no regrets even though I may have been deceived by Hōnen and by thus uttering the nembutsu, I may fall into the hells. . . . If the Fundamental Vows of the Buddha Amida are true, then Śākyamuni's sermons cannot be untrue. If the Buddha's words are true, then Shan-tao's comments cannot be untrue. If Shan-tao's comments are true, then how can what Hōnen has said be false?[11]

This is Shinran's later response to his disciple's questions about how to attain Pure Land rebirth. Besides expressing his own ideas, he refers to those of Hōnen at least three times. The nature of this master-disciple relationship begins to emerge, and the course of the development of Shinran's own thought in terms of Hōnen's guidance can be more fully appreciated if it is noted that Hōnen permitted Shinran to copy his writings and subsequently honoured him by writing the title sections to his copy manuscript. This could have happened only in a situation of complete harmony between master and disciple.

Shinran describes his life as a member of Hōnen's movement when he wrote the *Kyōgyōshinshō*, in his later years:

In the second year of Genkyū (1205), with the master's permission I copied his *Senjaku-hongan nembutsu-shū.* On the fourth day in early mid-summer in that year, the master Genkū [Hōnen] kindly wrote the following title phrases on the inside of my copy: "Senjaku-hongan nembutsu-shū," "Namu Amida-butsu," "Namu Amida-butsu ōjō shigō nembutsu i hon" ["The Source for the Process of Pure Land Rebirth is the Nembutsu"], and "shaku-Shakkū" [the Buddhist "Shakkū"—Hōnen's own name for Shinran]. On this same day I borrowed the master's portrait and copied it. On the ninth day of the seventh month in this same year, he [Hōnen] wrote the following words on it: "Namu Amida-butsu" and "If after I [the Buddha Amida] have attained Buddhahood, the sentient beings of the ten directions should pronounce my name—making even as few as ten utterances—and if they are not reborn [in the Pure Land], may I never attain complete and perfect enlightenment (anuttara-samyak-sambodhi). He [who said this] has now achieved Buddhahood [as the Buddha Amida]. You should realize that his fundamental vows have never been untrue. Any sentient being who utters the nembutsu will unfailingly attain rebirth in the Pure Land." On the same day he also wrote my new name "Zenshin" on the portrait according to the revelation in my dream, and this is how my former name Shakkū was changed. The master was then seventy-three years old.[12]

Shinran copied Hōnen's work and painted his portrait, which Hōnen signed as a gesture of approval. One can begin to realize the significance of this experience by considering a Ch'an and Zen school practice known as shih-tzu siang-ch'êng (Japanese: shishi sōjō, "master-disciple transmission").

Master-disciple transmission involves the passing on of a tradition's authentic lineage from master to disciple, a pedagogical experience which apparently originated in ancient India.[13] One often comes across a reference in a Chinese or Japanese biography to the effect that he made up his mind at the age of such and such, became a disciple of the master so and so, studied for many years, and finally left. This process of becoming a disciple, with long-term study, practice, and eventual departure, signifies the intensity of the traditional master-disciple relationship. In a mediaeval Western sense, this would mean the disciple as religious, artistic, or craft apprentice, not only attending a master's lectures, but also living daily life in the closest exposure to the master and his teachings. Hōnen constantly observed, evaluated, and guided Shinran's ideas and behaviour in the traditional master-disciple manner. After many years of the disciple learning the master's teachings in word and witnessing them in action, a master would eventually discuss his teachings and their ramifications with the disciple, much as a testing experience and review. When a disciple's questions were exhausted and discussion completed, a master usually recommended either that

the disciple find a teacher different or greater than himself or that
the disciple now continue to practise on his own. At this point the
master would either give or allow his disciple to make a daiken
("model text"), a copy of the master's major work which the disciple
had laboured to learn for the majority of his discipleship. Sometimes
a disciple would then return to his birth place and open his own
practice or school or he might go on to study with a new master by
recommendation and introduction from his former master. Within
the context of the master-disciple relationship, a master allowing a
disciple to copy his work took on the formal significance that the
master was fully confident of his disciple's abilities in properly
carrying on his ideas and methods. The daiken implies that the
disciple has received his master's trust through his demonstration of
personal devotion, sincerity, and aptitude to continue the lineage of
his master's tradition.

Hōnen's *Senjaku-hongan nembutsu-shū* was written at the
request of his patron Kujō Kanezane, and as a radically new technical
examination of Buddhist doctrine, it was not meant to be widely read.
"Once read, let it lie tucked away from the eyes of others"—still this
was not a legendary statement made from any motive of exclusion or
secrecy:

> In order for those who do not easily comprehend the
> doctrines of Buddhism not to fall into evil ways . . .[14]

It was clearly a difficult work intended for long-term disciples and
serious initiates. The *Senjaku-hongan nembutsu-shū* strongly
criticized both the rationale and the actual effectiveness of past and
then-contemporary Japanese Buddhism. It also disputed a great many
accepted teachings in the Buddhist tradition. For this reason Hōnen
permitted only those disciples who truly comprehended his ideas and
goals to study and copy the manuscript. The work was not revealed
to the public before his death, and only six of his disciples—Kōsai,
Benchō, Ryūkan, Shōkū, Chōsai, and Shinran—were allowed to copy
it.[15] Deeply conscious of the importance of the master-disciple
transmission and the honour bestowed on him by Hōnen, Shinran
wrote of this experience of copying his master's work in moving
terms:

> Out of the thousands of people who received his
> teachings, personally or in other ways over so many days
> and years, very few were ever allowed to read and copy
> his book. Yet I was allowed to copy the text and also his
> portrait.[16]

One may also conclude from this statement that Shinran saw this
transmission as a spiritual relationship which he believed assured him
rebirth in the Pure Land. Joyful gratitude would constantly surface
in his writings, and was responsible for the strengthening of the
master-disciple bond and the importance of Pure Land advocacy.

C. Shinran's views of his relationship with Hōnen

Five months before he copied Hōnen's *Senjaku-hongan nembutsu-shū*, Shinran had already demonstrated his sincerity and faithfulness as a major disciple in Hōnen's movement. On November 7, 1204, Hōnen decided to answer charges made by the Tendai school monastic headquarters at Enryakuji on Mt. Hiei. The Enryakuji monastic office had sent Hōnen a warning that "the behaviour of Hōnen and his disciples as Buddhist monks has become outrageous."[17] Hōnen received these charges and invited all of his disciples to join him in signing a statement of reply. This statement is known as the previously mentioned Seven Article Pledge (Shichikajō no kishōmon), and its purpose was to defend his Pure Land movement's advocacy and the propagation of nembutsu practice.

In signing the pledge, Shinran used the name "the monk Shakkū" (sō-Shakkū). This signature with the prefix *sō* ("the monk") has often been taken as evidence which proves that Shinran had not yet married Eshinni.[18] The conclusion was reached simply because the term *sō* designates a fully ordained monastic. Yet Hōnen's disciples Shinkū and Shōkū, who strictly observed monastic regulations and were considered among the most pious of his followers, did not prefix their signatures with the term *the monk*. Of the 193 monks who did put their signatures to the Seven Article Pledge within a three-day period, there were nine, including Shinran, who signed with the prefix *the monk*.[19] The biographies of these other eight monks who signed their names in this manner are somewhat uncertain, but one point should be noted: the prefixed signatures are concentrated in a single section of the pledge statement. Sonren's signature appears as the first of those written in this way, on the second day (and the eighty-first of the total signatures), followed by those of Sonren, Senun, Kengan, Busshin, Saijun, Ryōshin, Shakkū [Shinran], and Zenren, all of which included the prefix. The ninth and last prefixed signature is Keien's, which appears on the third day (as signature 183).

One cannot conclude that the prefixed signatures indicate any special or advanced degree of acknowledged accomplishment or spiritual ability. Junkō Matsuno notes that it may only have been a matter of copying the style of the signature of those immediately preceding one's own.[20] This small matter of a prefixed signature does hold greater significance when Shinran's motives and goals are taken into consideration. He writes in the *Kyōgyōshinshō*:

> Thus I have taken the true teachings and explained them, collecting the essentials of the Pure Land. I can only think of the profoundness of the Buddha's concern, yet feeling no shame at any constant ridicule by people. If someone reads or hears this text [Shinran's *Kyōgyōshinshō*]—either by the primary cause which is tied to faith [in the Pure Land] or by indirect reasons that provoke doubt and abuse [concerning the Pure Land]—to that person trust in the happiness [of the Pure Land] will be manifested by the power of the vows [of the Buddha

Amida] and the mysteries in the result [of the Pure Land
rebirth] will be revealed by the nourishment of peace
[that is the Pure Land].[21]

Shinran viewed opposition to Pure Land advocacy as both a test of
faith and a stimulus to greater dedication for more energetic
propagation. The prefixing of "monk" to his signature did not simply
reflect his sense of a celibate or advanced monastic status, but was
instead an opportunity which Shinran used to express the depth of his
commitment to master and movement.

Hōnen's Seven Article Pledge was a rather courageous response
to the Tendai school headquarter's charges. One could suppose that,
by inserting the prefix to his signature, Shinran attempted to
challenge the charge that Hōnen's disciples were nothing but a group
of novice or delinquent ex-monks. As Erik Erikson has pointed out in
his studies of adolescent psychology, when a young man places his
trust in a person, he in turn wishes to demonstrate that he too can be
trusted to the object of his trust.[22] Therefore, about two years after
Shinran joined Hōnen's group, he was given this first major
opportunity to express the extent of his dedication to Hōnen and his
movement.

One important element of a strong master-disciple relationship
is a close tie of mutual respect. Beyond the genuine gratitude,
respect, and sense of the Buddhist tradition that Shinran had shown
toward the Chinese and Japanese Pure Land masters, his writings
provide evidence of an extraordinary emotional bond with Hōnen
based on the master-disciple transmission and a mutual belief in their
present efforts and future Pure Land destiny. Hōnen was the subject
of at least twenty of Shinran's wasan (hymns), and among these are
some of Shinran's most literate and moving examples of the hymn
form.

> Although Shan-tao and Genshin did advance Pure Land
>   teachings, if our master Genkū [Hōnen] had not
>   propagated it,
> How could any of the people of a distant island in a
>   defiled world ever learn of the true purpose of the
>   Pure Land teachings?[23]

If there is one individual that Shinran affirms in his writings as the
ultimate inspiration for his conversion to Pure Land faith and all his
later efforts to spread the teachings, it was not the predecessors he
knew only through legend writings, but his master Hōnen, whose
advocacy and example he experienced daily. Yet it remains to be
seen how Shinran's experience from this master-disciple relationship
with Hōnen would influence the spiritual and doctrinal maturity of his
own Pure Land thought and practice.

D. Shinran's studies with Hōnen

One step Shinran had to take in order to fully comprehend Hōnen's teachings was an examination of the earlier Pure Land thought of the great Chinese master Shan-tao. As previously mentioned, Hōnen's own teachings were based on Shan-tao's *Amitāyur-dhyāna sūtra* commentary, the *Kuan-wu-liang-shou-ching-shu*. Shinran capsulized his opinion of the Chinese master in this statement: "He was the only one who made the Buddha's true intentions perfectly clear."[24] Here Shinran means that Shan-tao was the only Chinese Pure Land master he knew who properly advocated Pure Land Buddhism in the context of the Buddhist tradition. Besides the twenty-six hymns he wrote specifically about Shan-tao, he also included him in his listing of the seven patriarchs or most significant masters and transmitters in the transmission of the Pure Land tradition, as we can see in the following table.

Table 5
The Seven Patriarchs of the Pure Land Transition

Patriarch	Period	Nationality and School
1. Nāgārjuna	c. 2nd-3rd centuries A.D.	Indian Mahāyāna Buddhist (Mādhyamika)
2. Vasubandhu	c. 4th century A.D.	Indian Mahāyāna Buddhist (Yogācāra)
3. T'an-luan	476-542	Chinese Pure Land (Ching-t'u)
4. Tao-ch'o	562-645	Chinese Pure Land (Ching-t'u)
5. Shan-tao	613-681	Chinese Pure Land (Ching-t'u)
6. Genshin	942-1017	Japanese Tendai
7. Hōnen	1133-1212	Japanese Pure Land (Jōdo)

Material was discovered in 1943 which indicates that Shinran did study Shan-tao's work during his six year discipleship with Hōnen. This evidence is contained in his commentary on two of the three Pure Land sūtras, which is entitled the *Kangyō-amidakyō-shūchū* ("Annotated *Amitāyur-dhyāna sūtra* and *Sukhāvatī-vyhūha sūtra*"). It is a rare and valuable document on this period of his life because it does concern work he did while with Hōnen (most of his later studies were based on pre-Hōnen, Mt. Hiei doctrinal beginnings), and it is among the earliest of all his extant writings, written in his own handwriting.

Shinran's interpretation of the two sūtras in this commentary lacks the originality of thought so characteristic of his later works. It is a commentary essentially written as a review compendium citing earlier works and interpretations.[25] He quoted from Tan-luan's

Wang-shêng-lun-chu ("Commentary on [Vasubandhu's] Sukhāvati-vyūhopadesa") and Pai-chih Tsung-hsiao's (1151-1214) Lê-pang wen-lei ("A Variety of Texts on [the Pure Land of] Ultimate Happiness") in his Amitāyur-dhyāna sūtra section, and cited Kumārajīva's Sukhāvatī-vyhūha sūtra translation (the Ch'eng-tsan ching-t'u-fo-shê-shou-ching) and Kuei-chi's O-mi-t'o-ching i-shu ("Essentials of the Sukhāvatī-vyhūha sūtra") in his commentary on the Sukhāvati-vyhūha sūtra. Shinran also often referred to most of Shan-tao's writings, his Kuan-wu-liang-shou-ching-shu ("Commentary on the Amitāyur-dhyāna sūtra"), Fa-shih-tsan ("Hymns to Matters of the Dharma"), Kuan-nien fa-men ("Approach to the Dharma of Meditation [on the Buddha Amida]"), Wang-shêng li-tsan-chieh ("Gathā Honouring [Pure Land] Rebirth"), and Pan-chou-tsan ("Hymn to Rebirth based on Pratyutpanna-samādhi").[26] The large number of Shan-tao citations has led some to the conclusion that Shinran based his understanding of the two Pure Land sūtras on Shan-tao's commentaries.

There is one point of doubt regarding the texts which Shinran quoted in his writings from this period, and this concerns Pai-chih Tsung-hsiao's Lê-pang wen-lei. It was compiled during the southern Sung dynasty about the year 1200, when Shinran was twenty-eight years old and still studying at Mt. Hiei. It is not certain when this text reached Japan but Shinran apparently did not use it as a reference until about 1207 (that is, until he was thirty-five years of age). While it may seem curious, it is still possible in the Japan of seven and one-half centuries ago that a book published in China could be used for reference within ten years of its publication. It could well have been that Shinran was both aware of and eager to comprehend any new developments in contemporary Buddhism, particularly those concerning the Pure Land. His uncle Munenari was a noted Confucian scholar, and his influence may have secured the text for Shinran very quickly.[27] Shinran's purpose in citing the Lê-pang wen-lei appears to have been as a recent or contemporary verification of the earlier Pure Land doctrine he used so extensively. The Lê-pang wen-lei was soon cited by another of Hōnen's disciples, Seikō, in his Jōdo-shū yōshū ("Collection of Pure Land School Essentials") written thirty years later in 1237.

E.　Shinran's Kangyō-amidakyō-shūchū

Turning to his Kangyō-amidakyō-shūchū itself, the text was composed on a total of thirty-six sheets of paper, each 28.8 cm wide and 29.7 cm long, and when laid end to end, twenty-eight sheets or 77 percent consist of Amitāyur-dhyāna sūtra text. Taking into account the slim margin used to attach each sheet-page to the next, each sheet actually measures 28.2 by 38.8 cm. Each sheet has a 1.9 cm top and bottom margin, and seventeen Chinese characters of the sūtra text are copied on each line (which runs vertically from top to bottom in traditional style). There is a 2.4 cm space between each of the sixteen lines per page. Shinran wrote his commentaries about each word or phrase of the Buddhist Chinese original by using the empty space of the top and bottom margins, between the lines, and also on the back of the pages. Due to lack of space, the lines of the commentary text were written not in an easily readable single direction but wherever these would fit in. Red ink was employed to denote important sūtra passages, and some portions of the commentary text were written in such small calligraphy that a magnifying lens would be required to clearly read them. This thirty-six sheet-page scroll therefore measures more than ten metres in length. Its size and the intensely cluttered appearance of its text evidence great energy, and the novelist Yasushi Inoue recorded his own impression of the work: "Whoever has seen this text, even a three-year-old child, would be amazed and respectful of the magnitude of the work."[28] The entire commentary was later copied by Shinran's great-grandson Zonkaku (1290-1373), forty-six years after Shinran's death. This copy exists today, and Zonkaku notes in the postscript that he spent nineteen months completing the copy, from March 1317 to September 1318.[29] This easily suggests the enormous concentration and effort Shinran must have used in writing the original.

It is my opinion that this massive work on two of the three Pure Land sūtras is an excellent indication of his labour at concentrating all his efforts in search of a clear-cut understanding of the spiritual tension which had arisen from his earlier Tendai studies and his conversion experience and sudden intense exposure to Pure Land faith.

F. Shinran's attitude toward Hōnen

". . . for a hundred days, rain or shine and regardless of the obstacles, Shinran heard the master teach . . ."

It is said that as a result of this experience, Shinran asked Hōnen to take him as a formal disciple. The significance of this meeting was not simply that Shinran was satisfied with Hōnen's mastery of Pure Land doctrine in answering his questions, but that the intense emotional commitment he was feeling for Hōnen would stand side by side as he developed his study, practice, and advocacy of the necessity of every person totally committing heart and body to the Buddha Amida in Pure Land faith.

Shinran often mentioned in his writings that to him true faith meant believing in its potential meaning and results for actual individuals—faith as the act of a human being rather than an intellectual abstraction within a vast doctrinal system. Thus he twice referred to the following quotation from the *Mahāparinirvāṇa sūtra* in his *Kyōgyōshinshō:* "There are two kinds of faith. One is belief that the way exists. The other is belief that a person is capable of achieving this way."[30]

Shinran repeatedly stated that in his opinion the one person who had accomplished the way was his master Hōnen.[31] There is also Eshinni's description of this attitude in her letter to her daughter.

And just as he had confined himself for a hundred days at
the Rokkakudō, he visited Hōnen every day for a hundred
days, rain or shine and regardless of the obstacles. He
heard the master teach that the way to break the bonds of
eternal rebirth in one's future lives, regardless of whether
a person was good or evil, was simply a single speaking of
the nembutsu. The teaching he received penetrated
deeply in his heart, and when others asked about this he
would reply that wherever the revered master [Hōnen]
would go, regardless of what others might say and even if
he would have to cross into ways of evil [i.e., paths of the
Buddhist hells] he would follow, because he had already
wandered through countless rebirths and that now he had
only his delusion to lose.[32]

In his *Kangyō-amidakyō-shūchū* Shinran cites a passage from
the *Lê-pang wen-lei*.[33] The passage is the story about the rebirth of
an animal slaughterer in mediaeval China. In those times a butcher
was held in general contempt because it was commonly believed that
anyone who practised this act would never be able to die a peaceful
death. Shinran quoted the story to show that it was entirely possible
for a butcher to be saved through Pure Land faith. Here we can see a
beginning of Shinran's own future interpretation of the Pure Land
theory, which he would call 'akunin-shōki' ("the wicked person as the
true opportunity")—that anyone, regardless of the merit of their
daily actions and circumstances in life, could be saved by the
compassion of the Buddha Amida. In later talks with his disciples:

He [Shinran] also said, "If the Fundamental Vows are to be
trusted only through the observance of ethical rules, how
could anyone ever escape the bonds of eternal rebirth?
We certainly are wicked beings but it is only when we
meet with the Fundamental Vows that we can actually
trust in anything. Besides, no evil can ever be committed
that does not have its true origin within ourselves." Again
the master [Shinran] said, "There is no difference at all
among those who live by casting nets or fishing in the
oceans or the rivers, or those who earn their living by
hunting the beasts and birds in fields and mountains, or
those who pass their lives by trading or tilling the soil.[34]

The point is that, from his writings during early days with
Hōnen, one can trace ideas which Shinran received from Hōnen and
then examined and gradually developed in his commentaries by
discovering scriptural and commentary support, ideas which would
mature to become major aspects of Shinran's own future Pure Land
teachings.

In a letter he wrote at the age of eighty-eight, Shinran
mentioned his remembrance of Hōnen's gentleness toward his
followers:

I can certainly call to mind the words of the late revered master Hōnen, who said, "A faithful adherent of the Jōdo school gets born into the Pure Land as a person of ignorance." Besides, I often remember situations where he would smile pleasantly as he met quite simple people who could remember very little of anything. He would tell each of them when they spoke with him that each would unerringly be born into the Pure Land.[35]

Much of Shinran's discipleship with Hōnen would involve careful consideration of human nature and its possibilities and limitations in terms of Pure Land doctrine and faith. One could characterize this disciple training as an emphasis upon translating Pure Land doctrine in its written form into a living soteriology aimed at the basis of human experience and the direction of heart and mind toward a total emotional commitment to Pure Land faith.

The thrust of Shinran's attitudes and efforts from this time with Hōnen through the end of his life can be summarized by his famous statement of faith in the Pure Land: "Shinran abandoned all types of [self-effort-based salvation through] action, to take refuge in the Fundamental Vows."[36] It was twenty-nine years from childhood to his time with Hōnen that Shinran found the direction to which he would commit himself.

As has been stated, this early commentary work does not show the same depth of understanding of Pure Land Buddhism and maturity of faith as do his later writings. But just as a tension arose between his former Mt. Hiei Tendai ("self-effort") practice and his new Pure Land commitment, so an artistic struggle had to be overcome in articulating the predominance of pure faith over such self-effort structures as intellectual activity and traditional Buddhist practice. Here Shinran had to function creatively within the tradition of Far Eastern Buddhism of doctrinally justifying any innovation through constant scriptural and commentary examination and allusion. Thus the mode involved doctrinal exposition but the subject and purpose were the total direction of human emotion, and Hōnen's example and tutelage and Shinran's own Tendai training would serve him well in this effort.

G. Shinran and Hōnen's other disciples

In terms of the influence of this period on the development of his character and thought, one other possible source should be considered, and this is his interaction with Hōnen's other disciples.

Shinran joined Hōnen as one of his later disciples in 1201, for the movement had already been in existence for twenty-seven years. At the time the group was at its summit in membership and energy. This can be seen, for example, in the writings of the Tendai master Jien, the chief abbot of Mt. Hiei, where he wrote: "Hōnen is preaching from all four corners of Kyoto, and his nembutsu teachings are spreading and flourishing among people more every day."[37] When

Shinran joined Hōnen his movement was in its final period, for only six years later Hōnen would be banished from southern Japan (Kansai) and the group would functionally disband. In another seven years Hōnen died at the age of eighty and the movement was without a master.

The group that the impressionable twenty-nine-year-old Shinran joined consisted of a combination of disciples and followers who were both monks and laity. We have noted that at least 193 monks signed the Seven Article Pledge, and a suggestion of the range of types and capacities among Hōnen's adherents can be found in the quotation above. Shinran occasionally touched on the nature of Hōnen's earliest followers:

> Saburō Tamemori of Tsunoto was a man from Musashi. The three, Ōgo Sanehide [a warrior], Shinoya, and Tsunoto Tamemori [a warrior], were Hōnen's first disciples.[38]

According to Toshihide Akamatsu, Hōnen's disciples Shinkū, Junsai, and Genchi were peripheral members of the imperial family.[39] Junkō Matsuno claims that such warrior, aristocratic, and monastic followers "lived happily and harmoniously" as a community. These are not Matsuno's own words but an expression of admiration by a contemporary of Hōnen, the noted Kegon-school monk-scholar Myōei (1173–1232), who did not see Hōnen's new Pure Land movement as a threat or a heresy in the Japanese Buddhist tradition.[40] Matsuno discusses Myōei's description: "Hōnen's hermitage in Yoshimizu undoubtedly formed the kind of samgha or Buddhist community that the Buddha himself had attempted to develop. Distinctions of the mundane world, such as social status and age, simply did not exist here."[41] The disciples got along well with one another by expressing frankly their opinions and reactions, describing their experiences, and being totally dedicated practitioners. Shinran lived a healthy Buddhist life with his fellow adherents within this environment of mutual encouragement. In an excellent religious community atmosphere, it was possible for Shinran to grow spiritually, and it must have been one of the happiest periods of his life.[42]

Scholars of this period must carefully qualify such suppositions because only material indirectly useful for verification exists. There is one piece of writing, the *Tannishō* ("Summary of Regrettable Differences") by Yuiembō (dates unknown), one of Shinran's immediate disciples, written after Shinran's death but quite reliable in characterizing Shinran's attitude toward the community life of the Pure Land movement, both among Hōnen's followers and those of Shinran in later life. Here is a dialogue about the profession of faith:

> When Shinran said, "Zenshin's [Shinran's] faith and the revered master's [Hōnen's] faith are one," his fellow disciples such as Seikambō and Nembutsubō refuted him strongly by saying, "How in the world can Zenshin's faith be the same as the master's faith?" "It would be absurd," Shinran replied, "if I had claimed that our revered

master's extensive wisdom and learning were one with mine. But as to faith for rebirth in the Pure Land, there can be no difference at all, and his faith and my faith are identical." Since they still doubted how this could ever be possible, there was nothing to do but discuss his meaning with the master [Hōnen] to decide which side was right. When they explained the entire matter to him, the revered master Hōnen said, "Genkū's [Hōnen's] faith is the faith given by the Tathāgata [Amida] and Zenshin's faith is also the faith given by the Tathāgata. Hence they are one. Those who have a different faith will not possibly go to the same Pure Land where I, Genkū, shall be born."[43]

This conversation treats basic issues of Pure Land faith, but also illustrates the intense discussion that often occurred based on different interpretations of such issues and the way such differences were resolved. As Junkō Matsuno points out, the dedication of Hōnen's followers is obvious.

To my mind, however, Shinran develops as a very radical Buddhist in Hōnen's group. This is the case in the above passage because it was Shinran and his interpretation that initiated the dialogue, and this radical creativity and intensity would characterize his own Pure Land movement, eventually giving it pre-eminence over those of all of Hōnen's other disciples. Additional signs include the way he prefixed his signature to the Seven Article Pledge and the fact that he would be one of the seven disciples of Hōnen to be exiled in 1207. (There were four followers who would receive the death penalty at this time as well.) Of those disciples who would become leaders of Pure Land movements, only Chōsai, Kōsai, and Shinran would be exiled. Again as recognition of the transmission of his teaching, Hōnen allowed only those disciples he felt truly understood his teachings to copy his *Senjaku-hongan nembutsu-shū:* Kōsai, Benchō, Ryūkan, Shōkū, Chōsai, and Shinran. (Only Kōsai and Shinran in this group were exiled.) It can easily be seen, in comparison with fellow disciples, that Shinran interpreted Hōnen's Pure Land teachings in a more radical manner than most. One could say that he revealed an impatience and haste typical of an intense young person who felt he had to make up for time lost in joining Hōnen's group so late.

Assuming that Shinran was a genuine radical among Hōnen's disciples, the important issues would then be determining what evidence supports this conclusion in his interpretation of Hōnen's teachings.

H. Controversy over nembutsu practice among Hōnen's disciples

Hōnen's definition of Pure Land practice, the way to salvation in the era of the decay of the Dharma, was Pure Land rebirth through the nembutsu (one's attitude and utterance of the basic Pure Land testament of belief—namu Amida-butsu, "Praise and Dedication to the Buddha Amida"). Hōnen prescribed no hard and fast rule of practice, leaving the manner up to individual will and capacity. This led to an intense debate among his disciples over the quantity and quality of nembutsu practice—known as the ichinengi ("significance of a single invocation") versus the tanengi ("significance of many invocations").[44] Dispute over the validity of the two interpretations on the nembutsu was one excuse which would be used by opposing schools to suppress Hōnen's Pure Land movement.

One of the leaders who upheld the many-invocation interpretation was Ryūkan (1148-1227), who was twenty-five years older than Shinran. Due to a lack of material on Ryūkan's life, we can only estimate the year in which he joined Hōnen.[45] It is known, however, that he was at Mt. Hiei from an early age.[46] Ryūkan was a disciple of such brilliance that Hōnen spoke of him and another disciple, Seikaku (1167-1235), as followers who would carry on his nembutsu teaching.[47] Much later Shinran would speak of Ryūkan and Seikaku in a discussion with his own disciples about nembutsu doctrine:

> They are blessed persons on this earth. As they have already been born in the Pure Land, their writings are among the very best—actually second to none. They are people who know exactly the words of the revered master Hōnen.[48]

Ryūkan's work, the *Jiriki-tariki* ("Self-effort, Other-power") and Seikaku's *Yuishin-shō* ("Summary of 'Only-faith'") were highly esteemed by Shinran, as can be seen from the following statement to his disciples:

> To be born in the Pure Land is beyond any power we possess as sentient beings. Even those who fortunately possess great wisdom never take it for granted. Even the sages of the Mahāyāna and the Hīnayāna do not rely on their own efforts, but fully trust in the power of the vows [of the various Buddhas]. Especially with people like us, there will be only a happy few who can hear about the vows and who will know about the nembutsu. Therefore, never simply think about this or that, but look carefully into the *Yuishin-shō* and the *Jiriki-tariki* which I introduced to you some time ago.[49]

At the age of seventy-eight in 1250, Shinran himself wrote a commentary known as the *Ichinen tanen fumbetsu no koto* ("Matters of Distinguishing between Single-Invocation and Many-Invocations").[50] Ryūkan advocated the many-invocation theory of nembutsu practice which involved repeated voicing of invocation to Amida.[51] He believed and practised this throughout his life.[52] He taught that the many-invocation nembutsu was a constant psychological expression of an individual's strong desire to be reborn into the Pure Land and that the threefold mind (sanshin)—the "trusting mind" (shijō-shin), the "profound mind" (jin-shin), and the "mind aspiring toward rebirth by dedicating merit" (ekō-hotsugan-shin)—was an absolute prerequisite for true nembutsu practice. To Ryūkan, one's attitude during nembutsu chanting was the crucial issue, and no matter how many times hypocrites would voice it, they could never be rewarded with Pure Land rebirth without fervent belief but would only succeed in being reborn in a lesser situation.[53]

There were many who denied the possibility of a person desiring Pure Land rebirth as well as the efficacy of nembutsu practice in attaining this rebirth. These people held the single-invocation theory, which claimed that it is not the practitioner who makes any act toward salvation but rather that only Amida's compassion to save sentient beings is responsible for Pure Land rebirth, and, further, that the power of Amida's compassion (as we can know it through his fundamental vows in the three Pure Land sūtras) is what causes a person to invoke the name of Amida and to be reborn in the Pure Land. They considered nembutsu practice to be a truly preordained experience (in the sense that it could not be initiated by human effort or human will). In other words, a person invokes the nembutsu by the power of Amida's compassion, by the result of spiritually being drawn to the fundamental vows of Amida.[54] When Amida's desire that a sentient being be reborn in the Pure Land meets with a person's plea to be reborn and the two become one, the person truly experiences the nembutsu. It was Seikaku (mentioned by Hōnen as one of his major disciples) and Kōsai (who was exiled along with Shinran) who advocated this theory.

Shinran also favoured the single-invocation theory, as clearly seen in the following:

> When we believe that we are to be born in the Pure Land based upon the Buddha Amida's inconceivable vows, there rises up within us the desire to utter the nembutsu. At that moment we share in the benefits of being embraced and not being forsaken. We should know that Amida's fundamental vows do not discriminate whether one is young or old, good or malevolent, and that faith alone is of supreme importance, for it is the vows that will save sentient beings burdened with grave malevolence and fiery passion. Thus, if we do have faith in the fundamental vows, no other kind of good could be needed because there is no good which surpasses the nembutsu. And evil should never be feared, because there is no evil capable of obstructing Amida's fundamental vows.[55]

Interpretations of questions Hōnen left unanswered concerning nembutsu practice would lead to dissension and schism. Such clashes over essential doctrine by intense and dedicated disciples upset the harmony and unity of the movement after Hōnen's death. Some of the single-invocation nembutsu proponents slandered those who advocated the many-invocation nembutsu interpretation, claiming that multi-repetition nembutsu showed doubt in the complete power of the Buddha Amida's compassion and the efficacy of the nembutsu. They saw nembutsu repetition as a qualitative and quantitative evaluation of human self-effort over the total reliance upon Other-power so essential to Pure Land rebirth.[56] They even claimed that, after making the true single invocation, a person would be saved by Amida even if that person committed the traditional serious Buddhist moral offenses of the Five Evil Acts (go-aku) and the Ten Evil Acts (ju-akugo).[57]

I. Shinran's views on nembutsu practice

Shinran wrote a letter in which he stated his position on nembutsu practice:

> First of all, when it is said that the cause of birth in the Pure Land is perfected by a single nembutsu, this will certainly happen. But this still does not mean that we should never recite the nembutsu more than one time. This point is minutely covered in the *Yuishin-shō*. Please examine this work carefully. When it is said that any nembutsu recited more than a single time is for the welfare of all other sentient beings in the ten directions, this could also be. The emphasis here is on "for the welfare of all other sentient beings in the ten directions," but I would have to say that you are mistaken if you think that the nembutsu repeated twice, three times, etc., would harm your own rebirth in the Pure Land. Since the "vow [of Amida] guarantees that our birth in the Pure Land through the nembutsu does exist," it makes little difference whether we say it a single time or say it several times. Any of these will result in our rebirth in the Pure Land. This is what I have heard. We can never really say that because a single nembutsu unfailingly assures us birth in the Pure Land, then any nembutsu repeated several times will hinder it. Please examine the *Yuishin-shō* carefully.[58]

How did the single-invocation and many-invocation controversy arise in the first place? Each of Hōnen's prominent disciples who succeeded him and propagated his teachings had spent much of his life in the austere environment of intense study and practice either at Nara or on Mt. Hiei.   Consequently, whether consciously or otherwise, these disciples' experiences of study and practice would serve as the basis for their developments and interpretations of Hōnen's teachings.[59] As one of these disciples, Shinran took a strong stand on the single-repetition side of the debate among the disciples. What made Shinran support the more radical doctrinal interpretation of the single-invocation theory was the fact that, although he had spent twenty years in Tendai practice on Mt. Hiei, his early chanting meditation had not given him the satisfacton or the depth of spiritual experience that Pure Land practice did. He thus felt that many-invocation practice could not be the way to feel faith truly, and concomitantly, that to claim that nembutsu could ever exist without faith was meaningless. To Shinran faith in the Buddha Amida came first, and only then would any practice thoroughly grounded in true faith, such as the nembutsu, be spiritually rewarding. Once a person made the total commitment of faith in Pure Land rebirth, a many-invocation practice was not essential for salvation, it was merely accessory to the central role of faith. This was the reasoning process behind Shinran's advocacy of single-invocation nembutsu.

Hōnen and all of his major disciples, including Shinran, were attacked not because of their respective single-invocation or many-invocation interpretations but because they adamantly denied any validity to the practices of other Buddhist schools in the era of the decay of the Dharma, for other schools ignored faith in the Buddha Amida. To outsiders, Hōnen's entire group was a major heresy in terms of the traditions of Japanese Buddhism in those times.

J. Government suppression of Hōnen and his followers

There were numerous debates over Hōnen's teachings within the group. Such contention was rooted in a variety of interpretations and commitments to Hōnen's teachings which his followers held. These viewpoints ranged from solid acceptance of all of his ideas, to disagreement over minor points, through outright rejection of some teachings or clever amoral justifications based on them. Hōnen himself wrote about the existence of possible heresies within his group in the last portion of the Seven Article Pledge of 1204. He said, "In these ten years there have been some whose conduct has been rather unbecoming as Buddhist adherents."[60] Yet among new members of the group during the same period between 1194 and 1204 would be some of his brightest disciples, who would be instrumental in developing Pure Land movements after his death.[61] Occasionally this vast disparity in the behaviour of disciples caused Hōnen great anguish.

Before discussing the attacks and suppression of Hōnen's group and their effects on Shinran, we should develop a general outline of how the suppression developed. Individual followers of Pure Land teachings had already suffered persecution well before the formal and direct ban against Hōnen's movement.[62] Attempts at stopping the movement occurred on two separate occasions, the latter leading to Hōnen's sentence to exile. The first incident happened in 1204, when Hōnen wrote the Seven Article Pledge to refute the charges made by Mt. Hiei Tendai authorities. The charges were that nembutsu teaching was not founded on major doctrines of the prevalent Tendai and Shingon schools and therefore it was a fallacy; that it was heretical for the nembutsu practitioners to deny all practices other than the nembutsu and to advocate discarding other Buddhist sūtras; and that the Pure Land attitude of disregarding all teachings and practices except the nembutsu was a rejection of

Buddhist morality.[63]
The first and fourth articles of the Seven Article Pledge were
in response to the charges laid:

> Article 1. I will forbid any of my followers who lacks
> extensive learning and thorough preparation from
> criticizing Tendai and Shingon doctrine, and from
> slandering any Buddhas or bodhisattvas. Article 4. I
> forbid my followers from drinking alcohol or eating meat
> despite any claim that there could be no such prohibitions
> in nembutsu teachings, and in spite of the fact that they
> reject outsiders and those who follow typical [Buddhist
> self-effort] practices; and I finally also forbid them to
> indulge in any negative actions because they believe in
> the [certainty of salvation through the power of the]
> Buddha Amida.

In addition to the Seven Article Pledge, Hōnen dictated a letter of
apology to Mt. Hiei authorities.
His disciples reacted to his apparent capitulation with
unexpected resistance. They resented what they thought was a
surrender of principle by Hōnen, saying, "The master now advocates
the opposite of what he has taught us and is a little two-faced. No
matter what the probable interpretations people make of the Seven
Article Pledge, our master's true intentions are different."[64]
The second attempt at repression took place eleven months
after the Seven Article Pledge had been presented to Mt. Hiei. The
constant rash and often thoughtless advocacy of Hōnen's overzealous
disciples irritated several Buddhist schools, who together took a
request to the throne suggesting the abolition of the nembutsu
movement. Here they described the negligence and errors of the
Pure Land movement, itemizing them in nine articles. After some
questioning, Emperor Gotoba rejected their demands on the grounds
that Hōnen had earlier presented a genuine letter of apology.
Gotoba's decision seems to have been made by judiciously separating
Pure Land teachings from the offensive conduct of a few of Hōnen's
followers.
In October 1205, the major Nara monastery and headquarters of
the Hossō school, Kōfukuji, filed a brief in Nara against Hōnen's
movement, a complaint which became known as the *Kōfukuji-sōjō*
("Kōfukuji Report to the Throne"). The purpose of this complaint was
to invoke government suspension of Hōnen's group by forbidding any
nembutsu practice. This report was compiled by all eight important
Buddhist schools—the Sanron, Jōjitsu, Hossō, Kusha, Kegon, Ritsu,
Tendai, and Shingon schools.
The Kōfukuji Report consisted of nine articles which charged
Hōnen and his followers with the following transgressions unbecoming
a Buddhist school:

> 1) He had founded the Jōdo school without any authorized
> transmission of the tradition (from a Chinese master to

himself as disciple) and without imperial permission or official sanction (chokkyo).

2) His followers had made a recent portrait of the Buddha Amida, by which they claimed that only Pure Land practitioners would be illuminated by Amida's light, to the exclusion of Buddhists of other schools.

3) Pure Land believers did not pay respect to any other Buddha than Amida, not even to the Buddha Śākyamuni.

4) Pure Land adherents insisted that sūtra-recitation was not only a worthless but actually a harmful activity that would cause rebirth in the Buddhist hells, and included even the *Lotus sūtra* in their condemnations. They also despised such traditional acts of piety as the construction of temples, pagodas and the sculpture of Buddhist iconography.

5) Pure Land followers did not pay proper respect to the Buddhist teachings and practices of the other Japanese schools.

6) Pure Land practitioners denied some doctrines explicit in the *Sukhāvatī-vyūha sūtra*, upon which their own movement was based, affirming only nembutsu practice and the avoidance of blaspheming the Pure Land.

7) Pure Land practice emphasized only nembutsu recitation, which was the least important of several traditional Pure Land nembutsu recitations and meditations. Here the critics went back to earlier Chinese Pure Land studies, either distinguishing between orally praising the Buddha Amida (kōshō) and visualizing Amida in meditation (shinnen) or distinguishing between nembutsu meditation (kannen, or meditating upon the formal characteristics of the Buddha Amida in the Pure Land) and nembutsu chanting (kōnen, or chanting the name of Amida). Within such categories, nembutsu chanting was a minor and simple practice, and the critics felt that Hōnen's people were ignoring too much of overall Pure Land practice.

8) Pure Land adherents ignored and violated several monastic regulations of discipline such as those forbidding gambling, clandestine romance, and eating meat.

9) Pure Land followers did not get along with members of the other schools and did not attend national Buddhist ceremonies. Here the concern was voiced that, if Pure Land practice became extremely popular throughout the country, there would no longer be ceremonies conducted for the security of the nation and its people.[65]

The architect of these accusations was the noted Hossō school monk-scholar Jōkei (1155-1213). He did not overtly criticize the Pure Land movement itself; instead he criticized specific instances of what he saw as harmful non-Buddhist behaviour, in preaching method, doctrinal interpretation, and the everyday actions of some followers. When he discussed the eighth article about the proper observance of monastic discipline, he carefully qualified his criticisms: "Such actions which transgress against the way of the Buddha have been committed not only by Senju-nembutsu believers but also by some monks of the path of the sages [traditional Buddhism] in the era of the decay of the Dharma. Some Senju-nembutsu believers certainly do observe Buddhist rules of discipline and morality."[66] His arguments were quite persuasive, for he did not condemn the entire group (in any specific article) for the identified faults of some, and on the surface, his charges were directed against some eccentric and ignorant wrongdoers rather than against Hōnen himself and the movement. However, the final result, of course, was a repression of the entire Pure Land group.

When the government did finally decide to break up the movement and send its chief advocate into exile in 1207, Shinran wrote about the persecution:

> Then the Kōfukuji scholars presented a petition to the throne in early spring in the year Hinotonō of the Shōgen era during the reign of Emperor Gotoba-in (Takanari by name) or during the reign of Emperor Tsuchimikado-in (Tamehito by name). Lords and retainers who cared little for the Dharma and justice bore indignation and resentment against the nembutsu teaching. Thus, master Genkū [Hōnen], the great advocate of the true teaching, and his disciples were, without any proper investigation of their accusations, indiscriminately sentenced to death, deprived of their monkhood and exiled with the reputation of criminals. I was one of them. I am neither a monk nor a layperson.[67]

At this point Shinran was clearly disturbed over such hostile official response to the growth of the Pure Land movement.

K. Reasons for the suppression of the Pure Land movement

A number of obvious questions come to mind about this suppression and Shinran's response to it. After Kōfukuji representatives filed their suit in October 1205, why did it take fifteen months for the government to issue an official decision banning nembutsu practice—which was announced in February 1207? Why was the suppression so severe? After the exile decision was passed, why did Shinran make such a cryptic remark as "I am neither monk nor layperson"? What precisely did he mean by the word *layperson*? An understanding of the group's suppression and its influence on the next stage of Shinran's life will better indicate the course of his subsequent growth as a Buddhist master.

The *Sanchō-ki* ("Record of Three Talents") diary of Sanjō Nagakane (dates unknown), the chief court judicial officer (kurōdo no tō) responsible for lawsuits and judgements, throws much light on the issue of the delay in an official response to the Kōfukuji report. Nagakene was the fifth generation of the Sanjō family to be appointed to the office. His diary as it exists today unfortunately has several pertinent entries missing. First, the portion related to March 1206 and the months after October 1206 during the fifteen-month period from the filing of the Kōfukuji report to the court's decision is absent. This is probably due to an imperial court intrigue which occurred during March of 1206. In addition, the entry relating to the four months immediately before the official decision was reached has been destroyed. The second shortcoming is the fact that Nagakane, as the author of the diary, was a sympathizer toward the Pure Land movement, and thus the objectivity of the diary's viewpoint could be questioned.[68] There is yet a further point to bear in mind. Kujō Ryōkei, the second son of Kujō Kanezane, was regent when Kōfukuji filed its report. Kujō Kanezane had been an early convert to Hōnen's teachings and was said "to have died upon learning of Hōnen's exile."[69] It is safe to assume that Kujō Ryōkei as regent was somewhat sympathetic toward Hōnen's movement. Keeping all this in mind, we will now examine the stance adopted by the court toward the movement and the final decision in favour of exile.

One can begin with the expressed attitudes of both Nagakane and Ryōkei about the report itself. In his diary entry for February 14, 1206, Nagakane writes:

> Even though the behaviour of the followers may be heretical, the leader Hōnen's teachings are the way to rebirth into the Pure Land. This means that any success of the nembutsu is a flowering of Buddhism, and having to be in a position of penalizing the movement weighs heavily on my heart. . . . I must have been reborn of a terribly wicked previous life.[70]

Regent Ryōkei also writes:

> The present criticism of the Senju nembutsu arises from the shallow knowledge of a few of its followers and accordingly, the teachings of the leader Hōnen should not be criticized. Only those followers whose views are heretical should be punished.[71]

It is apparent that these two men are very sympathetic toward the nembutsu movement, but Hōnen's teachings are not specifically discussed in any terms. On February 19 in 1206, Nagakane had a meeting with Jōkei, the author of the Kōfukuji report, but here again the diary gives no evidence of any concrete discussion in terms of specific doctrinal issues.[72] The meeting between Nagakane and

Jōkei took place after a lapse of four months from the time the report was filed. Two days later, on February 21, 1206, in order to expedite the decision from the throne, Kōfukuji attempted to bypass Nagakane by dispatching envoys directly to Regent Kujō Ryōkei to request a conference. Ryōkei denied the request on the grounds "that he could not disregard routine regulations," insisting that the envoys go through proper channels, which meant seeing Nagakane first.[73] Nagakane explained the emperor's position to the envoys with the following:

> Your request concerns the glory of the Buddhist tradition and is therefore presently under careful consideration. Nevertheless, your claim that Hōnen and his group will destroy Buddhism is not easy to understand because nembutsu practice is also a Buddhist teaching. The two men Anraku and Gyōkū will be penalized as heretics.[74]

After this, there are no entries for March and, in the following two months, Nagakane makes no reference whatsoever to the incident.[75]

Reference to the Pure Land problem in the diary is next made on June 13, 1206. Emperor Gotoba delivered a mandate to the members of his court:

> Kōfukuji filed a suit claiming that Hōnen and his disciples have slandered other Buddhist schools in order to propagate their own nembutsu teachings. This is an act that could seriously harm Buddhism. If the court agrees with the request and penalizes the Pure Land movement, it would mean that we would ourselves participate in the crime of destroying nembutsu practice which is one of the teachings of Buddhism. Your deliberations on the matter are required.[76]

Nagakane was commissioned to undertake this task and diligently met with court officials to solicit their individual opinions, but his efforts appeared to be in vain, and he "returned home utterly exhausted."[77]

The names of five people appear in Nagakane's diary in connection with the Kōfukuji brief.[78] Matsudono Motofusa thought that it would be well to approve the Kōfukuji report because the heretics of the Pure Land school had already been sentenced (for heresy), but that care should be taken not to penalize any good nembutsu followers. Sanjō Sanefusa believed that, since the heretics of the nembutsu movement were to be punished, this was reason enough that the report should be approved, and that the action in itself would not mean any serious destruction of Japanese Buddhism. Ōinomikado Yorisane had the same opinion as Motofusa, while Kazan-in Tadatsune agreed with Sanefusa. The fifth person, Takatada, expressly said that, due to his illness, he would be unable to give his opinion on the matter. Views given by the members of the imperial judiciary never did mention any nembutsu doctrine. It is most probable that none of them had any understanding of Pure Land teaching or practice.

While establishing the Pure Land school as an independent Japanese Buddhist school, Hōnen had specifically narrowed it in teaching and practice to the nembutsu—in his words, "discarding, closing off, sealing up, and abandoning" the teachings of other schools. His underlying intention was for nembutsu practice to eventually predominate in the era of the decay of the Dharma, and this would naturally involve the decline of other Japanese Buddhist schools. The imperial court, however, both attempted to preserve the existence of his nembutsu movement and to keep an overall balance among all Buddhist schools. Never really understanding the Pure Land teachings and therefore much of the nature of what was being deliberated, the discussions continued and the court's decision was delayed for fifteen months. The decision which finally did emerge in February 1207 was to spring from a quite unexpected event.

This occurrence which gave the deliberation a sudden turn was the discovery that sexual relations had taken place between the two condemned Pure Land adherents Anraku and Gyōkū (who had been tried for heresy on February 20, 1206) and Emperor Gotoba's ladies-in-waiting. The adulterous episode had occurred toward the end of the year, after December 9, 1206, when the emperor was absent from court.[79] Upon his return on December 28, the emperor learned of the incident and was furious. He immediately took action to force a court decision in the Kōfukuji suit, and seven days later on January 24, 1207, he proclaimed the ban on the nembutsu movement. On February 18, Anraku and Gyōkū were executed, and during the same month Hōnen, Shinran, and several other important disciples were banished. The Pure Land group as a new Buddhist movement was suddenly suppressed by secular authorities on the basis of the immoral conduct of two troublesome followers.

As Shinran remarked, this suppression by the government was clearly a personal act by the emperor, strongly supported by the Kōfukuji and Mt. Hiei monastic authorities. Yet this account of the group's suppression based on the emperor's personal resentment does not entirely explain why its leader Hōnen was so severely punished. Not only the troublemakers but the entire movement was penalized, so to understand these events more fully, we must consider Shinran's allusion to himself as "neither monk nor layperson."

L.   Exile and Shinran's changing attitude toward his society

By the time the ban was submitted, the Pure Land movement's activities were actually feared by some of the Kōfukuji and Mt. Hiei petitioners, who commonly described them as "the black robes" and the "tumult of hymns."[80] It was written that the tremendous echoing of the chanting of Pure Land followers sounded like "an eerie haunting of a ruined nation."[81] This fear was a gradual change in what had been the positive image of the spiritual movement—the image which had been formed, for example, among the imperial court women who were so favourably impressed by the sad beauty of the melodious chanting, the numerous female converts, and the comparatively easy practice of the nembutsu. As the movement had quickly grown, however, followers began to crowd "around Kiyomizudera, the Gion area and the many temples in Kyoto" and a great number of them "formed parties or swarmed together in groups" appearing to take great pride in the strength of their increasing numbers.[82] Thus the public image of the movement slowly changed from an initial eccentricity, to a sincere fervency, to a menacing boisterousness as numbers increased to what was perceived as a threatening level.

The overall Pure Land movement was not restricted simply to the court city of Kyoto, for it was also growing in the warrior capitol of Kamakura in spite of a bakufu ban on nembutsu practice there.[83] In May of 1200 Minamoto no Yoriie (1182-1204) had burned the robes of fourteen monks. In Kyoto, the imperial court had no military force to support its titular authority, so the religious atmosphere was generally more liberal, and it was only the severest of measures that would force an allied effort from the Kyoto court and Kamakura military government.

Japanese political authority in the late Heian period had been in court hands but was strongly influenced by the great Mt. Hiei and Nara Buddhist institutions.[84] When either of these two centres of power acted, the other necessarily had to support the action for the good of their mutual influence. If the political chaos of Japan in the twelfth and thirteenth centuries had been centred only within the imperial institution itself, in such situations as court rivalry or usurpation of political power, for example, the nobility might have acted independently of Mt. Hiei and Nara monastic co-operation and found an opportunity to revive the classical monopoly of political power. However, the chaotic political situation at this time was deep-reaching enough to completely upset the existing social superstructure and, as already discussed in the introduction, the new warrior political institutions of the Kamakura shogunate (the bakufu) replaced the classical court rulers. The new political superstructure was the seizure of ruling power by the warrior, whose justification was the increasing need of their function as protectors of the property and estates of the nobility.[85]

In such a political scenario, anyone involved in the exercise of power, either in title alone or in actuality, could not afford to make a move of any consequence without the participation of others in power. This was especially the case with the court and the Kyoto and Nara Buddhist institutions, who had to co-operate to retain what little influence they still had, in light of the warrior domination of the country. Basically this type of co-operation meant not simply consulting one another, but compromising or acquiescing to the goals of one by the other when such goals were particularly important. Thus during the Anraku and Gyōkū heresy affair and when the Kōfukuji report was submitted, court officials could obstruct the fierce opposition of the Buddhist institutions against Hōnen's group, but when Emperor Gotoba suddenly supported suppression, the balance between partners had decidedly tipped against court Pure Land sympathizers.

It was in this political and social context that the unfortunate adultery by the two nembutsu followers appeared, and the court rendered its verdict of repressing Pure Land practice and banishing its leader Hōnen. In the earlier imperial proclamation of June 13, 1206, the emperor had viewed Hōnen's teachings and the conduct of the two erroneous followers as separate subjects, an approach that seemed based on a perception of Hōnen's Pure Land movement as a harmful distortion of Buddhist teachings, values, and practices that affected Japanese Buddhism. The emperor had broken the stalemate of indecision for purely personal reasons. Therefore, it was this combination of Buddhist institutional power plus the idiosyncrasies of court and social relations which resulted in the severe punishment, and this experience made Shinran intensely disillusioned about institutionalized power in society, in his view of the significance of Pure Land Buddhism for the Japanese nation and his role in its propagation. He began to distinguish strongly the course he saw himself taking (as he began his exile), divorcing himself from the temporal power of the Buddhist tradition in Japan ("I am neither monk") and equally from the nobility or warriors as any truly superior class ("nor layperson"). The effect of this experience would emerge in his Buddhist future with profound consequences for his career, his teachings, and the course of Japanese Buddhism.

From the day his exile was decided, Shinran was treated as a criminal by court and warrior authorities. To Shinran this meant that his humanity had been denied by Japanese authorities. From this day on, he would begin a fierce struggle to regain this lost humanity, and this would entail an intense determination and ceaseless energy to survive by living the principles of Pure Land teachings and practice. This can first be seen in the actual period of exile and its influence on his subsequent ideas and activities.

Chapter 3 Notes

1. Senjaku-hongan nembutsu-shū, Shinran-shōnin zenshū, vol. 6, p. 6.

2. See Leon Hurvitz, Chih-I (538-597), An Introduction to the Life and Ideas of a Chinese Buddhist Monk (Belge: Melanges Chinois et Bodhiques series, vol. I:12, 1963), p. 214.

3. "Discarding, closing off, sealing up, and abandoning" (sha-hei-kaku-hō): This four-word phrase is an abbreviation for Hōnen's summary of his philosophical and spiritual process of analysis and qualification—discarding the [self-effort] path of the sages; closing off the approach to meditation and positive acts [for better rebirth]; sealing up this approach to the path of the sages; and abandoning the myriad practices.

4. Tadao Doi, Hichiso shōgyō gaisetsu (Kyoto: Hyakkaen, 1957), p. 37.

5. Ibid., p. 44.

6. Senjaki-hongan nembutsu-shū, Shinran-shōnin zenshū, vol. 6, p. 33.

7. Kuroda no hijiri-ni nokosu-sho, Shinran-shōnin zenshū, vol. 5, pp. 294-296.

8. Ibid., p. 275.

9. Kyōgyōshinshō, Shinran-shōnin zenshū, vol. 1, p. 382.

10. Tannishō, Shinran-shōnin zenshū, vol. 4, p. 30.

11. Ibid., p. 4.

12. Kyōgyōshinshō, Shinran-shōnin zenshū, vol. 1, p. 381.

13. Dr. Masatoshi Nagatomi of Harvard University has kindly given me this information on the Indian origin of this master-disciple-transmission phenomenon.

14. Senjaku-hongan nembutsu-shū, Shinran-shōnin zenshū, vol. 6, p. 184.

15. Toshihide Akamatsu, Shinran (Tokyo: Yoshikawa Kōbunkan, 1961), p. 89.

16. Kyōgyōshinshō, Shinran-shōnin zenshū, vol. 1, p. 382.

17. Hajime Nakamura et al., Nihon bukkyo 2, Asia bukkyō-shi, vol. 4 (Tokyo: Kōsei shuppansha, 1972), p. 111.

18. Ryūshō Umehara, Shinran-den no sho-mondai (Kyoto: Kenshin-gakuen, 1951), p. 113.

19. "Hichi ka jō kishōmon," Ōhashi Shun'nō (ed.), Hōnen, Ippen Nihon

shisō taikei, vol. 10 (Tokyo: Iwanami shoten 1971), pp. 283-285.

20. Junkō Matsuno, Shinran (Tokyo: Sanseidō, 1959), pp. 41-42.

21. Kyōgyōshinshō, Shinran-shōnin zenshū, vol. 1, p. 383.

22. ". . . clearly the adolescent looks most fervently for men and ideas to have faith in, which also means men and ideas in whose service it would seem worthwhile to prove oneself trustworthy." Erik Erikson, Identity: Youth and Crisis (New York: W. W. orton, 1968), pp. 128-129.

23. Jōdo kōsō wasan, Shinran-shōnin zenshū, vol. 2, p. 128.

24. Shōshin nembutsu-ge, Shinran-shōnin zenshū, vol. 1, p. 90.

25. Kōdo Yasui, Kangyō amidakyō shūchū kaisetsu, Shinran-shōnin zenshū, vol. 7, p. 159.

26. The Pan-chou-tsan disappeared after it was imported to Japan and was only discovered at Ninnaji in Kyoto in 1217. Therefore, it is usually presumed that it had not been accessible to Shinran during his final period on Mt. Hiei. The year 1217 was five years after Hōnen's death, and Shinran left southern Japan (Kansai) for the north (Kantō) when he was about forty-five years old.

27. Enjutsu Ashikaga, Kamakura Muromachi jidai no jukyō (Tokyo: Nihon koten zenshū kankō-kai, 1932), p. 25. This study of mediaeval Japanese Confucianism mentions that mid-Kamakura period Confucian scholars were importing classical Chinese philosophy and literature at an amazingly rapid rate. For example, the great neo-Confucian philosopher Chu-hsi's Chuhg-yung chang-chu ("Commentary on the Doctrine of the Mean"), which was published in China in 1189, was already being examined in Japan by the year 1200.

28. Yasushi Inoue, "Kammuryōjukyō-san," The Honganji Shimpō, January 1, 1975.

29. Z nkaku's copy of the Kangyō-amidakyō shūchū is in the Senjuji collection, Mie prefecture, Japan.

30. Kyōgyōshinshō, Shinran-shōnin zenshū, vol. 1, p. 303.

31. Tannishō, Shinran-shōnin zenshū, vol. 4, p. 4.

32. Eshinni monjo, Shinran-shōnin zenshū, vol. 3, p. 189.

33. Kammuryōjukyō-shūchū, Shinran-shōnin zenshū, vol. 7, p. 203.

34. Tannishō, Shinran-shōnin zenshū, vol. 4, p. 20.

35. Mattōshō, Shinran-shōnin zenshū, vol. 3, pp. 74-75.

36. Kyōgyōshinshō, Shinran-shōnin zenshū, vol. 1, p. 381.

37. Jien, Gukanshō, vol. 86 in the Nihon koten bungaku taikei (Tokyo: Iwanami Shoten, 1962), p. 260.

38. Saihō-shinan-sho, Shinran-shōnin zenshū, vol. 5, p. 367.

39. Akamatsu, op. cit, p. 70.

40. Matsuno, op. cit., p. 135.

41. Ibid.

42. Ibid.

43. Tannishō, Shinran-shōnin zenshū, vol. 4, pp. 34-35.

44. Emperor Gotoba asked Seikaku, "There seem to be disputes among Senju-nembutsu followers recently about single-invocation and many-invocation. Tell me, which of these two is the correct interpretation?" Kokon chomon-shū, vol. 84 of the Nihon koten bungaku taikei series (Tokyo: Iwanami Shoten, 1957), p. 102.

45. Ryūchū, Kettō jushuin gimonsho jōdo-shū zensho, vol. 10 (Tokyo: Jōdo-shū seiten kankō-kai, 1913), p. 26.

46. Ryūkan-ritsushi ryaku-den, in Kettō jushuin gimonsho jōdo-shū zensho, vol. 17 (Tokyo: Jōdo-shū seiten kankō-kai, 1913), p. 586.

47. Moyōgi shingyō shū, quoted by Matsuno, op. cit., p. 228.

48. Mattōshō, no. 19, Shinran-shōnin zenshū, vol. 3, p. 108.

49. Ibid., p. 107.

50. Ichinen-tanen fumbetsu no koto, Shinran-shōnin zenshū, vol. 6, pp. 75-80.

51. Gokuraku jōdo-shū-gi, vol. 2, Ryūkan-ritsushi ryaku-den as cited by Shōkai Hirai, Ryukan-ritsushi no jōdokyō (Tokyo: Kanazawa bunko jōdo-shūten kenkyū-kai, 1941), p. 30.

52. Ibid., p. 63.

53. Ibid., pp. 27, 31.

54. Seikaku's Yuishin-shō, Shin-shū shōgyō zensho, vol. 3 (Kyoto: Kōkyō Shoin, 1951-1957), p. 740.

55. Tannishō, Shinran-shōnin zenshū, vol. 4, pp. 3-4.

56. Yuishin-shō, op. cit., p. 754.

57. The Five Evil Acts are (1) killing one's mother, (2) killing one's father, (3) killing an "arhat," (4) causing serious dissension in the monastic community, and (5) profanity. These five are the most serious offences against Buddhist morality and would result in the offender's rebirth into the Avici hell (the hell of never-ending pain). The Ten Evil Acts are (1) wilfully taking life, (2) taking anything not offered, (3) sexual misconduct, (4) lying, (5) profanity, (6) slander, (7) foolish chatter, (8) greed, (9) anger, and (10) heretical ideas.

58. Mattō-shō, Shinran-shōnin zenshū, vol. 3, p. 131.

59. Yuishin-shō, op. cit., p. 44.

60. Hichikajō kishōmon, Shinran-shōnin zenshū, vol. 5, p. 169.

61. For example, Genchi (joined 1195) was the founder of the murasakino monto faction; Seikaku (joined 1197) wrote the Seven

Article Pledge as Hōnen dictated it; Chōsai (joined 1202) led the Shogyō Hongangi faction; and Shinran would found the True Pure Land school (Jōdo shin-shū).

62. In 1199 the Kamakura shōgun Minamoto no Yoriie defrocked and burned the robes of fourteen monks at the military capital. This was three years before Shinran became Hōnen's disciple. See the May 12, 1200, entry in the Azuma-kagami, vol. 1 (Tokyo: Meicho kankō-kai, 1965), p. 490.

63. Chokushū-den, Jōdo-shū zensho, vol. 16 (Tokyo: Sankibō Busshoten, 1961), p. 99.

64. Akamatsu, op. cit., p. 106.

65. Kōfukuji-sōjō in Dainihon bukkyō zensho, vol. 61 (Tokyo: Kōdansha, 1972), pp. 13-17.

66. Ibid., p. 15.

67. Kyōgyōshinshō, Shinran-shōnin zenshū, vol. 1, p. 380.

68. According to Junkō Matsuno, Sanjō Nagakane was strongly patronized by the early Pure Land adherent, Kujō Kanezane. See Matsuno, op. cit., p. 101.

69. Jien, Gukanshō, op. cit., p. 296.

70. Sanchō-ki entry for February 14, 1206, Shiryō-taisei, vol. 31 (Kyoto: Rinsen Shoten, 1965), p. 86.

71. Akamatsu, op. cit., p. 110.

72. Sanchō-ki entry for February 19, 1206, op. cit., p. 87.

73. Sanchō-ki entry for February 21, 1206, op. cit., p. 88.

74. Sanchō-ki entry for February 22, 1206, op. cit., p. 89. Nagakane wrote of Gyōkū in detail as follows: "Gyōkū followed the single-repetition teaching (ichinen-gi), which maintained that, after a single utterance of the nembutsu, a person was allowed to transgress the ethical rules which forbade monks from killing and stealing. Gyōkū also criticized other schools and insisted solely on nembutsu practice." Sanchō-ki, entry for February 20, 1206, op. cit., p. 96.

75. The regent Kujō Ryōkei suddenly died in March 1206, and it was rumoured that he was assassinated. This may be the reason why Nagakane did not refer to nembutsu practice more often in his diary. See Nihon rekishi dai-jiten, vol. 4 (Tokyo: Kawade Shobō, 1968), p. 38.

76. Sanchō-ki entry for June 19, 1206, op. cit., p. 129.

77. Sanchō-ki entry for June 21, 1206, op. cit., p. 130.

78. Sanchō-ki entry for June 19, 1206, op. cit., p. 130.

79. Shijūhachi-kan-den, Jōdo-shū zensho, vol. 16 (Tokyo: Sankibō Busshoten, 1961), p. 964.

80. Nembutsu tsui-hō senji, Shōwa teihon nichiren-shōnin ibun, vol. 3

(Yamanashi: Sō-honzan Minobukuonji, 1953), p. 263.

81. Minamoto Arifusa, Nomori-kagami, vol. 2 as vol. 4 of the Nihon kagaku-taikei series (Tokyo: Kazama Shobō, 1956), p. 86.

82. Shinichi Satō and Yoshisuke Ikeuchi, Chūsei hōsei shiryō, vol. 1 (Tokyo: Iwanami Shoten, 1955), p. 101.

83. Azuma-kagami entry for May 12, 1200, op. cit., p. 490.

84. Shūichi Katō, Shinran—jūsan-seiki shisō no ichimen (Tokyo: Shinchōsha, 1960), p. 26.

85. Shō Ishimoda and Eiichi Matsushima, Nihonshi gaisetsu, vol. 1 (Tokyo: Iwanami Shoten, 1955), p. 171.

Chapter 4

Shinran's Exile and its Influence upon his Thought

A. The exile

Shinran had written that he became neither monk nor layperson with his exile, and further began to characterize himself as "Gutoku" ("the foolish and fuzzy-headed"). This epithet had been earlier used by Saichō, the founder of the Tendai school, in reference to himself. It is probable that Shinran had heard the colourful expression during his time on Mt. Hiei, but he has never written about its origin. His first recollection of his use of the characterization appears to have been the precise time of his exile.

His state of mind at the start of his exile could then be seen in his statement, "I called myself 'Gutoku'."[1] The term *toku* is based on the word *tokukoji* ("fuzzy-headed layperson") meaning a person whose appearance is that of a monastic but whose heart and conduct are not. To Japanese Buddhists of the time this pejorative epithet was commonly used to describe those who became monks or nuns to avoid starvation but with no intention of seriously practising Buddhism—those who apparently did not observe monastic morality and lived in a head-on clash with the Dharma. The term is found in the *Mahā parinirvāṇa sūtra,* which was the most frequently quoted sūtra in the *Kyōgyō shinshō* after the three Pure Land sūtras.[2] From the beginning of his exile in 1207, Shinran would constantly substitute the toku for his common name of Fujii Yoshizane, and in all his writings after exile he signed his name "Gutoku".[3] In traditional Buddhist doctrine the term *gu* meant "ignorance" and "stupidity" and, more significantly, "an inability to be repentant for a major crime or moral transgression."[4] In the *Kyōgyōshinshō*, one can sense a spirit of rebellion rooted in his deep faith in the Pure Land:

> Those who would abandon this defiled world and aspire to the Pure Land, those who are confused about practice and suspicious of beliefs, those whose mind is muddled and whose awareness is small, and those whose misdeeds are serious and whose excuses are many, should especially rely on the Tathāgata's urging [to take refuge], always returning to the superiority of the direct path and following only this practice and upholding only this faith.[5]

Shinran first came across the term *gutoku* in his study of the *Mappō tōmyō-ki* ("Record of the Bright Lamp amidst the Decay of the Dharma") traditionally attributed to Saichō. Shinran was so impressed by this apocryphal decay of the Dharma statement that he incorporated the entire text into his *Kyōgyōshinshō.*[6]

He had doubted his own capabilities at various times during his Buddhist career, and now the hard life he was forced to lead intensified these doubts even more. Comparing the two ways to salvation, he would write:

> There is a difference between the compassion of the path of the sages and that of the Pure Land path. The compassion of the path of the sages involves sympathy, pity, and care for sentient beings, but it is extremely difficult to save people in whatever way one might wish. It should be understood that the compassion of the Pure Land lies in achieving Buddhahood quickly through the saying of the nembutsu and giving benefit to sentient beings as we wish with the heart of the great compassion and the great mercy. It is difficult to respond to others the way we might wish, no matter how much love and pity we can feel in this life, for such compassion [of the self-effort path of the sages] never lasts very long.[7]

What one can sense here is the beginning of a change in his conception of compassion based on the radical change in experience during exile—both in the limitations of human compassion and the spiritual potential of Amida's compassion. A closer look at both the people and the environment of his site of exile, Echigo, will help explain the impact these had on Shinran's changing thought.

It is commonly believed that Shinran's exile lasted for five years. We do know that the place of exile was called Echigo or Kokufu in Echigo no kuni ("the Echigo district").[8] The circumstances surrounding these events are narrated in Yiuenbō's *Tannishō:*

> The revered master Hōnen and seven disciples were banished and four followers executed. The revered master was exiled to Hata in Tosa province with the criminal title 'Fujii Motohiko, male, age 76'. Shinran was exiled to Echigo province with the criminal title of 'Fujii Yoshizane, age 35'. Jōmonbō was exiled to Bingo province, Chōsai Zenkōbō to Hōki province, Kōkakubō to Izu province, and Gyōkū Hōhonbō to Sado province.[9]

B. Site of exile

According to the Heian period legal text, the *Engi-shiki* ("The Engi [Era] Formulary"), the three major traditional places of banishment were Kinru, Chūru, and Onru, and the type of punishment was determined by the distance of the exile site from Kyoto.[10] If the exiles were monks or nuns, they had to be stripped of all religious status prior to exile, for by law banishment was not applicable to monastics.[11] Exiles underwent severe treatment—regardless of age, sex, or social class, they were to be given only one daily meal, which consisted of small quantities of rice (isshō no kome) and salt (isshaku no shio).[12] In the spring they were given grain to grow and from the second year of exile they were expected to become self-sufficient, no longer dependent on any food or materials supplied by their government overseers.[13]

Shinran did not indicate his precise place of exile, but we are able to estimate the location by studying the topography of Kokufu in the Echigo area. It faces Kotahama on the Japan Sea coast, a section of Japan with some of the nation's heaviest annual snow and rainfall. Due to such monsoon weather conditions, Kokufu has winter weather for half the year and is quite overcast another third of the time. The other boundary of the Kotahama area is the Kubiki plain, from where one can see the high mountains of the Myōkō range. Shinran lived a simple farming life in these surroundings, something he had never done before. Good crops would, of course, depend mainly on favourable climate and soil conditions, and it was only after a decent harvest that one could hope to maintain a minimal existence.

In contrast to so many masters of other Japanese Buddhist schools, there are no statements in Shinran's works which glorify nature. However, the word *sea* appears ninety-four times in his *Kyōgyōshinshō*. it is reasonable to believe that he probably saw the Japan Sea often, and after a hard day of fieldwork it could well have reminded him of his master Hōnen, who had also been sentenced to exile in Tosa by the sea. The continual roar of the nearby sea must have stirred his heart, especially since he had grown up far from the Japan Sea in the inland city of Kyoto.

Shinran's life in Echigo was certainly a difficult one, living as he did in an isolated area where human relationships were so important and yet so tight and convoluted. One interesting fact about his exile is that the banishment itself was never officially recorded. Thus there is no official public substantiation for Shinran's own words when he declared "I have been sent to exile."[14] Exile was a drastic step taken against those who had violated the laws of the nation, and yet, despite the seriousness of the punishment, neither the fact of his exile nor even his name is found in the official record of the Kamakura period government, the *Azuma-kagami* ("The Mirror of Azuma"), nor is anything to be found in the diaries of aristocrats contemporary with him. A further discrepancy can be noted where the *Honganji-shōnin shinran dene* records the place of exile as Kokufu in Echigo, whereas the official government records on exiles in the *Engi-shiki* contain no mention of Shinran in connection with this area. It has been established that Sadogashima or Sado island was the designated place of exile in Echigo,[15] but Kokufu, which is mentioned in the *Honganji-shōnin shinran dene*, has a more healthy climate. In order to reconcile such discrepancies, the personalities of the Echigo functionaries of the time should be examined briefly.

Shinran's exile was proclaimed in February 1207.[16] The regional administrator of Echigo was Munenari, Shinran's uncle, who had just been appointed to this office on January 13, 1207.[17] It can be assumed that it was Munenari who arranged for Shinran to go to a place slightly more comfortable than Sado island. Kujō Kanezane, a devout follower as well as Hōnen's patron, knew Shinran and also possessed extensive land holdings in Echigo.[18]   It is known that Shinran was banished to a location where a benefactor of Hōnen owned some land. It is probable that it was through the intercession of these two court officials that Shinran served his exile at a site different than the officially designated one, and it is again probably this fact which caused any discrepancies in the records. Thus Shinran was not a simple martyr hounded by political and religious adversaries, but both a victim and a beneficiary of the aristocracy and its social system.

C.   The people of Echigo

It is easy to picture the kind of people Shinran would meet in his new daily life—simple peasants who subsisted on what they could cultivate and harvest themselves.   He would also have met hunters and fishermen as well as travelling pedlars who came through once a year at a regular time.[19]   According to the records of this period, a literate society looked down upon directly productive labour as a shameful occupation, so that farmers, fishermen, and the merchant class were held in very low esteem.[20]   Their occupations were the source of their social status, and these were considered as base as overt criminal activity.[21]   In addition to these people, Shinran probably met the slaves of the local gentry, known as genin ("subordinate people"), who were often bought and sold like animals.[22]   All of these ordinary people engaged in manual labour. Sometimes he probably bartered his produce with them for fish or meat, and he may have been taught how to cultivate the land in exchange for teaching elementary written Japanese, occasionally describing Kyoto and Kamakura and the life of the aristocracy to local children.

These people possessed few or no legal rights and could well be seen as an oppressed class, on whom the economic and productive structure of the Kamakura period was constructed. Since profession and social status were inextricably bound together in this early era of Japanese feudalism, there was no upward mobility (beyond Buddhist monasticism) for families who performed manual production because their occupations were hereditary. The nature of many of their occupations as hunters and fishermen gave them a social status of outcasts, so they had little hope of improving their lives. Basic family relationships and sexual activity were severely limited by the inherent restrictions of their lowly social status and fixed locality. Eshinni remarked in a letter to her daughter, Kakushinni, the following:

> The servants I have arranged to be transferred to you include the following: a woman named Kesa, age 36, her daughter Nadeshi who is 16 this year and another daughter nine years of age—which makes a total of three. Also there will be the daughter of Kesa's stepmother and her

daughter Inumasa, age 12, as well as a woman named Kotori, age 34, and a man named Antōji. I had the three-year-old boy born to Kesa and a male servant of another household taken by the father. The woman servants of our place usually have sexual relations with the male servants of other families, so it leads to complications. When all the above-mentioned people are added together, there is a total of seven people, six women and one man.[23]

The legal codes of the times had specific regulations governing the responsibility for raising newly born children among genin, and such sexual arrangements caused frequent family division and problems. For example, if a genin couple had a baby boy, the child's father was responsible for raising him, but if it was a girl, the mother had to bring up the child.[24]

In living and witnessing the oppression of these people, Shinran actually experienced for the first time a world in which mere survival involved the perpetual repetition of daily tasks which society needed while condemning its performers to the lowliest social status without right or privilege.

After reaching Echigo, Shinran no longer had a master under whom to study and practise Pure Land Buddhism. He must have searched for someone within the restrictions of his place of exile to receive instructions from or to converse about doctrine. Yet simply learning how to survive in the snow country of Echigo was of primary importance. He first had to get used to the life of a layperson which he was now forced to live. One reason why he had rejected his life at Mt. Hiei at the age of twenty-nine to join Hōnen's group was his feeling that Mt. Hiei, in spite of its great Tendai doctrinal and practice resources, was slowly becoming more and more degenerate and materialistic. In exile Shinran had none of the privileges of a high-ranking Buddhist monk or an aristocrat. He had to work hard for the food, shelter, and time to think which he had taken for granted in the past. It is ironic that Shinran had once given up the world for the security of a monastic life and that his spiritual course had now led him into being thrown back into the world by the same political and social forces he had originally sought to escape.

D. Shinran's marriage to Eshinni

Notwithstanding the absence of source material on how Shinran lived his daily life in Echigo, we do know for certain that he did live a married life. This marriage itself was an extraordinary event in the history of Japanese Buddhism, so it is of prime importance to examine what little is known about Eshinni, her personality and relationship with Shinran, her influence upon his life, and the effects of his marriage on his future as a Pure Land master. This first marriage of a Japanese Buddhist master would also involve numerous consequences of family life, children, and descendants, etc., which in turn would further affect the development of his Pure Land thought and practice.

First the woman Shinran married should be considered. It is known from the appallingly little available information that he married Eshinni and eventually fathered several children. 'Eshinni' is a Buddhist name ("Kind Faith"), but her family and personal name are unknown. She may have either adopted this Buddhist name after her marriage or already been a nun with that name when she married. The probability of the latter is greater because historical records show that nembutsu practice was very popular in the Hokuriku, Tōkai, and Tōsan regions of Japan about the year 1207, when Shinran was exiled to Echigo in the Hokuriku region, where a great many monks and nuns were active in the Senju-nembutsu movement.[25]

Ten letters written to Shinran by Eshinni exist today, from which we can extrapolate an understanding of the woman. These letters suggest that she kept a diary, and historians have concluded from the style, contents, and calligraphy of her letters that she was a cultured woman. Judging from her language, one is justified in assuming that she had lived in Kyoto. Two distinct speculations about her origin exist—either she was a member of the powerful Gōzoku family[26] or she was a capable and lively woman of the peasant class.[27] Umehara Ryūshō suggests that one reason for Shinran's marriage to Eshinni involved the financial support Shinran may have received from her parents while eking out an existence from the earth during his years in exile, and that for this reason she must have been of the Gōzoku family.[28] I believe that she was from a powerful clan because she brought along several genin servants of her own when the marriage took place. Furthermore, it is my opinion that she had been a nun before her marriage, first, because of the fine style of diction she used in writing her letters; second, from the frequent religious references in these letters (e.g., "I believe that my husband [Shinran] was a bodhisattva in his last life"); and third, because of the many monks and nuns in the Echigo region at the time.[29]

E. Shinran's family

Shinran and Eshinni are traditionally said to have been the parents of four boys and three girls. The dates of birth for two of these children are known—one son, Shinren, was born on March 3, 1211, and a daughter, Kakushinni, was born some time in 1224. Using common sense to estimate the probable length of pregnancy, we can estimate that Shinran and Eshinni were married at least around or before April or May of 1210. This year was his fourth in Echigo and he would have been thirty-eight and Eshinni, twenty-nine years of age. What records do exist, however, reveal that they already had three other children before Shinren. It is possible that four children, including Shinren, were born in the four years after Shinran came to Echigo, but this would mean that he and Eshinni were married immediately after his arrival. Therefore, some historians have suggested that

Shinran may have had more than one wife or that Eshinni was already married to him before he went to Echigo.[30]   Five genealogical records exist which cover the makeup of Shinran's family:
1. *Kuden-shō* ("Summary of the Oral Transmission [of Shinran]"), edited by Kakunyo in 1331.[31]
2. *Sonpi-bunmyaku,* edited by Tōin Kimisada in 1450.[32]
3. *Honganji keizu,* edited by Kujō Uemichi in 1536.[33]
4. *Hino-ichiryū keizu,* edited by Jitsugo in 1541.[34]
5. *Hogo-uragaki* ("Verifications on Scraps of Paper"), edited by Kensei in 1568.[35]

The *Kuden-shō* and *Hino-ichiryū keizu* agree in listing the same children's names in identical order.

Shinran
1. Hani (male)
2. Oguro no nyōbō (female)
3. Zenran (male)
4. Shinren (male), born March 1211
5. Masukata (male)
6. Takano zenni (female)
7. Kakushinni (female), born 1224

A minor point should be noted: these records do not follow the traditional Japanese style of grouping males and listing them before females.[36]   Since this customary format was not followed here, I presume that Hani and Oguro no nyōbō were the children of one mother, whereas Zenran, Shinren, Masukata, Takano zenni, and Kakushinni were of another mother. (If Oguro no nyōbō had been recorded after Masukata, there would have been no room for doubt.) Until the precise year of Shinran's marriage is clarified, both hypotheses should be kept in mind.

Regardless of whether he had one wife or more than one, Shinren was born in 1211 and three other children were born before him. It may be useful at this point to consider Shinran's life at the time of his marriage.

As has been earlier discussed, life in exile was so demanding of one's time and energy that it allowed for few other activities. Yet even in hardship Shinran eagerly awaited the news from Kyoto which came once a year with the travelling merchants. He would describe it as a showering of treasure which fuelled his hopes for the future. While he faced physical and intellectual deprivation, he also felt a strong desire for emotional and sexual support. In understanding Shinran as a combination of these essential human needs, we can see the interplay of the passions which would motivate the great religious master as he reached middle age. However, from his life of submission to state and the hardship of daily life in exile, he gradually developed courage and strength, as can be seen in the following passage, apparently written as a retrospective view of that period:

> To speak of an "ocean" is portraying it as the ocean—since the beginningless past the rivers and streams have flowed with the various practices and positive actions of ordinary people and of the sages, and the waters of the seas of ignorance have swirled with the Five Deadly Acts and obscenities against the Dharma by the unsavables as numerous as the sands of the Ganges, and these are converted into the great ocean waters of a myriad virtues of wisdom and truth as numerous as the sands of the Ganges, by the great compassion of the fundamental vows. Truly I know, just as the [unidentified] sūtra explains by stating, "The icy passions melt to become the waters of virtue." The ocean of the vows [of the Buddha Amida] does not shelter the corpses and bones of confused good deeds practised by middle and lower saintly beings of the two vehicles—how then could it ever shelter the corpses and bones of the fleeting and perverse actions of the [self-effort] heart confused with constantly-blending poisons [of greed and delusion]?[37]

Shinran's vigour and realization of his own limitations as an individual human practitioner stimulated the beginnings of his mature views on how sentient beings could truly relate to the Other-power of the Buddha Amida's compassionate vows.

F. The development of Shinran's thought from negation to affirmation

To appreciate the socio-historical factors which acted as the parameters for Shinran's developing thought, I have focused my attention on several aspects of his social environment during the first half of his life: his personal circumstances, the contemporary social environment which directly influenced his personal circumstances, and the temporal juncture in Japanese history that gave rise to the social environment. I have also stressed the role of Hōnen's ideas, his movement, and Shinran's participation in it because it is this experience which Shinran himself identifies as the greatest influence on the Pure Land tradition.[38] Under the guidance of Hōnen and his teachings, Shinran's thought matured during a process of conquering and transcending the spiritual and physical suffering he experienced in the first half of his life. Shinran saw his master Hōnen and his ideas as the primary factor which prevented his withdrawal into the soltitude and isolation of self-defeat and self-pity.

He was born into a family of court nobility, but he left this life during childhood to enter the monastic life on Mt. Hiei. He devoted twenty years to Buddhist meditation and study, which unfortunately did not open the way to spiritual salvation as he perceived it. After suffering severe disappointment in the Tendai nangyō-dō ("the path of difficult practice") which Pure Land advocates would qualify as self-effort practice or the attainment of enlightenment through one's own effort, Shinran finally abandoned Saichō's belief that "the practice of Buddhism should equally lead all sentient beings to the enlightenment of Amida's wisdom without any distinctions."39 He turned in desperation to Hōnen's movement, an act of intense faith which would ultimately result in his political exile and being defrocked as a Buddhist monk. At the same time he would confront basic human problems of physical and spiritual existence as he never had before while in exile, and his answers would evolve into the culmination of his mature thought. He would organize his experience into the doctrine he would develop to explain forcefully Pure Land Buddhism during the remainder of his life, and in these ideas can be found the attitudes he developed to resolve both earlier emotional and spiritual crises and the tremendous concentration of critical spiritual experience that occurred during his exile.

To Shinran, individuals could face their conditions only in a resolute and quiet manner. While people are tossed around by the circumstances of their existence, at the same time they react to them, influence these conditions, and create their own reality through their 'shukugō' or "prior karma." Thus all people exist in the same environment, but each will live a different life because of individual attitudes and values.

The problem of karma became a great intellectual and moral exercise for Shinran. He believed that karma was inherent in all human beings and that it endlessly resulted in wrongdoing and negative action throughout their lives. Humans are bound by it in every action:

> Suppose you could do anything you wanted—then you could kill, if you were told to kill a thousand people in order to be reborn in the Pure Land. But you do not kill because there are no karmic conditions within you to kill even a single person—not because your heart and mind are good. Even though you may have no thought of injuring others, it can happen that you could kill a hundred or a thousand people.40

The karma of one's present life is the result of accumulated karma from previous lives now manifested as environment and status in the present life. Prior karma from one's previous lives functions as the cause of one's present situation, while karma presently being accumulated as the result of present actions will become the causes of one's situation in the next life. The constant stream of karma from actions in one life exists as causes for action in the next life. In the longer view of a series of lives, the continual cycle of birth and death is Buddhist samsāra, a never-ending spiral of cause and retribution-effect from action as cause which becomes results that influence future action and future lives. Thus all human activity is nothing but the samsaric spiral of an individual conditioned by maturing karma.

> A good heart and mind arise due to the influence of
> inherent good [from positive karma ripening from prior
> acts of good], while negative actions are thought and
> committed due to [previous] acts of inherent evil [karma].
> We should realize that committing a trifling misdeed, as
> minute as a particle of dust on the tip of a single hair of a
> rabbit or a sheep, is without exception due to our inherent
> evil karma.[41]

Shinran believed that anyone who practised Buddhism in the
degenerate age of the decay of the Dharma was a monastic,
regardless of whether his head was shaven or his body cloaked in
clerical robes. In quoting the *Mappō tōmyō- ki*, which he believed to
have been written by Saichō, Shinran wrote in the *Kyōgyōshinshō*:

> Question: All the sūtras and the Vinaya completely
> prohibit transgression of the precepts, and those who act
> against them are not allowed to join the Samgha. The
> issue involves transgressing the precepts. In my opinion
> there is no observance of the precepts in this latter age
> [of the decay of the Dharma]. How could it be that a
> person can feel pain if he has no wound? Answer: All
> that has taken place in the age of the True and Complete
> Dharma, the age of the Artificial Dharma and the latter
> age [of the decay of the Dharma] is expounded in all the
> sūtras. Whether one is a Buddhist or not, what person
> cannot open his eyes and see that covering up his own
> misdeeds does not conceal the True and Complete
> Dharma? But in speaking of the latter age, there can only
> be monks who are barely monks in name because it is very
> difficult to perform good actions in this age. Because of
> this difficulty, the monk in name only will be made a true
> treasure of the world through the compassion of the
> Buddha Amida. If there is a single person who observes
> the precepts in this latter age, it is very strange indeed.
> It would be as if a tiger were loose in the streets.[42]

This line of thought shows the beginning of a new kind of logic.
Shinran was trying to make salvation more accessible with this
position. However, the development of his theory was strongly tied
to his own previous monastic existence and frame of reference, so it
would take his period of exile to refine these ideas to a point where
they would embrace all the Japanese people.

While Shinran lived with Hōnen's group, he had seen his master
chant the nembutsu seventy thousand times a day and keep all the
monastic precepts, even though the world around them was deep in
the degenerate age of the decay of the Dharma. Thus Hōnen's group
remained bound to traditional conceptions of Buddhist practice. In
Echigo Shinran was forced to exist among the poor and oppressed,

whose sustenance was tied to agriculture and the taking of animal
life. Since he had been obliged to leave Hōnen and the environment
of monastic practice, Shinran must have been forced to re-examine
constantly the premises of the precepts to find answers to the
challenges this new life posed to his former existence—"Can it be true
that unless these people are saved, I shall not be saved?" At this
point he was separated from his family and his social and monastic
background, so while experiencing the trauma of exile he once again
enlarged his conception of the Buddha Amida's compassion from what
he had firmly believed when he had joined Hōnen's movement.
Shinran could not remain an ambitious Buddhist monk or an
intellectual. In exile he could only exist as a believer of the
teachings of the Buddha if he shared daily labour with his neighbours.
This experience therefore forced him to identify with all people as a
common plurality. For example, he began to see people as "an ocean
of multitudinous beings"[43] or as "sentient beings in the worlds which
are as numerous as particles of dust."[44] He simply came to feel a
oneness with all people and the natural environment, and it was this
experience that broadened his idea of Amida's salvation from an
individual context to a great collective arena of all living things.
Thus, according to his evolving teachings, even the most treacherous,
anti-social and wicked of human beings was assured salvation through
the Buddha Amida's compassion.

> When we believe that we are to be born in the Pure Land
> based upon the Buddha Amida's inconceivable vows, there
> rises up within us the desire to utter the nembutsu. At
> that moment we share in the benefits of being embraced
> and not being forsaken.[45]

> The nembutsu is the unimpeded singular faith. The reason
> for this is that the gods of heaven and earth bow in
> reverence to the followers of faith and the maras and
> non-Buddhists cannot hurt them, nor can any wrong or evil
> exert karmic influence on them, nor can various good
> deeds surpass the nembutsu.[46]

He extended this kind of reasoning even further, going so far as to
state:

> We should know that Amida's fundamental vows do not
> discriminate whether one is young or old, good or
> malevolent, and that faith alone is of supreme
> importance, for it is the vows that will save sentient
> beings burdened with grave malevolence and fiery passion.
> Thus, if we do have faith in the fundamental vows, no
> other kind of good could be needed because there is no
> good which surpasses the nembutsu. And evil should never
> be feared, because there is no evil capable of obstructing
> Amida's fundamental vows.[47]

His mature teachings were not merely intended for a specific time in history but were to be a truly eternal doctrine to alleviate the grief and suffering of all people in every age, by asserting Amida's salvation through faith without discrimination of any kind.

Shinran taught people enduring a wretched existence that "human suffering was the only condition necessary for receiving the Buddha Amida's compassion."[48] He asserted that the Buddha Amida saw all beings as equal in their practice of the nembutsu. He did not take the dramatic role of a crusader or saviour, but rather viewed himself more like a support, as the cane of a blind person. He would re-emerge from exile as a creative and inspiring spiritual leader of the people whose hard life he had shared.

G. 'Shukugō' as karma-controlled human destiny

One of Shinran's disciples recorded this statement concerning the inevitable effects of karma:

> "We should realize that committing a trifling misdeed," said the late master [Shinran], "as minute as a particle of dust on the tip of a single hair of a rabbit or a sheep is without exception due to our inherent evil karma . . ."
>
> "Suppose you could do anything you wanted—then you could kill, if you were told to kill a thousand people in order to be reborn in the Pure Land. But you do not kill because there are no karmic conditions within you to kill even a single person—not because your heart and mind are good. Even though you may have no thought of injuring others, it can happen that you could kill a hundred or a thousand people."[49]

The above quotation refers to the evidence of our present circumstances and suggests that all acts are a result of misdeeds committed in the past. No matter how small these may be, they are still the result of some harmful action previously done. Shinran concludes that this world itself is hell, as can be seen in the following: "Since I am incapable of any practice whatsoever, hell would definitely be my abode in any case!"[50]

If it is said that a person lives in this world in the present as a result of inherent evil, then it logically follows that one also lives by committing wrongdoing. The meaning of the term *shukugō*, or "prior karma," which Shinran used in dialogue with his disciples, is this strong assertion that all human beings have been living in evil from the beginningless past.

The term *prior karma*, however, does not appear in any of his own writings or letters, and we must wonder how the term was embodied in his thought. Shinran said that living and acting in the present is a continuity from the beginningless past to the eternal future—from misdeed to misdeed. A passage from his *Kyōgyōshinshō* mentions this point:

The Buddha's intentions are difficult to understand. But I humbly presume his purposes to be as follows: From the beginningless past to this day and this moment, the ocean of multitudinous beings has been defiled as evil and filthy and does not possess the pure heart and mind; again, they have been deluded as flattering and deceitful and do not possess the true heart and mind.[51]

On the other hand, he also says:

All the ocean-like multitudinous beings, since the beginningless past, have transmigrated in the sea of ignorance, drowning in the cycle of existences, bound to the cycles of suffering, having no pure, serene faith. They have, as a natural consequence, no true serene belief.[52]

An awakening of our consciousness to this assertion is suggested by a comparison of wrongdoing and ignorance to the Buddhist teachings of absolute truth. For Shinran, the absolute or eternal truth is none other than the fundamental vows of the Buddha Amida. Becoming aware of one's wickedness can lead to realizing this eternal truth. The opposite can also be proved, and I believe that this is the substance of religious faith.

The profound mind is the mind of deepest faith. It has ... two aspects. The first aspect is believing deeply and with determination that we are really evil ordinary beings, fettered to samsāra, continuously drowning and transmigrating from innumerable kalpas in the past, having no means for emancipation. The second aspect is believing deeply and with determination that the forty-eight vows of the Buddha Amida embrace sentient beings, enabling those who trust in the power of his vows without doubt or apprehension to attain rebirth with certainty.[53]

This passage is often referred to as the two aspects of profound faith (nishu-jinshin), which is a term used in the Shin tradition to serve as the basis for its theory of salvation. The first aspect is called opportunity of profound faith (ki no jinshin), where a person fully comprehends the reality of his own wickedness, and the second is called the Dharma of profound faith (hō no jinshin), where one fully believes in the Buddha Amida's vows to unfailingly save all frustrated and evil beings. These two aspects of profound faith do not occur in the heart at separate times but rather arise simultaneously, born from faith. In other words, by becoming aware of the perpetuity of evil which is the opportunity for profound faith, one is able to believe in the Dharma of profound faith—Amida's vows. This is precisely the doctrine which establishes salvation in the Shin tradition as the faith of Other-power.

Shinran used the term *shuku* (as in "prior karma" or "shukugō") to mean "to dwell in" and "to possess" for the purpose of emphasizing the inherency of evil and ignorance in sentient beings. Although individuals typically see their actions in a manner Shinran characterizes as "when our minds and hearts are good, we think it is good; when our minds and hearts are bad, we think it is bad,"[54] each act is nothing more than a continuity whose source lies in previous action, and an action that will be a source of future acting. When people reflect upon themselves, a major object of consideration is usually their past action (one nuance of "shukugō"). Thus, despite the meaning "to dwell in" in the term *prior karma*, the phrase is also intended to reflect upon a person's present self as well. Subsequently, Shinran often told his disciples that it would only be through comparison with the absolute, eternal truth of Amida's vows that a person could attain understanding. The more one attempts to believe that Amida's vow is eternal truth, the greater the realization that one is in the midst of continuous wrongdoing. A sense of sadness and rejection at having one's back turned away from the Pure Land becomes a realization much like seeing one's self in a mirror from behind.

> It is hard to leave our native land of suffering where we have been transmigrating from time immemorial up through the present. We feel no longing for the Pure Land of serene sustenance where we are yet to be reborn. How powerful and how intense are our evil passions.[55]

This awareness, in turn, suggests that the more sinful a person is, the more the vows of the Buddha Amida are drawn to that person. Just as negative actions committed by human beings have continued from a beginningless past, so Amida's vows have also existed from beginningless time.

In one of the more scholarly but strongly emotional writings that Shinran composed, there is a passage in which he makes a frank confession and penitence. This is a passage which many have found to be the most unreserved confession in the history of Japanese Buddhism. It reads:

> Truly, I do realize. It is tragic that I, Gutoku [the foolish and fuzzy-headed Shinran], am overwhelmed in vast oceans of lust and bewildered among the enormous mountains of fame and profit, never rejoicing to belong to the multitudes who will strive to be reborn in the Pure Land nor enjoying any approach to the realization of true enlightenment. What a shame, what a terrible sorrow![56]

The more serious and profound the penitence and confession people make, the more joyful and elated they will be to realize the eternal truth of Amida's vow (which itself was offered for the salvation of sentient beings who are nothing more than wickedness themselves).

What a joy it is to place my heart in the ground of the Buddha [Amida's] universal vows and let my thoughts flow into the inconceivable sea of the Dharma. I deeply acknowledge the Tathāgata's compassion and sincerely appreciate the master's [Hōnen's] kindness in instructing me. As my joy increases, my feeling of indebtedness grows stronger and stronger.[57]

Shinran also states that the merit of Amida's vows would fill the ocean of multitudinous beings. He came to believe that the Buddha Amida even had mercy on those who had practised the Buddhism of the sages (which he had denied after twenty years of religious training). In a letter to his disciples, he wrote:

The path of the sages is the way by which those who are already enlightened attempt to lead us, and is represented by such superb Mahāyāna teachings as the school of the Buddha's mind, the Shingon school, the Lotus school, the Kegon school, the Sanron school, and others. The school of the Buddha's mind is the Zen movement that now flourishes so widely. The path of the sages is also represented by such teachings as those of the Hossō, Jōjitsu and Kusha schools as well as others, which are either pseudo-Mahāyāna or Hinayāna. These are all the path of the sages. We call these "pseudo" because the already enlightened Buddhas and bodhisattvas reveal themselves, for the moment, in various forms to urge us along the way.[58]

Shinran was thus able to find and accept the innate value of all aspects of Buddhism and all of its adherents. His turning point from a negative or critical position to a positive or all-encompassing logic centred on his prior-karma thought and its relationship to the power of Amida's vows. His profound sadness in realizing that he was living in never-ending evil was precisely what provoked his joy in realizing that the eternal truth of Amida's vows would completely embrace such sentient despair. This revelation he established as his rationale of salvation. His explanation to his disciples that they could continue living with confidence in spite of the knowledge that each was in the midst of continuous evil, has been discussed.

The nembutsu is the unimpeded singular faith. The reason for this is that the gods of heaven and earth bow in reference to the followers of faith and the maras and non-Buddhists cannot hurt them, nor can any wrong or evil exert karmic influence upon them, nor can various good deeds surpass the nembutsu.[59]

Only through faith can a person trapped in evil come to know the joy called the unimpeded singular path which is true freedom to

Shinran. This combination of the psychological awareness of one's sentient limitations and helplessness in the age of the decay of the Dharma (due to karmic-samsaric dilemma) and the all-encompassing, compassionate, saving power of the Buddha Amida became a central doctrine of Shinran's mature thought. While the exact term *prior karma/prior actions* was not explicitly mentioned in his letters and writings, it brilliantly suggests the purposes or rationale upon which the epitome of his Pure Land teachings was constructed.

H. Akunin shōki: "If a good person can attain salvation, how much more so a wicked person!"

As previously mentioned, the *Mahāparinirvāṇa sūtra* was the second most cited reference in Shinran's *Kyōgyōshinshō*, after the *Sukhāvati-vyūha sūtra*, which was one of the "three sūtras of the Pure Land" (jōdo sanbu-kyō).[60] The reason for such frequency was his recognition that the Buddha had various types of sentient beings in mind for salvation, particularly the nanke no sanki or "three types difficult to convert."[61] I have concluded that another reason for such frequent citation of the *Mahāparinirvāṇa sūtra* was Shinran's realization that he himself was one of the nanke no sanki, a most difficult person to save.

This idea is well characterized by his concept of 'akunin shōki' or the "true opportunity for the wicked person." An akunin, or wicked being, represents the greatest difficulty as a subject for the Buddha's salvation. Shinran's "true opportunity for the wicked person" as a view of humanity was integrally related to his concept of shukugō or "prior karma," and these became the starting point as well as the end result of the circular reasoning process of his mature thought.

Unlike the term *prior karma*, *akunin shōki* does appear in both the writings of Shinran and his disciples. The expression is found in his *Kyōgyōshinshō* as well as in T'an-luan's *Wang-shêng-lun-chu*, Genshin's *Ōjō-yō-shū* and the *Amitāyur-dhyāna* and *Mahāparinirvāṇa* sūtras.

In drawing together the relationship between human nature and Amida's power, Shinran often focused on the central role of trust and faith.

> Amida made his vows in compassion for us—we who are full of evil passion and who are unable to set ourselves free from samsāra by any kind of practice. Since the purpose of his vows is to enable wicked people to attain Buddhahood, the evil being who trusts in Other-power is in particular the one who has true cause for rebirth in the Pure Land. Therefore, the statement: "If a good person can be born in the Pure Land, how much more so can a wicked person!"[62]

It becomes evident in this type of thought that faith and trust are not limited to any single kind of person but transcend intellect, personality, social status, and moral circumstance. We should know what kind of people Shinran specifically had in mind in using this characterization of akunin, or wicked being. In one of his letters he provided a clue to this concept.

> So we should not think that we cannot be accepted by the Tathāgata because we are evil. We think that we are evil because we are by nature profoundly subject to delusion.[63]

In another letter, he said that such evil beings were the very people that the Buddha Amida was trying to save. It reads:

> Since we are in delusion, we may unknowingly be doing what we should not, saying what we should not and thinking what we should not. If we, on the basis that nothing hinders us, entertain dark thoughts toward others, do what we are not supposed to do, and say what we are not supposed to say, it is not because we are driven to evil by delusion but because we do so on purpose. How can this ever be.[64]

Shinran explains that human actions all stem from the spiritual darkness and ignorance of sentiency. He claims that a person is characterized by evil and that every action performed by human will is, in fact, not individual will but the inevitable interplay of karmic results which causes one to commit wrongdoing. This is the essence of Shinran's definition of the akunin or wicked one.

The term *shōki* refers to the true opportunity, the situation of the greatest spiritual potential for the soteriological power of the Buddha Amida. In the Shin tradition, the Chinese character *ki* (of *shōki)* is given exegesis as "sentient being" and is the source of a major Shin doctrine. *Ki*, or sentient being, is divided into three types: 'shobi no ki' or "to be capable of the opportunity"; 'juhō no ki' or "the opportunity of receiving the Dharma"; and 'shōtoku no ki' or "the opportunity of nature and accomplishment." 'Shobi no ki' affirms the wickedness of each individual, 'juhō no ki' is the faith of an individual, and 'shōtoku no ki' is a comparison of the individual with the absolute and eternal reality of the Dharma. Here again is Shinran's view of his nature in terms of the eternal reality of the Buddha Amida.

> The profound mind is the mind of deepest faith. It has ... two aspects. The first aspect is believing deeply and with determination that we are really evil ordinary beings, fettered to samsāra, continuously drowning and transmigrating from innumerable kalpas in the past, having no means for emancipation.[65]

To his disciples he explained this nature in terms of the self-effort basis of earlier Buddhism.

> I know absolutely nothing about good and evil. If I were able to know good so thoroughly that the Tathāgata would recognize it in his mind as good, then I could say that I do know good. If I were able to know evil so thoroughly that the Tathāgata would recognize it as evil, then I could say that I do know evil.[66]

In this way Shinran defined human existence (including his own) as evil in relationship to the Buddha Amida. He went on to write in his *Kyōgyōshinshō* that the person who is evil is the very object whom the Buddha seeks to save.

> Hereupon, the *Amitāyur-dhyāna sūtra* says, "Teach me how to observe the [Pure] land which results from the purest of actions." "Land resulting from the purest of actions refers to the [Buddha] Land of Reward established by [Amida's] fulfilment of the fundamental vows. "Teach me how to meditate" is his creative response to suffering [Sanskrit: upāya]. "Teach me how to receive properly" refers to the diamond-like reality of the mind. The words "clearly understand someone in the Pure Land who has accomplished the purest of action" mean that we should believe that the unobstructed light of the Tathāgata completely fills the ten quarters [i.e., all directions] due to his fundamental vows. "You are a common mortal whose mind and thought are inferior" reveals that even an evil man can be born in the Pure Land. . . . The words "the Buddhas and the Tathāgatas use different creative responses to suffering" show that the various meditations and positive actions are teachings of creative response to suffering. The words "she saw the land by means of the Buddha's power" imply that it was manifested through Other-power. The words "the many sentient beings after the Buddha's death" show that sentient beings in the future will have the true opportunity for rebirth in the Pure Land [i.e., will be the object of salvation].[67]

Shinran's ideological development of the 'akunin-shōki' concept resulted from his careful examination of the *Mahāparinirvāna sūtra* and became an extension of Saichō's 'convergence of time and opportunity' (jiki sō ō) which Shinran had studied at Mt. Hiei. This study originally served as a stepping stone to Pure Land teachings, and after experiencing his life in exile, he reached a new understanding of the dynamics of Amida's power and its relation to the hopeless nature of man. Shinran thus taught that the ordinary finite man can only be saved by Amida in his eternal truth and infinite compassion, that is, by the all-encompassing Buddhist Pure Land soteriology of Other-power. It was Amida's transcendental character that could offer merciful salvation to all, whether rich or poor, nobility or outcast, good or bad. Shinran's doctrine offered a democratic soteriology beyond monastic-lay distinctions for the possibility of enjoying the happiness of the Pure Land and experiencing the stability of true contentment, in a critical period for the efficacy of Japanese Buddhism.

Finding all previous Buddhist doctrine and practice to be strongly bound in some manner to self-effort, Shinran brought his religious training and experience together to find a Buddhist movement with the greatest accessibility for all Japanese people in the Kamakura period. His own version of Saichō's 'convergence of time and opportunity' was the result of his emotional and intellectual odyssey through the attitudes and values of the Japanese, the frustration of basic human passion, and the promise of the Buddhist tradition to reach salvation, for all who saw political and social change as well as decay in institutionalized Buddhism as a personal spiritual failure to meet the standards of traditional Buddhist accomplishment. It was at this stage in his life that Shinran began to show the great ability in religious thought that would earn him the title of a major religious reformer. His Pure Land interpretation of the 'convergence of time and opportunity' resulted from a deep awareness of history, of Buddhist teaching and practice, and of the depth of his own faith, and it would form the foundation for all of his later Pure Land thought. These ideas would exert a strong influence on the future of Japanese Buddhism by serving as a major impetus in Kamakura-period religion. Shinran was becoming one of the Buddhist masters of great understanding and vision who led what is known as the religious reformation of Japan.

Chapter 4 Notes

1. Kyōgyōshinshō, Shinran-shōnin zenshū, vol. 1, p. 381.

2. Mahāparinirvāna sūtra, Taishō 12:375, pp. 365-604. The term is found on pages 383-384.

3. There had been several Pure Land school (Jōdo-shū) followers before Shinran who called themselves Gutoku. See Yamada, op. cit., p. 109.

4. Sokusui Murakami, Shinran dokuhon (Kyoto: Hyakkaen, 1968), p. 21.

5. Kyōgyōshinshō, Shinran-shōnin zenshū, vol. 1, p. 5.

6. Ibid., p. 314. Modern scholars doubt that Saichō was the author of the Mappō tōmyō-ki, but Shinran did believe at the time that he was. See Mitsusada Inoue, Nihon kodai no kokka to bukkyō (Tokyo: Iwanami shoten, 1971), p. 125.

7. Tannishō, Shinran-shōnin zenshū, vol. 4, p. 8.

8. Shinran-shōnin kechimyaku-monjo (January 25, 1212 AD), Shinran-shōnin zenshū, vol. 3, p. 176.

9. Tannishō, Shinran-shōnin zenshū, vol. 4, p. 41.

10. Engi-shiki in Katsumi Kuroita, ed., Kokushi taikei, vol. 26 (Tokyo: Yoshikawa Kōbunkan, 1929-1966), p. 721.

11. Ibid.

12. An isshō no kome is 1.8 litres of rice; an isshaku no shio is .018 litres of salt.

13. Engi-shiki, op. cit., p. 669.

14. Kyōgyōshinshō, Shinran-shōnin zenshū, vol. 1, p. 381.

15. Engi-shiki, no. 29, op. cit., p. 721.

16. Kyōgyōshinshō, Shinran-shōnin zenshū, vol. 1, p. 381.

17. Danzō Hirano, Echigo to shinran eshinni no sokuseki (Niigata: Kakimurs shoten, 1972), pp. 120-121.

18. Dai-nihon shiryō-shū, vol. IV-8, edited by Teikoku daigaku shiryō hensansho (Tokyo: Teikoku Daigaku, 1912), p. 893.

19. Ōtani honganji yuisho tsūkan, no. 4 in Dai-nihon bukkyō zensho, vol. 132 (Tokyo: Bussho Kankō-kai, 1918-1930), p. 321.

20. Shūi-ōjō-den in Dai-nihon bukkyō zensho, vol. 51, op. cit., p. 86.

21. Zennen okitegaki for August 13, 1285 in Honganji monjo, quoted

in Junkō Matsuno, Shinran, op. cit., p. 180.

22. Shūi-ōjō-den, op. cit., p. 86.

23. Eshinni monjo, no. 1, Shinran-shōnin zenshū, vol. 3, p. 183.

24. Shinichi Satō and Yoshisuke Ikeuchi, ed., Goseibai shikimoku, Chūsei hōsei shiryō-shū: kamakura bakufu-hō muromachi bakufū-hō (Tokyo: Iwanami shoten, 1955), p. 24.

25. Saihō shinan-sho, Shinran-shōnin zenshū, vol. 5, pp. 267-272.

26. Kenmyō Nakazawa, Shijō no Shinran (Kyoto: Bunkendō shoten, 1923), p. 20.

27. Shisō Hattori, Shinran nōto (Tokyo: Fukumara Shuppan, 1967), p. 143. Notes made by the Marxist historian Hattori were based on letters such as the following, from which he pictured Eshinni as a robust woman with a highly positive attitude toward life:

> I myself do not have many more years left to live, so such things should not overly concern me, but I am not living alone . . . here we have with us the little girl and boy of my daughter Oguro, for they are without parents, and all of Masukata's children also live with me, so I somehow feel like a mother to them (Eshinni at eighty-three years of age).
>   I am very happy to be able to write you. I never thought that I could live this long, but I have already reached eighty-seven years of age . . . I have accumulated the years of an unbelievable age, but I never cough or drool. I have never yet had to have my back and legs massaged. I work just like a dog everyday. . . . There are many things I want to write about, but the messenger says that he is leaving early tomorrow morning, so I am writing this letter in the middle of the night . . . I will close now. . . . Please send me some needles. You may give them to the messenger by enclosing them within your letter to me (Eshinni at eighty-seven years of age).

28. Ryūshō Umehara, Shinran-den no sho-mondai (Kyoto: Kenshin Gakuen, 1951), pp. 219-220. This opinion is based on the premise that Shinran married after his arrival in Echigo.

29. Eshinni monjo, Shinran-shōnin zenshū, vol. 4, p. 89.

30. Takehiko Furuta, Shinran (Tokyo: Shimizu Shoin, 1970), p. 108.

31. Kuden-shō, Shinran-shōnin zenshū, vol. 4, p. 61.

32. Sonpi-bunmyaku, see note 23.

33. Honganji keizu, Zoku gunshoruijū, vol. 6 (Tokyo: Keizaizasshisha, 1903), pp. 745-751.

34. Hino-ichiryū keizu, Reizō Hiramatsu, ed., Shinshū shiryō shūsei,

vol. 7 (Kyoto: Dohōsha, 1975), pp. 504-544.

35. Hogo-uragaki, op. cit., p. 520-521.

36. Junkō Matsuno, Shinran—sono kōdo to shisō, op. cit., p. 160.

37. Kyōgyōshinshō, Shinran-shōnin zenshū, vol. 1, p. 78.

38. Tannishō, Shinran-shōnin zenshū, vol. 4, pp. 5-6. The belief which Shinran placed in Hōnen can be seen from his own words:

> I will have no regrets even though I may have been deceived by Hōnen and by thus uttering the nembutsu, I may fall into the hells. . . . If the fundamental vows of the Buddha Amida are true, then Śākyamuni's sermons cannot be untrue. If the Buddha's words are true, then Shan-tao's comments cannot be untrue. If Shan-tao's comments are true, then how can what Hōnen has said be false? (Tannishō, ibid., p. 4).

39. Ganmon in Dengyō-daishi zenshū, vol. 1, Tendaishū shūten kankōkai, ed. (Tokyo: Tendaishū shūten kankōkai, 1912), p. 2.

40. Tannishō, Shinran-shōnin zenshū, vol. 4, p. 21.

41. Tannishō, op. cit., p. 20.

42. Kōshō Yamamoto, trans., Kyōgyōshinshō (Tokyo: Karin bunko, 1958), p. 283.

43. Kyōgyōshinshō, Shinran-shōnin zenshū, vol. 1, p. 117.

44. Ibid., p. 127.

45. Tannishō, Shinran-shōnin zenshū, vol. 4, pp. 3-4.

46. Ibid., p. 10.

47. Ibid., pp. 3-4.

48. Ibid., p. 13.

49. Tannishō, Shinran-shōnin zenshū, vol. 4, p. 20.

50. Ibid., p. 6.

51. Kyōgyōshinshō, Shinran-shōnin zenshū, vol. 1, p. 116.

52. Ibid., p. 120.

53. Ibid., p. 103.

54. Tannishō, Shinran-shōnin zenshū, vol. 4, p. 22.

55. Ibid., p. 12.

56. Kyōgyōshinshō, Shinran-shōnin zenshū, vol. 1, p. 153.

57. Ibid., p. 383.

58. Mattō-shō, Shinran-shōnin zenshū, vol. 3, p. 61.

59. Tannishō, Shinran-shōnin zenshū, vol. 4, p. 10.

60. Shūkō Tsuchihashi, "Shinran shōnin to nehan-gyō" in <u>Ryūkoku daigaku ron-shū</u>, vols. 355-356 (Kyoto: Ryūkoku daigaku, 1961), p. 309.

61. The "three types difficult to convert" are (1) those who have committed the Five Evil Acts (see note 57, chapter 3); (2) those who mock the Buddhist tradition; and (3) those who cannot be saved (Sanskrit: icchantika).

62. <u>Tannishō</u>, <u>Shinran-shōnin zenshū</u>, vol. 4, p. 6.

63. <u>Mattō shō</u>, <u>Shinran-shōnin zenshū</u>, vol. 3, p. 64.

64. Ibid., p. 103.

65. <u>Kyōgyōshinshō</u>, <u>Shinran-shōnin zenshū</u>, vol. 1, p. 103.

66. <u>Tannishō</u>, <u>Shinran-shōnin zenshū</u>, vol. 4, p. 38.

67. <u>Kyōgyōshinshō</u>, <u>Shinran-shōnin zenshū</u>, vol. 1, p. 276.

Chapter 5

Shinran's Movement as
Buddhist Reformation

A. The significance of a new religious salvation in the Kamakura period

During the Kamakura period (1185-1333) traditional political power was given over to new authority. This process of change involved resistance and even revolt, while society experienced insecurity and hardship as its institutions faced severe challenge and often decay. Yet at the same time people were briefly liberated from the pressures of authority and found opportunities to awaken a sense of individual self-awareness and renewed co-operation. This was even apparent in the political system, where the older court structure and the new warrior-council structure both existed at the same time, a situation to be found in this period alone in Japanese history. Warriors who had originally been the bodyguards of the imperial court now came to possess the power to rule. Values and roles previously held were completely altered and this upheaval became the starting point of a social revolution.

The infiltration of the warrior into the ruling class had begun with the Heike clan, but the actual political power they possessed had remained within the court structure of authority under the emperor. By establishing kinship through marriage with the imperial family and by developing and leading a devoted military force, the Heike clan soon had a free hand within the sphere of imperial authority. As opposition to the solidification of power and the arrogance of the Heike clan increased, Emperor Goshirakawa, who wanted to regain complete imperial control, attempted to force the Heike from their position but was unable to do so alone, so he enlisted the aid of the rivals of the Heike, the Genji clan. This was the beginning of tragedy and the further decline of imperial power.

Minamoto no Yoritomo (1147-1199), whom the emperor mistakenly believed to be as obedient and trustworthy as a favoured watchdog, quickly changed into a wolf as the scent of power became stronger. Soon after the Heike were successfully subjugated in 1185, Yoritomo refused to remain any longer a docile servant of imperial will. The Genji had defeated the Heike, proving to themselves by this success that they could overwhelm imperial authority at any time as well, so the Genji eventually came to take from the emperor responsibilities for shugo (police and military power) and jitō (control of land ownership and collection of taxes) to establish a new national government in Kamakura.

With the rise of the Kamakura military (or bakufu) government, common warriors who ordinarily fought in the battlefields and were looked down upon by the aristocracy (as Azuma ebisu or illiterate men from the uncivilized east) were now assigned to positions of authority as military administrators, police officials, estate supervisors, and tax collectors. A class of people who had been ignored and castigated as lowly-born and whose work was seen as necessary but almost immoral was now given great opportunity to advance in society. An entire society had to realize a new order and a new identity.

It was also a time of change for religion, as institutions, teachings and practices, and monastic status were swept up in the development of a warrior culture. For those who now saw greater possibilities to participate effectively at broader or higher levels of society and power, a religious world-view that reflected more universal and humane possibilities for spiritual growth would be more attractive than a highly aristocratic and ritualized classical institution that had simply affirmed the previous order and the warrior's former subservient position in society. Thus the Kamakura period became a turning point in the history of Japanese Buddhism, when most people were searching for teachings and practices which reflected their changing attitudes and values. The warrior culture brought to the forefront an emphasis on strength, dedication, directness, and simplicity in daily affairs, in contrast to the sophisticated classical ceremonial and aesthetic cultivation of aristocratic life. This new culture influenced what people desired in religious values and activity, as trends toward strength and dedication in attitude and directness and simplicity in practice began to compete with the older forms of Buddhism and make way for a Buddhism of emotional commitment or faith to come to the forefront. The new way of the warrior in viewing and acting in the world to some extent influenced all the founders of the new Kamakura Buddhist movements, so a comparison of the basic approaches of Hōnen, Shinran, Dōgen, and Nichiren will next be examined.

B. A Buddhism relevant to the people and the period

Fumio Masutani has suggested one facet of the new Kamakura religious consciousness:

> In the Kamakura period, Japan, for the first time, discovered that Buddhism which was originally a foreign doctrine had become the accepted religion in the daily lives of the common Japanese people.[1]

This was made possible by a variety of doctrinal interpretations of Saichō's 'convergence of time and opportunity' (jiki sōō) by such Kamakura Buddhist masters as Hōnen, Shinran, Dōgen, Nichiren, and Ippen, all of whom had spent some time on Mt. Hiei. What would be most·productive at this point is some comparison of the legacies of the Sōtō Zen master Dōgen and Nichiren, the founder of the Nichiren school, with those of Hōnen and Shinran, particularly in observing their respective developments about religious faith and practice. It is after a comparison of how these masters developed such basic aspects of their Buddhist movements that Shinran's importance and uniqueness as a religious reformer in the Kamakura period can better be appreciated.

These four Kamakura masters had all at one time in their lives studied on Mt. Hiei—Hōnen from age thirteen to forty-three, Shinran from nine to twenty-nine, Dōgen from thirteen to fifteen, and Nichiren from age twenty-one to thirty-two. The traditions of thought developed by these four do share a common characteristic in that, from the vast Tendai encyclopedic organization of Buddhist teaching and practice, each chose a single teaching and practice to emphasize. (It is often suggested that the reason for this common development stems from the fact that all four did share a common background of early Tendai study and training on Mt. Hiei.)

The Tendai tradition on Mt. Hiei saw all Buddhist teachings and practices to be of equal spiritual significance. But it was from such a broad and eclectic position on Mt. Hiei that both Hōnen and Shinran left in search of stronger directions in Pure Land faith. Dōgen also left Mt. Hiei for a more meaningful life in a single system of practice (which he would find in Zen). Nichiren, whose practice centred upon the *Lotus sūtra* and who remarked that "those in Japan who are not followers of the great master Dengyō [Saichō] are evil men,"[2] himself left Mt. Hiei where the Lotus teachings and practices co-existed as equal components in the syncretistic atmosphere, rather than as the superior and only practices which he felt them to be.

These four men who "descended from the mountains" (as Far Eastern Buddhist painters often depicted Śākyamuni returning to teach in society) demonstrated their critical spirit and discernment toward the existing state of Japanese history, society, and the individual in the thirteenth century, each emphasizing a Buddhist teaching and practice to meet his perception of the actual spiritual needs of the people of his time. Each master re-interpreted and developed the Buddhist tradition based upon one chosen teaching and practice, and together these came to be known as the new Japanese or Kamakura Buddhism. This Kamakura Buddhism is also referred to as the religious reformation of mediaeval Japan, and such representative masters who formed important movements in this period are collectively known as the religious reformers of Japan.

The outstanding characteristic of Kamakura Buddhism was an emphasis on a specific teaching and practice to best fit the age, a spectrum of changing social classes and the nation itself. Each of these masters has in some way alluded to this necessity.

> In the practice of Buddhism, it is imperative to know oneself as thoroughly as the period in which one is living.[3] (Hōnen)

> The monks and laity of this age should consider their own limited capacities.[4] (Shinran)

The proper way to study Buddhism is first of all to always
examine the age and to see man and his times through the
eyes of the Buddhist tradition.[5] (Nichiren)

They further remarked on the Kamakura period in which they
lived, their contemporaries, and Japan:

The world has already entered the degenerate age of the
decay of the Dharma. Man is ignorance.[6] (Hōnen)

Two thousand five hundred years after the death of
Sākyamuni, this age has so much conflict that it is most
difficult to master any practice of Buddhism.[7] (Hōnen)

More than two thousand years after the death of
Sākyamuni, the ages of the True and Complete Dharma
and the Artificial Dharma have long passed. Believers in
Buddhism who attempt to practise after the death of
Sākyamuni are saddened.[8] (Shinran)

We are in far-off islands scattered in the ocean.[9]
(Shinran)

Contrasting we who are of a far-off island in the present
degenerate age with those in the ages of the True and
Complete Dharma and the Artificial Dharma, there are
all the differences between heaven and earth.[10] (Dōgen)

More than two thousand years have passed since we
entered the degenerate age—we are of a far-off island
and as well, human beings are ignorance itself.[11]
(Nichiren)

Each of these masters referred to his age as one of conflict, the
person as profound ignorance, and to Japan as an island nation far
distant in time and space from the life and teachings of the Buddha.
This special characteristic of the new religious consciousness of the
times was certainly shared by them, and it was their acute understanding and critical spirit of time, place, and people that led to their
interpretations of Buddhism and the radically new movements that
followed.

The Pure Land teachings and nembutsu practice chosen by
Hōnen have already been examined in chapter 3. He characteristically distinguished in his understanding of religion between "the
reality of this earth and the Pure Land" and between "the Buddha and
sentient beings." He turned his back on the secular world and
concentrated his teachings about Pure Land rebirth on the next or
subsequent life, also denying a person's ability to achieve salvation by
self-effort and teaching that people can appeal only to the mercy of
the Buddha Amida. In addition, Hōnen urged believers to abandon
many of the Buddhist practices which were considered spiritually
valid at the time. He stressed only the shōmyō nembutsu, the 'easy
path' which was the invocation of the nembutsu.

See the Buddha Amida with your eyes, invoke the name of
Amida with your mouth, await the coming of Amida in
your heart . . . and pray for your right-mindedness at your
deathbed.[12]

Dōgen opposed such teachings of Hōnen and in his sermons and
written works also questioned the existence of this type of afterlife,
clearly emphasizing the responsible performance of religious practice
through which enlightenment could be attained in this world and in
this life. In other words, Dōgen maintained that human ignorance
could be transformed into realization and that it was possible to seek
eternal truth in the everyday world. In order to attain such
enlightenment, Dōgen chose 'shikan-taza' ("only-sitting" or zazen
without any set theme for meditation), which he taught as the
practice of cultivating intense self-effort to break through individual
ignorance and frustration. He thus clearly took a completely
opposite stance to Hōnen, who taught that the attainment of a serene
and happy life was only accessible through Other-power and by the
practices of the "easy path." Dōgen argued for his position with
these words:

Rather than remaining sluggish by using the excuse that
the world is in a degenerate age, one should ask when a
person can ever be enlightened if he will not struggle for
the mind of realization?[13]

In denying the spiritual worth or efficacy of the easy path, Dōgen
also stated:

What the people of today mean by "practice" is the
performance of easy activity. This is clearly harmful and
inconsistent with the teachings of the Buddha. Which of
the Buddha's teachings popular among the people of this
age are easy to comprehend and to practise? It is neither
the laws of this world nor the Dharma of the Buddha. It is
nothing but a highly confused delusion of people.[14]

He made this comment specifically about the practice of the
nembutsu:

Do you know what merit or virtue could be attained by
such practices as chanting and saying the nembutsu? It is
truly sad that you can think of Buddhist merit or virtue as
the mere movement of your tongue and the voicing of
sounds. Nonstop moving your mouth and chanting can be
equated with frogs making incessant noise day and night
in a spring rice paddy, and there is nothing ever to be
gained.[15]

Dōgen thus strongly criticized the practice basis of the Pure
Land teaching of abandoning any possibility for spiritual success

through self-effort in this world and instead focusing on the nembutsu. He, like Hōnen, did refer to his era as the "degenerate age" and affirm man as corrupt and Japan as a far-off land. Dōgen contended that in such a social and historical matrix an individual's only choice would be to seek eternal and infinite truth more strenuously. His thought did not perceive the Buddha as a single figure whose power had to be appealed to for salvation.

There is a radical difference in Hōnen's and Dōgen's fundamental attitudes toward reality and the spiritual potential of the individual. In Hōnen's teachings, breaking-away from and transcending reality is emphasized, while to Dōgen, an active confrontation with reality can be the only fruitful possibility for the human condition.

Having examined Hōnen's and Dōgen's ideas, we are in a better position to appreciate Nichiren's religious views. The characteristics of his teachings are the importance he gives to one specific Buddhist sūtra, the *Lotus sūtra*. Nichiren had studied Tendai teachings on Mt. Hiei but strongly criticized the institution for submerging the Lotus doctrine (which is the central sūtra of the Tendai school) within the Tendai synthesis and development of other Buddhist teachings and practices. He therefore attempted to revive the singular importance of the *Lotus sūtra* while purifying and critically examining Buddhist doctrine as Hōnen and Dōgen had done. Nichiren also reflected on the degenerate age, the capabilities of the average person, and the remoteness of Japan. He maintained belief in and practice of the teachings of the *Lotus sūtra* as the ultimate way to attain eternal truth in this finite life. The efficacy of the *Lotus sūtra* hinged upon a strong dedication and spiritual commitment by the individual, thus turning the issue of practice to the pivotal question of faith.

> The basis upon which one enters the way of the Buddha is faith. Though without enlightenment, he who possesses faith is a person of true seeing, he who has enlightenment but not faith is one who cannot be saved.[16]

In other words, Nichiren placed emphasis upon faith as the central act of practice, much as Hōnen had done before him. However, the faith in the *Lotus sūtra* which Nichiren referred to was the degree or quality of practice as a concrete manifestation of faith. In other words, he claimed that strenuous practice was evidence of profound faith—hence practice per se could easily take priority over faith. In this way, Nichiren's emphasis on faith over practice was obviously different from the Pure Land faith which Hōnen had advocated.

Again, to distinguish this relationship between faith and practice among the teachings of the Kamakura reformers, Nichiren's conception of practice can be compared to Dōgen's. As previously mentioned, Dōgen proposed strenuous Zen meditation as the sole individual effort for the realization of eternal truth. Nichiren saw practice much more as a collective effort to build an ideal society in this world based upon the teachings of the *Lotus sūtra*. His teaching was strongly historical and nation-oriented, with revolutionary implications for Japanese society.

Nichiren's faith and practice can also be evaluated in terms of modern Buddhist scholarship. He claimed that he was the "activist or ascetic of the *Lotus sūtra*"(Hokke-kyō no gyōja), asserting this to his followers particularly during the latter half of his life.[17] This self-ideal does much to explain the social thrust of his energetic practice. The Nichiren scholar Shigemoto Tokoro summarizes the faith-practice relationship of Nichiren as follows:

> Nichiren never refers to himself as a "believer" (shinja) in the *Lotus sūtra*. For Nichiren, to believe means to express in action what he believes. The depth of faith is substantiated by practice. Nichiren, who calls himself the 'Hokke-kyō no gyōja' placed importance on practice over and above faith.[18]

A practice given significance over faith certainly differs from Hōnen's nembutsu practice. Hōnen's nembutsu was a practice which arose after faith, and it would be through such practice that an adherent could reach enlightenment. In strict doctrinal terms, Hōnen's nembutsu was an 'ōsō no gyō' ("practice toward Pure Land rebirth").

Nichiren's concept of practice, on the other hand, functioned as the foundation upon which faith was born and enlightenment achieved, and subsequent practice would serve to prove or certify the spiritual truth of an individual's enlightenment. His doctrine of practice could be referred to as a kind of 'gensō no gyō' or "practice to return (to this world) as response (to the sufferings of sentient beings)"—practice to save others. Nichiren speaks of this type of relationship between faith and practice in the following manner:

> One must labour for both the ways of practice and of learning. When practice and learning cease, there can be no Buddhism. By your own practice and learning, teach others. Practice and learning originate from faith. If you have any strength, be it a single word or a single sentence, do utter it.[19]

In another place, he writes:

> In reading the *Lotus sūtra*, some people only mouth the words and do not read it with their bodies—the heart may be reading but the body is not. Reading with both body and heart is certainly what is religious.[20]

Yoshirō Tamura speaks of the source of this social and historical characteristic in Nichiren's conception of practice, with the following:

It is the teachings found in Chapters 10 (entitled 'Hosshi-bon' or "Master or Teacher of the Dharma") through 22 (entitled 'Zokurui-bon' or "Entrustment" of the *Lotus sūtra).* Here, the sūtra praises: "Those who bear and embrace the sufferings of this world, exalt the truth and labour in the realization of the ideal society (such as the innumerable bodhisattvas springing up from the earth as indicated in Chapter 15—'Welling Up Out of the Earth') are bodhisattvas born to this world as messengers of the Buddha." Therefore, it teaches, "Never fear suffering and always pursue your practice."[21]

One of the reasons that Nichiren called himself the activist or ascetic of the *Lotus sūtra* and marshalled his energy for revolutionary activities in this world is derived from this passage. His consciousness with regard to his own words "the messenger sent to build a nation of Buddhist ideals in this world of reality" strongly motivated him to act as a prophet (which, needless to say, antagonized Kamakura rulers and administrators). This is the major reason why Nichiren was persecuted far more than Hōnen, Shinran, or Dōgen. This persecution provoked Nichiren to a moral attitude of righteousness—he saw his life as activist or ascetic from the *Lotus sūtra* as well as a fierce advocate of his teachings, almost bent on martyrdom to affirm the strength of his beliefs. Nichiren was perceived by the people as an unusually militant Japanese religious reformer whose ideal of a Buddhist state gave challenge to both the earlier aristocratic government and the new warrior administration.

C. Shinran's Faith: the "Inevitability of the Dharma as it is"

The conceptions of faith and practice of Hōnen, Dōgen, and Nichiren can be briefly summarized before a comparison with Shinran's ideas is attempted. Hōnen, Dōgen, and Nichiren each criticized and rejected earlier Buddhist views about the efficacy of institutionalized Buddhism in Japan and the spiritual possibilities these offered to the Japanese in the Kamakura period.

Hōnen denied the worldly or finite circumstances of people in their search for the eternal reality of the Buddha Amida and rebirth in the Pure Land. Dōgen and Nichiren also searched for an ideal in the Buddha as eternal truth. However, what distinguished Nichiren and Dōgen from Hōnen were the efforts of the former to realize the ideal they found in the present (phenomenal) world. In short, neither Dōgen nor Nichiren denied the reality of this life. Dōgen in particular attempted to break beyond his finite and ignorant individuality to experience the realization of Buddhist truth through a re-affirmation and restructuring of some of the most traditional kinds of Buddhist practice, for example, his "only-sitting" meditation (shikan-taza).

Nichiren attempted to transform this finite world into an ideal society, utilizing the faith and practice taught in the *Lotus sūtra* for this purpose. He interpreted the sūtra to preach social reform with the ultimate goal of establishing a Buddhist commonwealth of the Dharma. Because he saw in the Lotus teachings that action was the ultimate evidence of faith, he defined practice as the vigorous advocacy of his teachings for the reformation of an unconcerned and degenerate society, whatever the personal consequences might be. Such efforts by Dōgen and Nichiren to transcend their historical limitations through practice as struggle with the self (Dōgen) or as struggle with society (Nichiren) can be viewed as an essential Buddhist confrontation with the finite realities of the Kamakura period.

Shinran, however, followed in the footsteps of his spiritual master Hōnen in affirming the teachings of the nembutsu. He accepted Hōnen's absolute unbridgeable gap between this world and the Pure Land, between the ordinary sentient being and the Buddha Amida. But Shinran differed from Hōneh in his denial of human ability to attain Buddhahood through one's own efforts. In response to his disciple Jōshinbō, Shinran explained this complete denial of self-effort.

My dear Jōshinbō,

I fully understand what you are trying to say. Now, you have written to inquire about your doubts regarding religious questions and you state that since we are taken in and protected by the unobstructed light [of the Buddha Amida] the moment faith becomes established, the cause for birth in the Pure Land is always established. This is good. You thus express it properly, but this all may end in presumption on our part. When we are wonder-struck, there should be no more worry or presumption on our part. It is difficult to understand that there is so much desire to flee this world and yet less cause to be born in the Pure Land. The desire to escape from this world and the cause to be born in the Pure Land are both the same. Any other conclusion would simply be a halfway presumption. When your faith is set in the inconceivable wisdom of the Buddha Amida, you will not particularly need to worry about one thing or another. Please do not worry about what other people say. Only trust in the vows of the Tathāgata and never make assumptions about this or that.

With reverence, I remain
Shinran

P.S. Other-power means never presuming anything about this or that.[22]

Shinran, of course, emphasizes the significance of profound faith. One area where he moved beyond Hōnen's teachings was in rejecting nembutsu practice in terms of the Pure Land doctrine of 'rinjū shōnen' or "the final true thought" (completely abandoning frustration, ignorance and fear at death to truly realize the all-encompassing virtue of the Buddha Amida) and 'rinjū raigō' or "the final coming to welcome" (the Buddha Amida and his bodhisattvas coming from the Pure Land to welcome the person who makes a fervent deathbed desire for rebirth in the Pure Land).

> The followers of true faith sit in the truly established situation because of him who takes us in and never abandons us. Therefore, there can be no waiting for the last moment of life and looking for Amida's coming to accept us upon our deathbed. No sooner is faith established than birth in the Pure Land becomes a certain fact. There is no waiting for any set formality of Amida's coming to receive us at our deathbed. The word *right-mindedness* refers to the establishment of faith as pledged in the vows. Because of this faith, we unfailingly attain unsurpassed nirvāna. This faith is called the "singular mind." This "singular mind" is known as the "diamond-like mind." The "diamond-like mind" is called the "mind of the great enlightenment." This is the "Other-power" of Other-power.[23]

Here Shinran denies the possibility of any human spiritual accomplishment through the self-effort taught by Dōgen or Nichiren and instead insists upon absolute dependence on the compassion of Amida as Other-power. In Shinran's views:

> It is terribly wrong, when, with a mind of self-effort, a person says that he is equal to the Tathāgata.[24]

The shōmyō nembutsu practice which Shinran proposed was neither a practice to be undertaken for rebirth in the Pure Land nor a practice to return to this world for the purpose of saving others, but was in its most basic sense a sincere prayer of gratitude on behalf of all sentient life.

The culmination of Shinran's thought is found in this passage, which Shinran himself referred to as 'jinen hō-ni' or "the natural inevitability of the Dharma as it is"—the spiritual certainty of Amida's fundamental vows.

> We speak of 'jinen'. The 'ji' means "of itself." It has nothing to do with the effort of the person who practises the nembutsu. 'Nen' means "to cause to." "To cause to" has nothing to do with the effort of the person who practises the nembutsu. As it has been so vowed by the Tathāgata, we use 'hō-ni' [the Dharma as it is]. Because these are the vows of the Tathāgata, we speak of "to cause to" with 'hō-ni'. Since 'hō-ni' comes of the vows and because nothing is related to the effort of the person who practises the nembutsu, we can say by virtue of this Dharma that we are made "to be caused to." Overall, we

see for the first time that there is now no effort on our part which we can speak of. That is why it is described with "non-reason as reason." 'Jinen' means "to cause to" from the very beginning. The vows of the Buddha Amida from the very beginning have nothing to do with the effort of one who practises the nembutsu. His vows were so pledged that we must trust in his holy name, "Namu-amida-butsu," and he then takes us in. Therefore, when we think neither in terms of good nor evil, this 'jinen' is possible. So I have heard. What is vowed is to make us unsurpassed Buddhas. An unsurpassed Buddha has no form. As there is no form to conform to, we speak of 'jinen'. When things are described in terms of form, there can be no "unsurpassed nirvāna." To make us aware of this formlessness, first there came to be the Buddha Amida. So I have heard. We can hear of the Buddha Amida, and it is only to make us know this 'jinen'. When this fact is understood, we do have to talk about the 'jinen'. If we ever discuss 'jinen', it will mean that 'nonreason as reason' will still retain some reason. This will arise out of the unfathomable depths of wisdom of the all-enlightened one.

December 14, second year of Shōka
Shinran, at age eighty-six[25]

Shinran thus taught that the ordinary and finite person can be saved by Amida, the eternity of Buddhist truth, and the infinite embracing of Buddhist compassion, by the all-encompassing teachings of Other-power.

In seeking to break beyond any remnants of self-effort-oriented attitudes and practice in Pure Land thought, Shinran developed the full potential of faith among Kamakura Buddhist movements, by stressing the soteriological power of the Buddha Amida in direct proportion to the strongest possible individual realization of human spiritual limitations and the inability ever to know Buddhist reality through one's own efforts. The equality of human spiritual impotence meant at the same time the equivalence of all the Japanese people as potential adherents of the movement and as sentient beings able to be saved by Other-power, for the transcendental character of Amida by its nature offered salvation to all. One of the most significant accomplishments of Shinran's mature definition of the Pure Land tradition was the very accessibility it would offer as his creative response to the religious needs of the Japanese people.

Chapter 5 Notes

1. Fumio Masutani, Shinran, Dōgen, Nichiren (Tokyo: Shibundō, 1961), p. 24.

2. Senji-shō in Shōwa teihon nichiren-shōnin i-bun, vol. 2, Risshō Daigaku Nichiren Kyōgaku Kenkyūsho, ed. (Yamanashi: Sō-honzan Minobukuonji, 1953), p. 1016.

3. "Nembutsu tai-i" in Wago-tōroku, vol. 2, as contained in Jōdo-shū zensho, vol. 9 (Tokyo: Jōdo-shū Shūten Kankō-kai, 1908), pp. 510-511.

4. Kyōgyōshinshō, Shinran-shōnin zenshū, vol. 1, p. 313.

5. Senji-shō, op. cit., p. 1003.

6. "Nembutsu ōjō yōgishi" in Wago-tōroku, op. cit., p. 497.

7. "Nembutsu tai-i" in Wago-tōroku, op. cit., p. 511.

8. Shōzōmatsu wasan, Shinran-shōnin zenshū, vol. 1, p. 157.

9. Shōshin-ge, Shinran-shōnin zenshū, vol. 1, p. 91.

10. Eihei-kōroku, no. 5 in Dōgen zenji zenshū, vol. 1 (Tokyo: Chikuma Shobō, 1969), p. 539.

11. Kaimoku-shō in Shōwa teihon nichiren-shōnin i-bun, op. cit., p. 556.

12. Hichikajō kishō-mon, no. 5 in Wago-tōroku, op. cit., p. 509.

13. Shōbōgenzō zuimon-ki (Tokyo: Iwanami shoten, 1965), p. 24.

14. Gakudō yōshin-shū, chapter 5 in Dōgen zenji zenshū, vol. 1, op. cit., p. 474.

15. Ibid., vol. 6, p. 475.   Since a rice paddy does not exist after October harvest and rice fields remain bare until June, Dōgen intended to suggest the meaninglessness of the easy path.

16. Hokke daimoku-shō in Shōwa teihon nichiren-shōnin i-bun, vol. 1, op. cit., p. 392.

17. In his Kaimoku-shō ("Text on Opening the Eyes [of the People]") which Nichiren wrote at age fifty-one, he used the expression 'Hokke-kyō no gyōja' twenty-seven times.

18. Shigemoto Tokoro, "Nichiren," in Nihon shisō taikei, vol. 14 (Tokyo: Iwanami shoten, 1971), pp. 485-510.

19. Shōhō-jissō-sho in Shōwa teihon nichiren-shōnin i-bun, vol. 1, op. cit., pp. 728-9.

20. "Tsuchirō gosho," ibid., pp. 509-510.

21. Yoshirō Tamura, Nihon bukkyōshi nyūmon (Tokyo: Kadokawa shoten, 1969), p. 120.

22. Mattō-shō, Shinran-shōnin zenshū, vol. 4, pp. 84–86.

23. Ibid., p. 99.

24. Ibid.

25. Ibid., pp. 72–74.

Conclusion

We have attempted to trace the dynamic interaction of the influences and circumstances on Shinran in his early life until his forty-second year. Rather than restricting itself as a pure examination of his thought, this study has had the purpose of locating Shinran as a creative religious master within the social and political currents of his time. These have included the decline of the domination of the court and the aristocracy upon the national order and life as well as the rise of a new, self-confident, warrior-controlled mediaeval society. The conflict-laden position of a sensitive young Buddhist monk in quest of spiritual security and growth has also been described. Shinran's initial choice of career was not his own but was instead imposed on him by the circumstances of his youth and the decisions of others. Needless to say, the basis of any individual's personality is to some degree affected by personal circumstances and the surrounding historical situation, so there is always some compulsion present. In establishing an identity, individuals have to define themselves by action which both confronts and conforms to this partially heteronomous environment. The first forty-two years of Shinran's life can easily be divided into three distinct periods: his monastic life on Mt. Hiei; his conversion to the teachings of the Pure Land, as well as his experience with Hōnen and his followers; and his life of exile in Echigo. For Shinran, the earliest circumstances were the social and economic difficulties of his family in changing times, which caused his entry into Mt. Hiei, and then life within the vast Tendai monastic establishment itself.

Shinran was required to identify himself as a monk from the early and impressionable age of nine, and life in the monastery demanded austerity and dedication in religious practice. Before his entry into the monastery he had been under the tutelage of his uncle Munenari, who was a man always striving for personal improvement and advancement in the bureaucracy. He presented a strict ethical bearing which strongly influenced Shinran during his early years.

At the same time influences did exist in his youth which were completely opposite to such positive ones. Shinran's father abandoned his four-year-old son when he lost his position and had to retire. His grandfather had been a libertine who apparently caused such embarrassment to the family that he affected its social status and came to be omitted from the family genealogies. Shinran had to grow up while exposed to a variety of disparate family influences.

He also faced the terrible spiritual tension of perceiving the degenerate Buddhist age of the decay of the Dharma while having to live his daily life attempting to practise within changing religious institutions. Using the language of the psychologist Erik Erikson, the conflict between these two heteronomous adversities could be described as a "curse" which Shinran would have to overcome.[1] According to Erikson, this "curse" is formed between the ages of fifteen and thirty-three and is borne by the individual throughout his life as something that one day has to be squarely faced and resolved. Erikson describes this process in terms of an "account to settle."[2]

Shinran's "curse" consisted of his intense fears that he had inherited the laziness, weakness, and wickedness of his father and grandfather, for his uncle-stepfather Munenari gave Shinran a strong sense of responsibility, decency, and the possibility of concerted effort toward clear-cut goals. He must have known moments of deep spiritual despair on Mt. Hiei at the limits of his capabilities, continuously but unsuccessfully searching for some path to salvation in what he perceived to be a degenerate, disintegrating world. He must also have borne the full brunt of anxiety as a monastic, for he could never sublimate his spiritual angst through a pursuit of secular goals. In the anguished process of establishing his identity in the degenerate age of the decay of the Dharma, Shinran could be characterized as swinging like a pendulum between the one extreme of identifying the failures of his spirit with those of his disgraced grandfather and father and the other extreme of identifying with the strict ethics of his uncle and of exemplary Buddhist masters of the past.

His personal anguish in not achieving spiritual success in his own terms found expression in the Buddhist theory of the decay of the Dharma as it embraced the epistemological, soteriological, and institutional dimensions of Buddhist life at this time and his own personal and spiritual frustrations.

> So a time like ours is close to the final days of the age of the Artificial Dharma. What took place in the days already passed will be equal to those of the final age [of the decay of the Dharma]. Thus in the final age there can only be teachings in word, but no practice and no attainment. If there are any moral precepts at all, there will be only the transgression of such precepts. Already no precepts exist, so how can anyone say that the precepts are broken when there are no longer any precepts to break? There is already no transgression of the precepts, so how can there be any observance of the precepts? This is why the *Mahā-saṃnipāta sūtra* says that after the death of the Buddha, the non-observance of moral precepts will spread all over the country.[3]

Because of his troubled family background, his perception of the disappearance of moral precepts was not only an ethical dilemma within his practice of Buddhism but also a painful reflection of the insecurity of his growth and personal identification of self.

Shinran's life on Mt. Hiei lasted twenty years, but because he was only a young boy nine years of age when he entered, one can obviously question the degree or quality of his initial understanding of religious teaching and practice. There is no material which gives factual information about at approximately what age Shinran began his earnest and regular religious exercises in search of spiritual reconciliation, save for a single sentence from one of Eshinni's letters which reads: "Your father was an ordinary temple monk (dōsō) on Mt. Hiei."[4] No further references about Shinran's life on Mt. Hiei do exist, so any understanding of the development of his personal identity from boyhood to adolescence can only be found in the subsequent period when he had already joined Hōnen's group of Pure Land followers.

E. Victor Wolfenstein has defined a "revolutionary" in a hypothetical context as:

> one who escapes from the burdens of Oedipal guilt and ambivalence by carrying his conflict with authority into the political realm.[5]

If we apply this hypothetical definition to Shinran, it could be surmised that he was attempting to escape from the social and moral degradation of his father and grandfather while feeling deep personal guilt over his family's and his own failure to succeed. He also felt that the time itself was one of secular and religious moral collapse. From the systematic Tendai synthesis of Buddhist doctrine and practice in equivalence, Shinran selected Pure Land teachings to closely identify with and to see as the answer to his personal and familial difficulties as well as those of society, the political order, and the conditions of Buddhism in Japan. The solutions to all the problems he perceived could only be found in the universal salvation of the compassionate Other-power of the Buddha Amida. His strong sense of limitation and failure on so many levels led to his serious confrontation with the most fundamental issues of faith as the essential key to his Buddhist quest.

As a consequence of this concentration, confrontation, and definition of faith as the answer, Shinran prepared himself for leaving Mt. Hiei by engaging in a one-hundred-day dialogue with the Pure Land master Hōnen, after which his convictions were sufficiently clear to enable his departure.

To settle this confrontation over personal salvation, he began to use his energy as a new follower of Hōnen's movement to study and organize commentaries on Pure Land scripture, specifically his *Kangyō-amidakyō-shūchū* ("Annotated *Amitāyur-dhyāna sūtra* and *Sukhāvatī-vyūha sūtra*"). The intellectual effort required to complete this exegesis was as physically demanding as his earlier practices of Tendai asceticism on Mt. Hiei had been. The "Annotated *Amitāyur-dhyāna sūtra* and *Sukhāvatī-vyūha sūtra*" was the first step in examining all pertinent doctrinal issues found in scripture and in the great Pure Land commentary masters, and organizing these into the beginnings of his own systematic understanding of salvation through the compassionate Other-power of the Buddha Amida.[6]

Shinran constantly saw his Pure Land Buddhism as inextricably bound to society in the problems of daily life, so his teachings and actions had to grapple with the spiritual frustrations and everyday survival of monastic and lay Buddhist alike. His own personal salvation reflected this merging of spiritual experience and everyday living, no more so than with his marriage and his exile. The marriage can certainly be seen as a deliberate challenge to the psychological curse of his earlier life—the moral weakness of his father and grandfather and his fear about his own strength, as it was constantly questioned by his realization at Mt. Hiei of his basic inabilities and degeneracy as a human being. Just as completing the Pure Land sūtra commentaries was a major step in organizing the commitment of faith arising within him, so too his marriage was a drastic challenge to traditional Buddhism (and the efficacy of its self-effort salvation) and dramatic proof of his total faith in the inevitability of salvation by Amida. The marriage not only demonstrated the depth of his faith but also was a religious gesture whose social significance thoroughly blurred or eradicated monastic-lay distinctions in his teachings and opened the potential of salvation by Amida to all people.

As a result of political and religiously inspired opposition to Hōnen and his movement, Shinran was banished to Echigo, where he had to begin a completely new kind of existence. There he was integrated into the daily life of a class that constituted the very lowest strata of thirteenth-century Japanese society. It was a seminal encounter with ordinary people who were commonly described as "wicked creatures"—fishermen who "lived by casting nets or angling in the rivers and seas," hunters seen as "hunting the beasts in the mountains," farmers who "passed away their lives by trading and tilling the soil," and the lowliest of people, the genin (subordinate people) who were themselves traded like animals.[7]

The more earnestly Shinran had aspired to self-effort spiritual goals and the more strictly he kept to his religious practices as a monk, the more he became aware of his own limitations and wickedness. This made him all the more conscious that there could be no hope or escape except in completely resigning body and spirit to the compassion of the Buddha Amida. He lived his exile among the lowest classes of simple people whose only means of survival was characterized as evil by society, and this situation well paralleled Shinran's own existential condition—an ostracized monk who, no matter how hard he had tried, had failed to benefit from the orthodox and traditional Buddhist paths to spiritual fulfilment. The social conditions of these people in Echigo seemed to Shinran much like a living metaphor of his own brutal spiritual existence.

His struggles to overcome his intense fears and inabilities by dedication of will to the Other-power of faith in Amida necessitated a relentless and radical examination of his religion. This can be constantly seen in his own writings. The fact that most of his works are written in the first person singular instead of the common plural strongly suggests that he was not a man who stood before people to preach or to teach, but was instead one who listened and believed, and then tried to convince others to do so. Therefore, Shinran, who began within a sincere and difficult confrontation with his own faith, gained great sympathetic understanding of the dilemma of those whose position in society inevitably and cruelly denied them much opportunity for salvation within the orthodox religious institutions of the age. He remained in Echigo with these people some two years after his sentence of exile expired. Only in 1214, at the age of forty-two, did Shinran move to eastern Japan with his thirty-three-year-old wife and their three children, a move much like a welcomed summer after a long and hard winter and a brief spring.

Conclusion Notes

1. Erik H. Erikson, Insight and Responsibility: Lectures on the Ethical Implications of Psychoanalytic Insight (New York: Norton, 1964), p. 202.

2. Ibid.

3. Kyōgyōshinshō, Shinran-shōnin zenshū, vol. 1, pp. 317-318.

4. Eshinni monjo, Shinran-shōnin zenshū, vol. 3, p. 186.

5. E. Victor Wolfenstein, The Revolutionary Personality: Lenin, Trotsky, Gandhi (New Jersey: Princeton University Press, 1967), p. 307.

6. Kōdo Yasui, "Commentaries on the Kangyō-amidakyō-shūchū," Shinran-shōnin zenshū, vol. 7, p. 159.

7. Tannishō, Shinran-shōnin zenshū, vol. 13, p. 23.

Epilogue

Shinran's exile in Echigo ended on November 17, 1211, when he was thirty-nine years old. Having regained his freedom, he chose to remain in Echigo. Probable reasons for this decision are that his eight-month-old son Shinren (b. 1211) was too young to travel and the month of November was a difficult time for moving in the snow country of Echigo. It can be further surmised that the news of Hōnen's death (on January 25, 1212), reached him while he waited for spring. Whatever the reasons were, Shinran stayed in Echigo for another two years and only in 1214 did he begin his journey to eastern Japan (the Kantō district). No material exists which indicates why he chose to settle there. The Marxist historian Shisō Hattori conjectures that Shinran joined the farming population of the Hokuriku district (which included Echigo) in migration to Kantō, but there is no evidence to substantiate this theory.[1]

In eastern Japan at this time, the power of the Kyoto court aristocracy had definitely waned as the warrior bakufu government reorganized control over the provinces. The shift in power was not yet complete, for the nobility at court and in charge of major Buddhist institutions was still able to influence the warrior government to restrict the new Kamakura Buddhist reformers and even to banish them in some instances. On the other hand, records exist which show that the new warrior ruling class centred in Kamakura did shelter some of the people considered political or religious menaces by the aristocracy, one of whom, for example, was the Rinzai Zen master Eisai. This indicated that life in Kamakura society did differ from that in Kyoto in a few respects.

Kamakura was the home of a formidable warrior fighting force but its lack of culture made it turn to Kyoto for leadership in arts and letters. The politically and culturally developing Kamakura was a new environment for Shinran, but he did not find the protection or aid given to Eisai by the bakufu government. Hōnen's and Shinran's Pure Land teachings met with a largely hostile reception and were frequently opposed at high levels.

Shinran lived in the Kantō area from 1214 to about 1234, that is, from age forty-two to sixty-two. Throughout this twenty-year period, he spread the nembutsu doctrine among the farming population until his followers numbered approximately ten thousand. He was at the same time writing the six-volume compendium of his mature Pure Land thought, the Kyōgyōshinshō ("Teachings, Practice, Faith, Realization").[2]

When the number of followers in a new movement begins to reach sizeable proportions, two problems usually emerge—first, the question of enforcing some standard of orthodoxy, and second, the necessity to allay the suspicions of political authorities who fear the potential power of a strong new unified religious movement. The earlier suppression of the nembutsu group, which began in the Kantō area in 1234, had already existed in Kyoto for several years.

In 1234 Shinran left the Kantō area at the age of sixty-two to return to his birthplace in Kyoto and begin a productive period of intense writing. Most of the material he now wrote was directed toward spreading the Pure Land faith in the Kantō region. His absence in eastern Japan was soon felt. Many disputes arose over contradictory interpretations of his teachings as well as conflict among his followers and further oppression by ruling authorities. Shinran wrote, in a letter to a disciple who feared the suppression of the nembutsu:

> Now, I hear that you feel uneasy about what is happening to the nembutsu movement. It all sorrows me. Whatever reasons there have been for you to live where you do now seem to have come to an end. Please do not grieve at any obstacles thrown in the way of the nembutsu. What might not happen to those who create obstacles to the nembutsu? Yet no disheartening thing will ever possibly occur to those who say it. Please never try to spread the nembutsu with the assistance of any other people. It will all be by the will of the Buddha that the nembutsu will prosper in your area.[3]

Shinran avoided any suggestion that his followers should resist opposition and selected his son Zenran to go to eastern Japan.[4] Whether Zenran was actually sent as Shinran's deputy or not is uncertain. However, the knowledge that his next of kin would arrive in Kantō in the middle of conflict and oppression at first appeared to the adherents to be a guiding light, someone who would be capable of straightening up the movement.[5] But it turned out that several of the region's disciples were far superior to Zenran in leadership ability. Each was the head of a small group of followers, while in comparison Zenran lacked the charismatic personality needed to give sound advice and lead all the disciples. Zenran himself soon realized that he could never be the leader which the movement so desperately needed. He did not give up, however, and in order to unify and control all the disciples in the Kantō area, he claimed that as Shinran's son his instructions were the true desires of his father. He next filed a complaint with the Kamakura military government stating that any adherent who claimed himself a Pure Land leader in opposition to Zenran would cause disturbance to the civil order. Dismayed by this rather pretentious attitude, many of the Kantō Pure Land followers were thrown into deeper confusion. In desperation and in an attempt to bring some order to the movement, the disciples went to Kyoto to personally meet with Shinran. One of them, Yuien, noted Shinran's words on this occasion:

> Your only reason for making the long journey here, having crossed the borders of the more than ten provinces at the

risk of your lives, is to learn from me how to be reborn in the Pure Land. Yet you gravely err if you secretly suppose that I know of any other way to the Pure Land than through the nembutsu or know of passages in the scriptures [to facilitate rebirth in the Pure Land]. If that is what you are thinking, then you should go and visit the many fine Buddhist monk-scholars in Nara and on Mt. Hiei and question them intensely on the way to be reborn in the Pure Land.

As for me, Shinran, there is no reasoning—I believe only what my revered teacher taught: "Just call the name [of the Buddha Amida] and you will be saved by the Buddha Amida." The nembutsu may lead me to rebirth in the Pure Land or it may land me in the Buddhist hells—I simply don't know. But even if I were deceived by my teacher, the revered master Hōnen, and landed in the hells as a result, I would never come to regret it. This is the reason why. Were I the kind of person who could become a Buddha through other strenuous religious practices and yet would land in the hells because of the nembutsu, I might come to regret having been deceived by my teacher. But because I am absolutely incapable of any other religious practice, the hells are definitely my place.

If the fundamental vows of the Buddha Amida are true, then Sākyamuni's sermons cannot be untrue. If the Buddha's words are true, then Shan-tao's comments cannot be untrue. If Shan-tao's comments are true, then how can what Hōnen has said be false? And if Hōnen's words are not false, can the words which I, Shinran, speak, be in vain? That, in brief, is the faith of this ignorant person—more I cannot say. You yourselves must make the choice of whether to believe in the nembutsu or to cast it aside.[6]

Shinran's severe response perhaps reflected his disheartened sense of betrayal by his son Zenran. (Shinran later disinherited Zenran in order to reaffirm a proper and unified direction to his movement.)

Shinran was gradually approaching the final period of his life, and now in old age, he met another source of anguish. Just before he had sent Zenran to the Kantō area, his family began to break up—in 1254 his wife Eshinni left her son Zenran and daughter Kakushinni behind in Kyoto with Shinran and went to Echigo with her other children: Oguro no Nyōbō, Shinren, Masukata, and Takano zenni.[7] After Zenran went to eastern Japan, Shinran's widowed thirty-two-year-old daughter Kakushinni and her ten-year-old son Kakuei (1247-1307) returned to her father's home. At the age of eighty-five and one year after he had disowned his son, Shinran was practically blind, but a letter still remains addressed in a trembling hand to one of his disciples in the Kantō area, asking the disciple to take care of his widowed youngest daughter. The letter is dated November 12th. There also is a letter extant to his daughter Kakushinni, dated November 11th, informing her that he had written to a Kantō disciple asking him to look after her well-being.[8] Some historians consider these letters to be Shinran's will. If, in fact, these letters were written just before his death, the year would have been 1262 and the letters would have been dated only sixteen days before his death. For the sake of broadening the potential of his Buddhist experience and the thrust of his practice, Shinran had married and raised a family. Now in advanced old age, he underwent the sufferings of a family patriarch and died at the age of ninety on November 28, 1262, in a somewhat lonely and shabby manner.

Ten years after his death a grave was built by his disciples in 1272. Kakushinni was appointed its caretaker and her services were payed for by donations from the disciples of the Kantō area. Shinran's last wish, the security of his family, was thus fulfilled. The purpose served by the gravesite in the eyes of the followers in eastern Japan was its role as a unifying shrine for all of Shinran's nembutsu followers, so private control by a single subgroup would not be tolerated.

Because the grave became a collective symbol to all the Pure Land followers, the caretaker position gathered great prestige, and subsequently, at Kakushinni's death, a squabble began over who would assume the position. Kakuei, Kakushinni's first-born son, at first continued the work but was eventually deprived of the responsibility by his step-brother Yuizen (1253-1317). Yuizen managed to secure the caretakership by altering it into a private position instead of administering it in trust for the entire movement. He then started to forbid nembutsu followers from paying visits to the gravesite. Through the joint efforts of Kakushinni's first-born son Kakuei and many disciples, the grave was eventually placed under Kakuei's administration and once again became a collective responsibility. However, the problem of a future caretaker and administrator soon occurred once again. When Kakuei died in 1307, Kakunyo firmly believed that he should inherit his father's position. But many followers had been through a bitter experience with Yuizen and would not entrust the position to Kakunyo merely because he was related to Shinran as his great-grandson or even because he had rendered invaluable assistance to regain the gravesite from Yuizen. When his wishes to become caretaker and administrator of the gravesite were made public, Kakunyo was given a twelve-point contract by the movement to which strict and absolute adherence was demanded. Even with such precautions, Shinran's grave remained a central concern in the Pure Land movement; the disciples were extremely cautious and would not readily entrust the duties to Kakunyo or to any other single person.

With the co-operation of his own first-born son, Zonkaku (1290-1373),[9] Kakunyo went to the Kantō area to solicit the approval of local nembutsu followers about his plan to build a temple on the site and to be appointed to the administrator position.[10] To Kakunyo, having to seek such approval on top of being handed the twelve-point contract was extremely humiliating.

He constructed a temple called the Honganji ("Temple of the Fundamental Vows [of the Buddha Amida]") on the gravesite, not in the capacity of grave caretaker and administrator commissioned by the movement but solely as Shinran's successor.[11] He declared himself to be the successor of the Hōnen-Shinran-Nyoshin (1235-1300) lineage of the Shin Pure Land tradition.[12] Besides being Shinran's direct descendant, he saw himself as the third successor of Shinran's tradition after Nyoshin. All these events took place exactly fifty years after Shinran's death.

Such arrogance in attitude and action on Kakunyo's part began to resemble the earlier difficulties with Yuien to many of the movement's followers. The disciples thus wanted Kakunyo's oldest son, Zonkaku, to take charge of the gravesite. Zonkaku showed little interest in this position at first, but was so strongly encouraged by so many followers that he finally agreed to become the caretaker. Zonkaku felt that the responsibility would further the reputation of the Honganji. But he never did assume the position because Kakunyo became adamantly opposed to his own son assuming the responsibility and soon disinherited him, always persisting with the goal of organizing a religious body with Shinran's grave as its focal point and the Honganji as the caretaker institution.[13] Many of the disciples refused to comply with Kakunyo's plans and tried to consolidate the nembutsu followers into a decisive and unified opposition to confront Kakunyo and his Honganji. In order to establish the viability of such organized opposition, the disciples were forced to challenge the Honganji domination in limiting the succession of head abbots solely to Shinran's direct descendants. They also challenged the Honganji claim to inherit Shinran's teachings as originally taught and, above all, the claim to the administration of Shinran's gravesite. This tension divided the movement, which was further fractionalized as leaders of subgroups added new teachings and interpretations to Shinran's doctrines in order to attract new followers. Small nembutsu groups such as the Bukkōji, Gōshōji, Kinshokuji, Sanmon-to, and Senjuji sects did manage to form a united front against the Honganji, but an unhealthy stalemate resulted. (These were the sources from which the ten sects of the modern Shin tradition originated.) The Honganji lineage, established by its chief abbot Kakunyo (the self-declared third successor to Shinran) down through the fourth to seventh abbots who succeeded Kakunyo, continued to dismiss the teachings of all other nembutsu groups as heretical.[14] They strictly held to retaining the office within the blood lineage and restricted propagation to their inherited understanding of the teachings.

Needless to say, while these multiple subsects of Shinran's tradition were scrambling about competing with one another for new followers, the social and economic history of Japan continued to undergo change. The regional administrative power of police and military affairs (shugo) and control of land ownership and the collection of taxes (jitō) were separated. National stability led to a concentration of energy and administration on provincial government and regional development. Organization of resources coupled with improvements in agricultural techniques and production levels enabled the peasants to increase their standard of living. What they produced over and above taxation and their private needs was now sold in growing urban markets. These people increasingly engaged in direct production (which had so recently still been the object of denigration) and now formed self-governing communities which organized themselves under their own laws. They were thus able to protect their own lives and to control the development of their own regions to a much greater degree than in the past.

In periods when governments or social forces are so powerful that they dominate the individual or when chaos and change cause the same results, individual capabilities and everyday goals tend to be overlooked or dismissed. In such circumstances the people will view the immediate future with pessimism and will readily commit themselves to the promise of religious salvation after death (as a positive future for the individual). However, as the economic and social situation of the nation improved with an increase in organized community development, wealth, and limited power, the people began to reorganize their own potential for some degree of secular or worldly advancement. At the same time they began to require some comprehensive and tenable proof while still on this earth of their future spiritual salvation.

Shinran's teachings never contained such proof (for worldly proof directly contradicted the total commitment to the Buddha Amida based upon faith in the salvation of his Other-power). In one sense, brief and limited success at secular "self-effort" led some to question the tenets (or to become impatient with) religious Other-power. Nevertheless, several Shin groups (other than the Honganji) attempted to find some means to fulfill the desires of such people. To this end, some Shin leaders found in themselves the power to grant or deny the Buddha Amida's salvation to followers as well as the right to expel nonbelievers or dissenters from nembutsu groups. People saw such institutional measures as spiritual evidence in the present life of future salvation. In this way various new teachings and new interpretations of Pure Land doctrine were added to Shinran's original teachings. It is obvious that these teachings were inconsistent with Shinran's ideas to the point of heresy, yet so many followers in some Shin groups approved of and found these new directions consistent with their aspirations and values that few paid particular attention to the degree of change which was taking place. Instead it was the Honganji lineage itself which appeared to cling to Shinran's original teachings in an absurdly rigid and dogmatic manner, disregarding the changing religious needs of the people in the two centuries which by now had elapsed since Shinran's death.

Eventually, a dynamic Shin personality emerged who gave new and powerful interpretation to Shinran's original doctrines. This was the Shin leader Rennyo (1415-1499), the eighth chief abbot of the Honganji. He was born from an encounter of the seventh chief abbot Zonnyo (1396-1459) with a lady-in-waiting. The mother lived with Rennyo only until he reached six years of age, and after he would never have the opportunity to see his mother again. Rennyo married

Nyoryō when he was twenty-eight, but by this time conditions in the Honganji congregation had fallen into such decay that no one knew where the next meal would come from. Rennyo married five times during his lifetime and had thirteen sons and fourteen daughters.[15] His wives died one after another and at no time did he ever have more than one wife. Each of his wives was in her twenties at marriage and his last child was born when he was eighty-four years of age, the year before he died. Rennyo was a man of unusual vitality and a realist with a firm understanding of the changes in Japanese religious needs in the present and how these would probably develop in the immediate future.

The first step he took was to portray his own ideas in epistle form, which would eventually be compiled by disciples under the title, the *Gobunshō* (or 'Ofumi', "Honoured Explications"). This was not a traditional Buddhist sūtra commentary or a mere retelling of Shinran's words but was instead a contemporary interpretation of Shinran's teachings. In forming his statements, Rennyo turned back to the point when Shinran himself had expressed his Pure Land doctrines in writings and letters. Then Rennyo used this material as the basis for his own creative interpretations of the teachings. Rennyo's *Gobunshō* often included significant religious phrasing which had never been used by Shinran—for example, "we place complete reliance in you for all our lives to come."

Rennyo also eagerly read the *Anjin ketsujō-shō* ("Securing the Mind Without Doubt") at least seven times, a book by an unknown author which taught Shinran's Pure Land teachings in a strongly heretical light. Rennyo even said of this work, "I have never tired of reading this book over these forty or more years. It is like discovering gold."[16] Such efforts by the chief abbot of the Honganji lineage, whose predominant concern was purity of bloodline and the task of preserving the orthodox, to examine enthusiastically all extremes of interpretation must be seen as a major attempt to renew traditional Shin doctrine in fresh language for a new era. The *Gobunshō* was handed from follower to follower to be copied and, in this way, Rennyo's teachings were propagated among many adherents. Rennyo himself frequently read portions to the faithful, for it was purposely written in a language readily comprehensible to ordinary people. This was the first activity of this kind in the entire history of the Honganji Shin establishment, but the results did not necessarily coincide with Rennyo's objectives.

What had held great appeal to the common people throughout the centuries in Shinran's teachings was a thorough denial of all worldly power because of the transcendental nature of the compassionate Other-power of the Buddha Amida. A major factor in appeal, more precisely, was the denial of any kind of differentiation by wealth, social status, family heritage, etc., based on typical sentient attachment to material wealth and power—whether the adherent was a wealthy person, an aristocrat, a monk, a commoner or even the lowliest menial, all people were in essence equal within the Shin tradition, particularly in terms of salvation by the Buddha Amida. This concept of religion transcending all worldly circumstances was interpreted into a socio-political doctrine in Rennyo's time, to be used as a potent propaganda artifice in anti-government resistance movements by the populace.

Rennyo took advantage of the structural organization of communities in his energetic proselytism of the masses.[17] The past few centuries had seen an increase in the economic and political organization of the common people, and the consciousness also gradually made them aware of their potential to fight undue oppression by regional lords and warrior authorities. Some now began to use Shinran's teaching of the spiritual equality of all people before Amida as justification for armed opposition to a repressive political establishment. This type of militancy in turn helped to unite and thus strengthen the entire nembutsu movement. Coupling the concept of spiritual equality before Amida with the guarantee of salvation in future lives produced the radical new political interpretation that death in political and military conflict had no moral significance in obstructing one's ultimate future in the Pure Land (which proved very advantageous in battle). Isolated Pure Land resistance groups started to join together in an opposition so intense that feudal lords, such as dogō and kokujin, of relatively small areas could no longer control the rising mass movement. Instead of attacking with force, dogō and kokujin avoided any confrontation with this aroused opposition by themselves joining the new Pure Land insurrections.

In this way the Honganji began to count large numbers of warriors among its adherents, and these warriors, in turn, took advantage of their membership to manipulate fervent fellow Pure Land followers to increase their own political and economic power.[18]

Under such circumstances, Rennyo forbade his nembutsu followers from accepting the advice or leadership of any such power-hungry individuals. He also forbade the acceptance of any kind of warrior assistance in the peasant resistance movements. Rennyo taught his followers to obey their civil authorities and to pay appropriate taxes to the government, or in other words, to render unto Caesar what was Caesar's.

With only the institutional authority of the chief abbot, the Honganji headquarters lacked effective power of persuasion over the new warrior converts or over the peasant followers taking up arms. In order to prevent simple peasant followers from turning into the pawns of ambitious (and irreligious) Pure Land warriors in the constant struggle for political power, Rennyo took a dramatic but patently heretical stand. He gave himself the power to grant or deny salvation in the Pure Land and the power to expel followers from the nembutsu movement, powers which had been assumed by several regional group leaders in past years.[19] With this gesture Rennyo did achieve his first objective of stopping the more militant activities of the resistance groups, and at the same time, caused the number of followers of the Honganji institution to increase rapidly. The reason for the latter was that now salvation in the Pure Land was suddenly guaranteed by none other than the chief abbot of the Honganji, the direct descendant of Shinran and the definitive inheritor of Shin teachings and practice. This assertion of spiritual and institutional authority (and genuineness, to the people) overwhelmed any competition in leadership by other Pure Land groups, so most leaders and followers alike ended up by joining the Honganji in one great unified movement.

While the other small Pure Land subgroups had taken a century or more to establish themselves and to expand, Rennyo succeeded in forcing them to join the Honganji almost overnight. He retired at the age of seventy-five and died ten years later, yet even on his death there were impressions on his feet from the rope thongs of his straw sandals, clearly showing his indomitable energy in travelling far and near to propagate Pure Land teachings.

Rennyo's greatest achievement consisted of restoring the appeal and soteriological power of Shinran's teachings in a new age, as well as reasserting the dominance of Honganji leadership to the Shin tradition. Yet in many ways the new propagation of Pure Land doctrine through his *Gobunshō* and the economic and political expansion of Honganji power through compromise with the ruling class were clearly of a contradictory nature. In somehow managing to reassert Shinran's denial of worldly power while at the same time increasing Honganji wealth and influence and an accommodation to secular authority, Rennyo revealed great abilities in maintaining an apparent compatibility in accomplishing these objectives without contradiction.[20]

After Rennyo's death, the Honganji cultivated ever closer ties with political authority and the nobility, thus strengthening its position in society. There were already many warriors who had infiltrated the ranks of nembutsu followers to use their membership within the Honganji as a stepping-stone to personal power in the nation at large. For this reason more than any other, some seventy years after Rennyo's death, the Honganji institution itself was perceived as a powerful political rival and was challenged by the great mediaeval warrior generals who attempted to conquer and unify Japan. The first was Oda Nobunaga (1534-1582), who nearly controlled the entire country through manipulation of military alliances, overt warfare, and intrigue. Nobunaga thought that his achieving control of the Honganji-led Shin movement would result in his absolute and complete sovereignty over Japan, especially in view of the fact that many regional leaders had become Honganji followers (more out of opportunity than from sincere religious conviction, for Shin adherence at this time offered them breathing space to assess changes in the winds of political power and constantly shifting alliances).

Kennyo (1543-1592) was the eleventh chief abbot of the Honganji during this era. He ordered the nembutsu followers to challenge Oda Nobunaga in order to preserve and protect the Honganji tradition and the doctrines of the Pure Land sect. He declared that to shed blood in this fight for independence was to receive the seal of faith from Shinran's tradition and his teachings of Amida's salvation. Warfare between Oda Nobunaga and Honganji forces continued for eleven years until the Honganji fell in 1580. However, Kennyo's first-born son Kyōnyo (1558-1614) continued fighting despite his father's defeat.

Toward the end of this prolonged conflict, many of the warriors among Shin followers who had fought for the Honganji authority and independence in regional areas began to defect to the clearly emerging centre of power which held the greatest possibility for control of the entire nation. Nobunaga claimed complete military administrative authority over the country, and in time, the Honganji lost all of its military potential.

In 1592, the next great warrior general, Toyotomi Hideyoshi (1536-1598) called Kennyo to audience in Kyoto. By this time Kennyo was living his life as a fugitive chief abbot, constantly moving from one place to another as Honganji power dissipated. Hideyoshi allotted some land to Kennyo and ordered a new Honganji to be built upon it (which is the site of the present Nishi honganji—the "Western Honganji"). Kennyo, however, died in that year and was succeeded by his son Kyōnyo. Kennyo's wife Nyoshunni (d. 1598) insisted that their third-born son Junnyo (1577-1630) should succeed Kennyo as the twelfth chief abbot in accordance with her husband's will, and as a result Junnyo was given the position.

Many Pure Land adherents openly sympathized with Kyōnyo, who had unsuccessfully but loyally continued to fight in opposition to Oda Nobunaga and was now forced to give up the position of twelfth chief abbot. The third and greatest military general-unifier of Japan, Tokugawa Ieyasu (1542-1616), then allotted new land to Kyōnyo, ordering that a second Honganji be built in 1600 and making Kyōnyo its first chief abbot. (This is the origin of the present Higashi honganji —the "Eastern Honganji").[21] Ieyasu brilliantly divided the Honganji-led Shin tradition in two, virtually reducing the economic power and religious authority of the former institution by half.

When Ieyasu gained recognized sovereignty as shōgun of the entire nation of Japan in 1603, he incorporated all Buddhist temples into a system of feudal bureaucratic regulation, the tera-uke or "temple authorization system."[22]

Under the new totalitarian samurai reorganization of all aspects of Japanese political, social, and cultural life, all the Japanese people became tied by legal registration as Buddhists to the nearest Buddhist temple. All Buddhist temples themselves were organized into a hon-matsu or "main-branch" system. Each Japanese citizen without exception had to be officially registered as a member of a Buddhist parish and, when moving about, had to carry a certificate showing that he was a member of a specific temple parish. Because such a combination political-register and police-surveillance function was forced on Buddhist institutions and officially fixed the number of adherents in each locality (and guaranteed a set amount of financial support based on this fixed number of registered adherents), there was no further need for the Honganji or for any other Buddhist school or institution to propagate their teachings. The entire nation had been organized into adherents of Buddhist sects, and all individuals, regardless of personal religious belief, were forced by political authority to join the temple which held local territorial monopoly.

The hon-matsu system of national control ordered the numerous temples of a school which were randomly scattered throughout the country into a unified hierarchy with such bureaucratic distinctions as honzan (sect headquarters), honji (major temples), chū-honji (first rank major temples), choku-honji (second rank major temples), and mago-honji (third rank major temples), which established a tight vertical relationship among temples of any given sect. The temple authorization system and the "main-branch" temple organization structure were imposed as a combination to exercise tight supervision over temple activities and any expansion of Buddhist institutional power. In other words, Buddhist temples were made to watch or supervise the populace by the temple authorization system, and each temple was under the efficient surveillance of another within the main-branch structure. Therefore, the two systems easily made it possible for the Tokugawa military government to maintain close surveillance over Buddhist institutions and the general populace at the same time.

With the rise of the great military unifiers and political dictators in the final centuries of the late feudal period, the earlier secular wealth and power of the Pure Land tradition were destroyed. Even after the middle of the seventeenth century, when the Tokugawa feudal system was perfected under an ingenious political organization of samurai bureaucracy, the Honganji continued to restrict the succession of its chief abbots to direct blood descent. As the modern age dawned and all aspects of traditional Japanese civilization underwent challenge and renewal or reform from the introduction of Western civilization, it was never possible for the Shin Pure Land tradition to flourish as mightily as it once had in the mediaeval ages. With the coming of the age of modern nations and the Second World War, the Shin tradition was repeatedly subjected to secular political domination, such as having to amend its readings of Shinran's *Kyōgyōshinshō* and other Pure Land writings in line with current political propaganda. However, there were dynamic chief abbots during the late feudal age and in modern times who attempted to bring new life and power to Shinran's teachings and to begin fundamental reformation of the Honganji itself. For example, in the Nishi honganji tradition, there were its twenty-first chief abbot Myōnyo (1850-1903) and his fourth son Sonyū (1886-1939), and its twenty-second chief abbot Kōzui (1876-1948). Each tried to reform the management of the Honganji and assert religious independence by criticizing government policies on the control of religion in Japan. At times they did succeed in affecting and altering these policies. However, none was forceful enough to achieve the position of influence for the Honganji that Rennyo had made possible. While these individuals accomplished some progress in influencing government religious policy, more often than not it was modern Japanese governments that affected influence and control on Shin tradition policies. Again various chief abbots chose to hold high government positions and encouraged Shin adherents to support the Japanese government. Few did possess the consummate skills of Rennyo in both existing within the political and social order while offering spiritual guidance to Pure Land followers and transcending sectarian interpretations and divisions to forge a united Shin religious voice.

The real key to the vitality of the Shin movement in spreading the power of Shinran's teachings lies in the tension between Shin tradition and innovation. Either the lengthy Shin tradition can serve as the mature foundation from which to develop Shinran's message creatively in terms of modern spiritual problems and needs, or it can exist as a moribund institution preserving the remnants of past religious accomplishment over future spiritual promise. A healthy future for the movement begun seven centuries ago in radical response to Japanese religious needs can only develop if its followers carefully listen to Shinran's original declarations of the tremendous compassion of the Buddha Amida for the past, present, and future suffering of sentient existence.

Epilogue Notes

1. Hattori, op. cit., p. 356.

2. Kazuo Kasahara, Shinran to tōgoku nōmin (Tokyo: Yamakawa Shuppan, 1957), p. 272.

3. Shinran-shōnin goshōsoku, Shinran-shōnin zenshū, vol. 3, pp. 147-148.

4. Kakuei Miyaji, Shinran-den no kenkyū (Kyoto: Hyakkaen, 1968), pp. 211-245.

5. Ibid., pp. 211-245.

6. Tannishō, Shinran-shōnin zenshū, vol. 4, pp. 4-6.

7. Ichimu Tanishita, "Kazoku no mondai" in Shinran-shōnin no kyōgaku to denki (Kyoto: Hyakkaen, 1963), p. 278.

8. Akamatsu, op. cit., p. 344.

9. Kazuo Kasahara, Kakumei no shūkyō (Tokyo: Jimbutsu Ōraisha, 1964), pp. 93-95.

10. Circulating among Shinran's immediate disciples, Kakunyo gathered a great deal of first-hand information about Shinran's life. This was the material he used to write the Honganji-shōnin shinran dene.

11. Kakunyo wrote the Honganji-shōnin shinran dene in part to establish a reputation for the Honganji.

12. Kakunyo was Shinran's great-grandson, and Kakunyo's father, Kakuei, is Nyoshin's cousin.

13. Zonkaku did not follow Kakunyo as the fourth successor. Instead, his younger brother Zennyo became the chief abbot of the Honganji.

14. The fourth through seventh chief abbots of the Honganji were Zennyo (1333-1389), Shakunyo (1350-1393), Gyōnyo (1376-1440), and Zonnyo (1398-1459).

15. The five wives were Nyoryō (d. 1455), Renyū, Nyoshō (1448-1478), Shunnyo, and Rennō (1475-1518).

16. Rennyo shōnin goichidaiki kikigaki, in Shinshū shōgyō zensho (Kyoto: Kōkyōshoin 1951-1957), vol. 3, and for an English translation see Kōshō Yamamoto, The Words of St. Rennyo (Yamaguchi: Karin bunko, 1968), p. 88.

17. By making use of clan and village community structure, it was easy to maintain control of the followers, and it was quite convenient

to use such units to collect and channel donations to Honganji headquarters.

18. The major resistance movement led by the Honganji and based on existing peasant social structures was known as the Ikkō-ikki or "Single Direction—Singular Mind." Later during the Edo period there were a great number of peasant uprisings but these were not related to Ikkō-ikki ideology.

19. The leaders of such small nembutsu groups as the Bukkōji, Gōshōji, Kinshokuji, Sanmon-to, and Senjuji sects had previously asserted such powers among their adherents.

20. Enjun Miyazaki, "Shinran to sono kyōdan" in Nihon no bukkyō— Kōza bukkyō, vol. 5 (Tokyo: Daizō Shuppansha, 1967), p. 180.

21. Kyōnyo is referred to as the twelfth chief abbot of the Higashi-honganji lineage.

22. The terauke seido or "temple authorization system" originated in 1613 when Japanese Christians in Kyoto got Buddhist temples to certify that they were legitimate Buddhists as proof of their renunciation of Christian belief and papal allegiance.

**Glossary, Bibliography, Appendix
and Index**

Glossary

1. General

-A-

Akunin
悪 人

Akunin shōki
悪人正機

Amida butsu
阿弥陀仏

Amitābha (Amidabutsu)
阿弥陀仏

Avalokiteśvara
(Kannon)
観 音

Azuma ebisu
東 夷

Azuma-kagami
吾妻鏡

-B-

Bakufu
幕 府

Bingo
備 後

Bodhisattva (Bosatsu)
菩 薩

Bodhisattva
Mahāsthāmaprāpta
大勢至菩薩

Boki-eshi
慕帰絵詞

Bosatsu (Bodhisattva)
菩 薩

Buddha
仏 陀

Bukkōji
仏光寺

-C-

Chiao-p'an (Kyō-han)
教 判

Chiba
千 葉

Chinzei-ha
鎮西派

Chokkyo
勅 許

Choku-honji
直本寺

Chū-honji
中本寺

Chūru
中 流

-D-

Daijō kyōten
大乗経典

Daiken
題 検

Dharma (Hō)
法

Dogō
土 豪

Dōshū
堂 衆

Dōsō
堂 僧

-E-

Echigo
越 後

Ekayāna śila (Ichijōkai)
一乗戒

Ekō-hotsugan-shin
迴向発願心

Engi-shiki
延喜式

Enryakuji
延暦寺

Eshinni monjo
恵信尼文書

-F-

Fudan nembutsu
不断念仏

-G-

Gakushō
学生

Genin
下人

Gion
祇園

Genkyū
元久

Genpei seisui-ki
源平盛衰記

Gensō no ekō
還相の廻向

Gensō no gyō
還相の行

Goaku
五悪

Gobunshō (Ofumi)
御文章

Gōshōji
毫摂寺

Gōzoku
豪族

Gozokushō
御俗姓

Gu
愚

Gukanshō
愚管鈔

Gunsho-ruijū
群書類従

Gutoku
愚禿

Gyokuyō
玉葉

-H-

Hata
番多

Heian
平安

Heiji
平氏

Hieizan (Mt. Hiei)
比叡山

Higashi honganji
東本願寺

Higashiyama
東山

Hīnayana (Shojō)
小乗

Hinoke honganji keizu
Fujiwara hokke
日野家本願寺系図　藤原北家

Hinoto no U
丁卯

Hino ichiryū keizu
日野一流系図

Hino-uji keizu
日野氏系図

Hō (Dharma)
法

Hōgen
保元

Hogo-uragaki
反古裏書

Hōki
伯耆

Hokke-kyō no gyōja
法華経の行者

Hokuriku
北陸

Honchō-kōsō-den
本朝高僧伝

Honganji
本願寺

Honganji keizu
本願寺系図

Honganji shinran-shōnin
dene
本願寺聖人親鸞伝絵

Honganji-shōnin
本願寺聖人

Honganji-shōnin dene
本願寺聖人伝絵

Honganji-shōnin shinran
dene
本願寺親鸞聖人伝絵

Honji
本寺

Honmatsu
本末

Hō no jinshin
法の深心

Honzan
本山

Hōon-kōshiki
報恩講式

Hōryaku
方略

Hossō
法相

Hōunji
法雲寺

Hua-yen (Kegon)
華 厳

-I-

Ichijō shisō
一乗思想

Ichijōkai (Ekayāna śila)
一乗海

Ichinen gi
一念義

Ichinen tanen funbetsu no koto
一念多念分別事

Isshaku no shio
一寸の塩

Isshō no kome
一升の米

Izu
伊 豆

-J-

Jiki sōō
時機相応

Jinen hō-ni
自然法爾

Jinshin
深 心

Jiriki
自 力

Jiriki-tariki
自力他力

Ji
時

Jitō
地 頭

Jōdo
浄 土

Jōdo-mon
浄土門

Jōdo sanbu-kyō
浄土三部経

Jōdo shin-shū
浄土眞宗

Jōdo-shū
浄土宗

Jōdo shin-shū kyōdan
浄土真宗教団

Jōgū-taishi gyoki
上宮太子御記

Jōgyōdō
常行堂

Jōgyō zanmai
常行三昧

Jōgyō-zanmai-dō
常行三昧堂

Jōgyō-zanmai-in
常行三昧院

Jōgyō-zanmai no hō
常行三昧の法

Jōjitsu
成 実

Jūaku
十 悪

Juhō no ki
受法の機

Jūshichi-jō kenpō
十七条憲法

-K-

Kai
戒

Kamakura
鎌 倉

Kannon
(Avalokiteśvara)
観 音

Kannen
観 念

Kannon bosatsu
観音菩薩

Kannon-dō
観音堂

Kanoto no tori (Shinyu)
辛 酉

Kanpaku
関 白

Kantō
関 東

Kanzeon
観世音

Karma (Gō)
業

Kegon (Hua-yen)
華 厳

Kengyō
検 校

Kennin
建 仁

Keshin
化 身

Keshindo kan
化身土巻

Ki
機

Kigai
癸亥

Ki no jinshin
機の深心

Kinoto no ushi
乙丑

Kinru
近流

Kinshokuji
錦織寺

Kiyomizudera
清水寺

Kōfukuji
興福寺

Kōfukuji-sōjō
興福寺奏上

Kokubunji
国分寺

Kokufu
国府

Kokujin
国人

Kokushi
国師

Kōnen
口念

Kōsai
高才

Kōshō
口称

Kotahama
居多浜

Kōtaigōgū gon no daishin goi no ge
皇太后宮 権の大進 五位の下

Kōtaishi shōtoku hōsan
皇太子聖徳奉讃

Kuan-yin (kannon)
観音

Kubiki
頸城

Kuden-shō
口伝鈔

Kuroda no hijiri
黒田の聖

Kuroda no hijiri-hi nokosu-sho
黒田の聖にのこす書

Kurōdo no tō
蔵人の頭

Kusha
倶舎

Kyō (Sūtra)
経

Kyō-han (Chiao-p'an)
教判

Kyō-shū
経宗

Kyōdan
教団

Kyōsōhanjaku
教相判釈

Kyoto
京都

–M–

Mago-honji
孫本寺

Mahāyāna (Daijō)
大乗

Mahāyāna sūtra (Daijō kyōten)
大乗経典

Mahāvairocana (Shanagyō)
庶那業

Mahāsthāmaprāpta
大勢至

Makura no sōshi
枕草子

Makashikan (Mo-ho shih-kuan)
摩訶止観

Mappō
末法

Meigetsuki
明月記

Mie
三重

Mimurodo no daishin nyūdō
御室戸の大進入道

Mo-ho shih-kuan (shishu-zanmai)
四種三味

Monto
門徒

Mt. Hiei (Hieizan)
比叡山

Mujō
無常

Mukoku
夢告

Murasakino monto
紫野門徒

Myōkō
妙高

–N–

Nagaoka
長岡

Namu amida butsu
南無阿弥陀仏

Namu Amida-butsu ōjō
shigō nembutsu i hon
南無阿弥陀仏往生之業念仏為本

Nangyō-dō
難行道

Nanke no sanki
難化の三機

Nara
奈 良

Nembutsu
念 仏

Nichiren shū
日蓮宗

Nirvāṇa (Nehan)
涅 槃

Nishi honganji
西本願寺

Nish jōgyō dō
西常行堂

Nishi jōgyōzanmai dō
西常行三昧堂

Nishu jinshin
二種深心

Nembutsu zanmai no hō
念佛三昧の法

Nyorai (Tathāgata)
如 来

-O-

Ōjō
往 生

Ōsō no gyō
往相の行

Onjōji
園城寺

Onru
遠 流

Ōtani-ichiryū keizu
大谷一流系図

-R-

Rinzai zen
臨済禅

Rinjū raigō
臨終来迎

Rinjū shōnen
臨終正念

Rinne (Saṃsāra)
輪 廻

Ritsu
律

Ritsuryō-kokka
律令国家

Rokkakudō
六角堂

Rokuharamitsuji
六波羅密寺

Ron (Śāstra)
論

Ron-shū
論 宗

Ryōgōn-in
楞厳院

Ryōgon-zanmai-dō
楞厳三昧堂

-S-

Saishō
宰 相

Sado ga shima
佐渡ケ島

Śākyamuni (Shakamuni)
釈迦牟尼

Samādhi (Sanmai)
三 昧

Saṃgha
僧 伽

Saṃsāra (Rinne)
輪 廻

Samurai
侍

San-chieh-tsung (Sangai shū)
三階宗

Sanchō-ki
三長記

Sangan tennyū
三願転入

Sangi
参 議

Sanmonto
三門徒

Sanrō
参 籠

Sanron
三 論

Sanshin
三 心

Śāstra (Ron)
論

Seizan-ha
西山派

Sendai
闡 提

Senjuji
専修寺

Senju-nembutsu
専修念仏

Sha-hei-kaku-hō
捨 閉 閣 抛

Shakamuni (Śākyamuni)
釈迦牟尼

Shaku
釈

Shana-gō
(Mahāvairocana)
庶那業

Shêng-ching erh-men-
p'an (Shōjō nimonhan)
聖浄二門判

Shichikajo no kishōmon
七ケ条の起請文

Shih-tzu siang-ch'êng
(Shishi sōjō)
師資相承

Shijō no Shinran
史上の親鸞

Shijō-shin
至誠心

Shikan-gyō (Chih-kuan)
止観業

Shikan taza
只管打座

Shimotsuke engi
下野縁起

Shinaga
磯長

Shinbutsudo kan
身仏土巻

Shingon
眞言

Shinnen
心念

Shinran dene (Shinran-
shōnin dene)
親鸞（聖人）伝絵

Shinran muki
親鸞夢記

Shinran-shōnin hisseki
no kenkyū
親鸞聖人筆跡の研究

Shinran-shōnin seitō-
den
親鸞聖人正統伝

Shinran-shōnin-ron
親鸞聖人論

Shinran to sono kyōdan
親鸞とその教団

Shinshū
信州

Shinshū kyōdan
眞宗教団

Shishu-zanmai
四種三昧

Shintō
神道

Shinyū (Kanoto no tori)
辛酉

Shirakawa monto
白川門徒

Shishigatani
鹿ケ谷

Shishi sōjō (Shih-tzu
siang-ch'êng)
師資相承

Shobi no ki
所被の機

Shōbō
正法

Shōdō-mon
聖道門

Shōganji
照願寺

Shōgen
承元

Shōgun
将軍

Shōgyō
正行

Shogyō hongan gi
諸行本願義

Shōhō
正法

Shōjō nimon-han
(Shêng-ching erh-men-
p'an)
聖浄二門判

Shōka
正嘉

Shōki
正機

Shōmyō
称名

Shōmyō nembutsu
称名念仏

Shōtoku no ki
性得の機

Shugo
守護

Shugyōgyō
修行業

Shūi kotokuden
拾遺古徳伝

Shukugō
宿業

Sō
僧

Sō (Sung)
宋

Sōhei
僧兵

Sonpi-bunmyaku
尊卑分脈

Sōto zen
曹洞禅

Sung (Sō)
宋

Sūraṃgama-samādhi
(Ryōgon zanmai)
楞厳三昧

Sūtra (Kyō)
経

-T-

Taishi byōkutsu-ge
太子廟窟偈

Taishi shinkō
太子信仰

Takada Senjuji
高田専修寺

Takada kaisan seitō den
高田開山正統伝

Takaozan
高雄山

Tandoku-mon
嘆徳文

Tanengi
多念義

Tathāgata (Nyorai)
如来

Teiji-ryū fujiwara
nanke
貞嗣流藤原南家

Tendai (T'ien-t'ai)
天台

T'ien-t'ai (Tendai)
天台

Tendai no shōshikan
天台の小止観

Tera-uke
寺請

Tōdaiji
東大寺

Tōkai
東海

Toku
禿

Tokukoji
禿居士

Tongyō ichijō
(Tun-chiao i-ch'êng)
頓教一乗

Tosa
土佐

Tōsan
東山

Tun-chiao i-ch'êng
(Tongyō ichijō)
頓教一乗

-U-

Upāya (Hōben)
方便

Uchimaro
内麿

-W-

Wasan
和讃

-Y-

Yamato
大和

Yokawa
横川

Yoshimizu
吉水

Yuishin-shō
唯信鈔

Yūzū nembutsu
融通念仏

-Z-

Zen
禅

Zennin
善人

Zenshin-shōnin dene
善信聖人伝絵

Zenshin-shōnin shinran
dene
善信聖人親鸞伝絵

Zōhō
像法

2. Names of persons

-A-

Akamatsu Toshihide
赤松俊秀

Anraku
安 楽

Antōji
あんとうじ

Antoku
安 徳

Arikuni
有 国

Arinori
有 範

Arinobu
有 信

-B-

Benchō
弁 長

Busshin
仏 眞

-C-

Chien-chên (Ganjin)
鑑 眞

Chih-I (Chigi)
智 顗

Chigi (Chih-I)
智 顗

Chōsai
長 西

Chōsai zenkōbō
澄西禅光房

-D-

Dengyō-daishi (Saichō)
伝教大師（最 澄）

Dōgen
道 元

Donran (T'an-luan)
曇 鸞

Dōshaku (Tao-ch'o)
道 綽

Dōzui (Tao-sui)
道 邃

-E-

Eisai (Yōsai)
栄 西

Eizon
叡 尊

Eji
恵 慈

Ekan
恵 灌

Eikū
恵 空

Enchin
円 珍

Engyō
円 行

Ennin
円 仁

Enō
依 能

Erikson Erik H

Eshinni
恵信尼

Eun
慧 運

-F-

Fa-ts'ang (Hōzō)
法 蔵

Fujii Motohiko (Hōnen)
藤井元彦（法 然）

Fujii Yoshizane
(Shinran)
藤井善信（親 鸞）

Fujiwara
藤 原

Fujiwara no Michinaga
藤原道長

Fujiwara no Motofusa
藤原基房

Fujiwara no Motohisa
藤原基久

Fujiwara no Motomichi
藤原基道

Fujiwara no Tashi
藤原多子

Fujiwara no Teika
藤原定家

Fujiwara no Teishi
藤原呈子

Fujiwara no Tokuko
藤原得子

Fujiwara Yūsetsu
藤原猶雪

Fujishima Tatsurō
藤島達郎

Fukui Kōjun
福井康順

-G-

Ganjin (Chien-Chên)
鑑真

Genchi
源智

Genji
源氏

Genkū (Hōnen)
源空 (法然)

Genshin
源信

Gishūmonin Tōko
宜秋門院任子

Goshirakawa
後白川

Gotoba
後鳥羽

Gutoku ran (Shinran)
愚禿鸞 (親鸞)

Gyōhyō
行表

Gyōkū
行空

Gyōman (Hsing-man)
行満

Gyōnyo
巧如

-H-

Hani
範意

Hanen (Shinran)
範宴 (親鸞)

Hattori Shisō
服部之聡

Heiji
平氏

Heike
平家

Hino
日野

Hiramatsu Reizō
平松令三

Hirohashi
広橋

Hirono
広野

Hōnen (Genkū)
法然 (源空)

Hōzō (Fa-ts'ang)
法蔵

Hsin-hsing
信行

Hsing-man (Gyōman)
行満

Huai-kan
懐感

Hui-ssū
慧思

-I-

Ienaga Saburō
家永三郎

Inoue Mitsusada
井上光貞

Inoue Yasushi
井上 靖

Inumasa
いぬまさ

Ippen
一 遍

-J-

Jien
慈 円

Jitsugo
実 悟

Jōgyō
常 暁

Jōkei
貞 慶

Jōmonbō
浄聞房

Jōshinbō
浄信房

Jūkaku
従 覚

Junnyo
准 如

Junsai
遵 西

Junshin
順 信

-K-

Kakuei
覚 恵

Kakunyo
覚 如

Kakushinni
覚信尼

Kamatari
鎌 足

Kanmu
桓 武

Karasuma
烏 丸

Kazan-in Tadatsune
花山院忠経

Keien
慶 宴

Kengan
顕 願

Kennyo
顕 如

Kensei
顕 誓

Kenshunmonin
建春門院

Kenyū
兼 有

Kesa
け さ

Kikkōnyo
吉光女

Kiso no Yoshinaka
木曽義仲

Kōkakubō
好覚房

Konoe
近 衛

Kōsai
幸 西

Kotori
ことり

Kōzui
光 瑞

Kuei-chi
元 照

Kujō Kanezane
九条兼実

Kujō Ryōkei
九条良経

Kujō Uemichi
九条植通

Kūkai
空 海

Kumārajīva (Kumarajū)
鳩摩羅什

Kyōnyo
教 如

-M-

Masukata
益 方

Masutani Fumio
増谷文雄

Matsudono Motofusa
松殿基房

Matsuno Junkō
松野純孝

Minamoto no Yoriie
源 頼家

Minamoto no Yorimasa
源 頼政

Minamoto no Yoritomo
源 頼朝

Minamoto no
Yoshichika
源 義親

Miyazaki Enjun
宮崎円遵

Mochihitoō
以仁王

Munenari
宗 業

Munemitsu
宗 光

Murakami Sokusui
村上速水

Myōei
明 恵

Myōnyo
明 如

-N-

Nadeshi
なでし

Naganuma Kenkai
長沼賢海

Nāgārjuna (Ryūju)
龍 樹

Nagatomi Masatoshi
永富正俊

Nakamura Hajime
中村 元

Nakazawa Kenmyō
中沢見明

Nichiren
日 蓮

Nijō
二 条

Ninshō
忍 性

Noritsuna
範 綱

Nyoryō
如 了

Nyoshin
如 信

Nyoshunni
如春尼

Nyoshō
如 勝

—O—

Oda Nobunaga
織田信長

Ogurono Nyōbō
小黒の女房

Ōinomikado Yorisane
大炊御門頼実

—P—

Pai-chih Tsung-hsiao
(Shūgyō)
百芝宗暁

—R—

Rennō
蓮 能

Rennyo
蓮 如

Renyū
蓮 祐

Ryōchū
良 忠

Ryōgen
良 源

Ryōkū
良 空

Ryōnin
良 忍

Ryōshin
良 信

Ryūju (Nāgārjuna)
龍 樹

Ryūkan
隆 寛

—S—

Saichō (Dengyō)
最 澄 (伝 教)

Saijun
西 遵

Sanjō Sanefusa
三条実房

Sanjō Nagakane
三条長兼

Sanjō Takatada
三条隆忠

Sanemitsu
実 光

Saneshige
実 資

Sanetsuna
実 綱

Seikaku
聖 覚

Seikan bō
誓観房

Sei shōnagon
清少納言

Senun
仙 雲

Shakkū (Shinran)
綽空 (親鸞)

Shaku-Shakkū
釈 綽空

Shakunyo
綽 如

Shan-tao (Zendō)
善 導

Shiban
師 蛮

Shinbutsu
眞 仏

Shinkū
信 空

Shinran
親 鸞

Shinren
信 蓮

Shōkō
聖 光

Shōkū
証 空

Shōtoku-taishi
聖徳太子

Shūei
宗 叡

Shunkan
俊 寛

Shūnyo
宗 如

So Shakkū (Shinran)
僧 綽空 (親 鸞)

Sonren
尊 蓮

Sonyū
尊 由

Sukemitsu
資 光

Sukenaga
資 長

Sukenari
資 業

Suzuki Daisetsu
鈴木大拙

-T-

Tadamori
忠 盛

Taira
平

Taira no Kiyomori
平 清盛

Taira no Shigeko
平 滋子

Takano zenni
高野禅尼

Takakura
高 倉

Tadataka
忠 隆

Tamura Yoshirō
田村芳郎

T'an-luan (Donran)
曇 鸞

Tao-ch'o (Dōshaku)
道 綽

Tao-sui (Dōzui)
道 邃

Tenjin/Seshin
(Vasubandhu)
天 親 (世 親)

Tōin Kimisada
洞院公定

Tokugawa Ieyasu
徳川家康

Tokuko
徳 子

Toyotomi Hideyoshi
豊臣秀吉

Tsuchimikado
土御門

Tsuji Zennosuke
辻 善之助

Tsunetada
経 尹

-U-

Uramatsu
裏 松

Umehara Ryūshō
梅原隆章

-V-

Vasubandhu
(Tenjin/Seshin)
天 親 (世 親)

Vimalakīrti (Yuima)
維 摩

-W-

Wake no Hiroyo
和気広世

Washio Kyōdō
鷲尾教導

Wolfenstein, E. Victor

-Y-

Yamada Bunshō
山田文昭

Yamamoto Kōshō
山本晃紹

Yanagihara
柳 原

Yōmei
用 明

Yūi
有 意

Yuienbō
唯円房

Yuizen
唯 善

Yukikane
行 兼

-Z-

Zendō (Shan-tao)
善 導

Zennyo
善 如

Zenran
善 鸞

Zenren
善 蓮

Zenshin (Shinran)
善 信 (親 鸞)

Zonkaku
存 覚

Zonnyo
存 如

3. Buddhist text with Japanese equivalents

Abbreviations: Chinese (Ch)
Japanese (Ja)
Sanskrit (Sk†ˋ

-A-

Amitāyur-dhyāna sūtra (Skt)
観無量寿経

Anjin ketsujō-shō (Ja)
安心決定鈔

An-lo-chi (Ch)
安楽集

Aparimitāyus sūtra (Skt)
無量寿経

Avataṃsaka sūtra (Skt)
華厳経

-C-

Ch'eng-tsan ching-t'u-fo-she-shou-ching (Ch)
称讃浄土仏摂受経

-D-

Daimuryōjukyō (Ja)
大無量寿経

-F-

Fa-shih-tsan-(Ch)
法事讃

-I-

Ichinen tanen funbetsu no koto (Ja)
一念多念分別事

-J-

Jakkōdo-ki (Ja)
寂光土記

Jōdo-shū yōshū (Ja)
浄土宗要集

-K-

Kakuzen shō (Ja)
覚禅鈔

Kangyō-amidakyō-shūchū (Ja)
観経 阿弥陀経集註

Kanjin ryakuyō-shū (Ja)
観心略要集

Kuan-nien fa-men (Ch)
観念法門

Kuan-wu-liang-shou-ching-shu (Ch)
観無量寿経疏

Kubon ōjō-gi (Ja)
九品往生義

Kyōgyōshinshō (Ja)
教行信証

-L-

Lê-pang wen-lei (Ch)
楽邦文類

-M-

Mahā-dhāraṇī
大方等陀羅尼経

Mahāparinirvāṇa sūtra (Skt)
大般涅槃経

Mahāprajñāpāramitā sūtra (Skt)
大般若波羅密多経

Mahā-saṃnipāta sūtra (Skt)
大集経

Mahāvairocana sūtra (Skt)
大日経

Mappō tōmyōki (Ja)
末法燈明記

-O-

Ōjō-yō-shū (Ja)
往生要集

O-mi-t'o-ching-i-shu (Ch)
阿弥陀経義疏

-P-

Pañcaviṃśatisāhasrikā Prajñāpāramitā sūtra (Skt)
大品般若経

Pan-chou-tsan (Ch)
般舟讃

Prajñāpāramita sūtra (Skt)
般若波羅密多経

Pratyutpanna-samādhi sūtra (Skt)
般舟三昧経

-S-

Sangyō-gisho (Ja)
三経義疏

Saptśatikā-prajñāpāramitā sūtra (Skt)
文殊師利説般若波羅密経

Senjaku-hongan nembutsu-shū (Ja)
選択本願念仏集

Śrīmālā-devi sūtra (Skt)
勝鬘経

Sukhāvatī-vyūha sūtra (Skt)
阿弥陀経

Sukhāvatī-vyūhopadeśa (Skt)
浄土論

Suvarṇaprabhāsa sūtra (Skt)
金光明経

-T-

Tannishō (Ja)
歎異抄

Ta-ch'eng ch'i-hsin-lun-i-chi (Ch)
大乗起信論義記

-V-

Vimalakīrti sūtra (Skt)
維摩経

-W-

Wang-shêng li-tsan-chieh (Ch)
往生礼讃偈

Wang-shêng-lun-chu (Ch)
往生論註

Wu-liang-shou-ching (Ch)
無量寿経

-Y-

Yuishin-shō (Ja)
唯信鈔

Bibliography

This bibliography includes all cited works as well as works which were consulted and found relevant. The macron indicates a long vowel; however, it has been used only in authors' names and titles of books or articles.

1. Shinshū materials
Collection of materials relating to Shinran and his tradition

Genten kōchū, shinshū seiten (原典校註 真宗聖典 全1巻 Collated and annotated, Shinshū sacred text). Ed. by Kaneko, Daiei (金子大栄 編). Kyoto: Hozokan, 1969, 1 volume.

Honganji shi (本願寺史 全3巻 The history of Honganji). Ed. by Honganji shi hensansho (本願寺史編纂所 編). Kyoto: Nishi honganji, 1961, 3 volumes.

Shinshū shiryō shūsei (真宗資料集成 全13巻 Collection of Shinshū historical materials). Ed. by Ishida, Mitsuyuki and Joryū Chiba (石田充之 千葉乗隆 他編) and others. Kyoto: Dohosha, 1974, 13 volumes.

Shinshū shogyō zensho (真宗聖教全書 全5巻 Collection of Shinshū sacred text). Ed. by Shinshū shōgyō zensho hensansho (真宗聖教全書編纂所 編). Kyoto: Kokyo shoin, 1951-1957, 5 volumes.

Shinshū zensho (真宗全書 全46巻 続28巻 Compendium of Shinshū text). Ed. by Tsumaki, Naoyoshi (妻木直良 編). Kyoto: Kokyo shoin, 1912-1916, 46 volumes, 28 additional volumes.

Shinran-shōnin zenshū (親鸞聖人全集 全9巻 Complete collection of Shinran-shōnin). Ed. by Shinran-shōnin zenshū kankōkai (親鸞聖人全集刊行会 編). Kyoto: Hozokan, 1969, 9 volumes.

2. Complete works of the Masters of Japanese Buddhist sects

Dengyō-daishi zenshū (傳教大師全集 全3巻 Complete collection of Dengyō daishi). Ed. by Tendaishū shūten kankōkai (天台宗 宗典刊行会 編). Tokyo: Tendaishu shuten kankokai, 1912, 3 volumes.

Dōgen-zenji zenshū (道元禅師全集 全3巻 Complete collection of Dōgen zenji). Ed. by Ōkubo, Dōshū (大久保道舟 編). Tokyo: Chikuma shobo, 1969, 3 volumes.

Jōdoshū zensho (浄土宗全書 全42巻 Complete collection of Jōdo sect). Ed. by Jōdoshū zensho kankōkai (浄土宗全書刊行会 編). Tokyo: Sankibo busshorin, 1961, 42 volumes.

Shinran-shōnin zenshū (親鸞聖人全集 全9巻 Complete collection of Shinran-shōnin). See Shinshū materials.

Shōwa teihon Nichiren-shōnin ibun (昭和定本日蓮聖人遺文 全4巻 Complete collection of Nichiren Shōnin's writings, showa edition). Ed. by Risshō daigaku (立正大学 編). Yamanashi: Sohonzan Minobu Kuonji, 1953, 4 volumes.

3. Buddhist scriptures

Dainihon bukkyō zensho (大日本仏教全書 全151巻 補遺10冊 A compendium of Buddhist texts of Japan). Ed. by Bussho kankōkai (仏書刊行会 編). Tokyo: Bussho kankokai, 1912-1930, 151 volumes and 10 supplementary volumes.

Taishō shinshū daizōkyō (大正新修大蔵経 全100巻 Newly revised Tripitaka of the Taishō period). Ed. by Takakusu, Junjirō (高楠順次郎 他編) and others. Tokyo: Taisho issaikyo kankokai, 1924-1932, 100 volumes.

4. Collections of historical materials

Shintei zōho kokushi taikei (新訂 増補 国史大系 全66巻 Newly revised and enlarged compendium of Japanese history). Ed. by Kuroita, Katsumi (黒板勝美 編). Tokyo: Yoshikawa kobunkan, 1929-1966, 66 volumes.

Shinkō gunsho ruijū (新校 群書類従 全24巻 Newly revised gunsho ruijū [Nation's writings put in order by kind]) revised by Ueda, Kazutoshi et al. (上田万年 他). Tokyo: Naigaishoseki kaisha, 1928-1937, 24 volumes.

Zoku gunsho ruijū (続 群書類従 全72巻 Second series gunsho ruijū). Ed. by Hanawa, Hokiichi (塙 保己一 編). Tokyo: Zoku gunsho ruiju kankokai, 1931-1933, 72 volumes.

Zoku shiryō taisei (続 資料大成 全22巻 Continued complete historical materials). Ed. by Takeuchi, Rizō (竹内理三 編). Kyoto: Rinsen shoten, 1958, 22 volumes.

5. Dictionaries and chronological tables

Bukkyō daijii (仏教大辞彙 全6巻 Encyclopedia of Buddhist terms). Ed. by Ryūkoku daigaku (龍谷大学 編). Kyoto: Ryukoku daigaku, 1940, 6 volumes.

Bukkyō daijiten (仏教大辞典 全5巻 Buddhist encyclopedia). Ed. by Mochizuki Shinkō (望月信亨 編). Kyoto: Sekai seiten kankokai, 1954-1963, 10 volumes.

Butten kaidai jiten (仏典解題辞典 Encyclopedia of summaries of Buddhist scriptures). Ed. by Mizuno, Kōgen (水野弘元 他編) and others. Tokyo: Shunjusha, 1966, 1 volume.

Japanese-English Buddhist dictionary, ed. by Daitō shuppan sha (大東出版社 編).
　　Tokyo: Daito shuppansha, 1965, 1 volume.

Nihon rekishi dai jiten (日本歴史大辞典 全20巻 別冊2巻 An encyclopedia of
　　Japanese history). Ed. by Nihon rekishi dai jiten henshūiinkai
　　(日本歴史大辞典編集委員会 編). Tokyo: Kawade shobo, 1956-1961, 20 volumes,
　　2 additional volumes.

Shinshū nempyō (真宗年表 Chronological table of Shinshū). Ed. by Ōtani daigaku
　　(大谷大学 編). Kyoto: Hozokan, 1973.

Shinran-shōnin gyōjitsu (親鸞聖人行実 Life and events of Shinran-shōnin). Ed. by
　　Ienaga, Saburō (家永三郎 編). Kyoto: Hozokan, 1962.

Nempyō, chizu (年表 地図 Chronological table, maps). Ed. by Kodama, Kōta
　　(児玉幸多 編). Nihon no rekishi, extra number 5. Tokyo: Chuo koronsha,
　　1972.

6. Other books and/or articles

Akamatsu, Toshihide and Kazuo Kasahara, ed. (赤松俊秀 笠原一男 編). Shinshūshi
　　gaisetsu (真宗史概説 An outline of the history of Shinshū). Kyoto: Heirakuji
　　shoten, 1963.

Akamatsu, Toshihide et al., eds. (赤松俊秀 他編). Shinran-shōnin shinseki shūsei
　　(親鸞聖人真蹟集成 全9巻 別巻2 Collection of Shinran-shōnin's own writings).
　　Kyoto: Hozokan, 1973-1974, 9 volumes, 2 additional volumes.

_____. Shinran (親 鸞 Shinran). Tokyo: Yoshikawa kobunkan, 1961.

_____. Kamakura bukkyō no kenkyū (鎌倉仏教の研究 A study of Buddhism in the
　　Kamakura period). Kyoto: Heirakuji shoten, 1957.

_____. Zoku-kamakura bukkyō no kenkyū (続 鎌倉仏教の研究 Continued study of
　　Buddhism of the Kamakura period). Kyoto: Heirakuji shoten, 1966.

Allport, Gorden W. Basic Considerations for a Psychology of Personality. New
　　Haven: Yale University Press, 1955.

_____. The Individual and his Religion. New York: The Macmillan Co., 1950.

_____. Becoming. New Haven: Yale University Press, 1955.

Anesaki, Masaharu. Nichiren, the Buddhist Prophet. Cambridge: Harvard
　　University Press, 1960.

Araki, Yoshio. (荒木良雄). Chūsei bungaku no keisei to hatten (中世文学
　　の形成と発展 Formation and development of mediaeval literature). Kyoto:
　　Mineruva shobo, 1953.

Ashikaga, Enjutsu (足利衍述). Kamakura Muromachi jidai no jukyō
　　(鎌倉 室町時代の儒教 Confucianism in the Kamakura and Muromachi periods).
　　Tokyo: Nihon koten zenshū kankōkai, 1932.

Azuma kagami (吾妻鏡 The mirror of Azuma). Tokyo: Meicho kankokai, 1965.

Bandō, Shōjun. "The Significance of the Nembutsu." Contemporary Religions in Japan, 7. Tokyo: International Institute for the Study of Religions, September 1966.

Beardsley, Richard K. and John W. Hall, ed. Twelve Doors to Japan. New York: McGraw-Hill, 1965.

Bitō, Masahide (尾藤正英). Nihon ni okeru rekishi ishiki no hatten (日本における歴史意識の発展 The development of historical consciousness in Japan). Tokyo: Iwanami shoten, 1963.

Blok, Marc. Feudal Society. Chicago: University of Chicago Press, 1961.

Bloom, Alfred. "Shinran's Philosophy of Salvation by Absolute Other Power." Contemporary Religions in Japan, 5. Tokyo: International Institute for the Study of Religions, June 1968.

_____. The Life of Shinran-shōnin: The Journey to Self-Acceptance. Leiden: E. J. Brill, 1968.

_____. "Shinran: His Life and Thought." Thesis, Harvard University, 1963.

Bohner, Hermann. "Shōtoku taishi." Deutsche Gesellschaft für natur- und volderkunde Ostasiens, Mitteilungen, supplement 15. Tokyo: Deutsche Gesellschaft für natur und volderkunde Ostasiens, 1940.

Brecher, Michael. Nehru: A Political Biography. London: Oxford University Press, 1961.

Bukkyō Daigaku, ed. (仏教大学 編). Hōnen shōnin kenkyū tokushūgō No. 1 (法然上人研究 特集号 Special edition for the study of Hōnen shōnin). Kyoto: Bukkyo daigaku kenkyukiyo, 1960.

Chiba, Jōryū (千葉乗隆). Shinshū kyōdan no soshiki to seido (真宗教団の組織と制度Organization and system of Shinshū kyōdan). Kyoto: Dohosha, 1978.

Coates, H. Harper, and Ryūgaku Ishizuka, tr. Hōnen, the Buddhist Saint: His Life and Teaching. Kyoto: Chionin, 1962.

Coulborn, Rushton. "The Origin and Early Development of Feudalism in Japan and Western Europe." Coulborn, Rushton, ed. Feudalism in History. Princeton: Princeton University Press, 1956.

Doi, Tadao (土井忠雄). Hichiso shōgyō gaisetsu (七祖聖教概説 An outline of sacreds of seven patriarchs). Kyoto: Hyakkaen, 1955.

Eisenstadt, S. M. From Generation to Generation: Age Groups and Social Structure. London: Collier-Macmillan, 1964.

Eliot, Charles. Japanese Buddhism. London: Routledge and Kegan, 1964.

Engishiki (延喜式 Engi code), Kokushi taikei, vol. 26. Tokyo: Yoshikawa kobunkan, 1955.

Erikson, Erik H. Gandhi's Truth on the Origins of Militant Nonviolence. New York: W. W. Norton, 1969.

_____. Identity: Youth and Crisis. New York: W. W. Norton, 1968.

_____. Insight and Responsibility: Lectures on the Ethical Implications of Psychoanalytic Insight. New York: W. W. Norton, 1964.

_____, ed. Youth: Change and Challenge. New York: Basic Books, 1963.

_____. Childhood and Society. New York: W. W. Norton, 1963.

_____. Young Man Luther: A Study in Psychoanalysis and History. New York: W. W. Norton, 1958.

_____. Psychoanalysis and Religion. New Haven: Yale University Press, 1950.

Erwitt, Shinjune Boris. "Shinran-shōnin and the Pure Land Sect of Japan." Maha bodhi, 72. Calcutta: May 1964.

Fromm, Erich. The Crisis of Psychoanalysis. New York: Holt, 1970.

Fugen, Daien (普賢大円). "Anrakushū ni okeru gyō no kōsatsu" (安楽集における行の考察 Study of religious practice in An-lo-chi), Shūgakuin ronshū, vol. 31. Kyoto: Shugakuin, 1939.

Fujiki, Kunihiko (藤木邦彦). Heian jidai no kizoku no seikatsu (平安時代の貴族の生活 The life of the aristocracy in the Heian period). Tokyo: Shibundo, 1960.

Fujishima, Tatsurō (藤島達郎). "Shinran-shōnin dene kaisetsu" (親鸞聖人伝絵解説 Commentary to Shinran-shōnin's biography), Shinran-shōnin zenshū, vol. 4. Kyoto: Hozokan, 1969.

_____. "Shōtoku taishi to Shinran-shōnin" (聖徳太子と親鸞聖人 Prince Shōtoku and Shinran-shōnin). Nihon bukkyō shigaku nempō, vol. 29. Kyoto: Nihon bukkyo shigakukai, 1963.

_____. Eshinni kō (恵信尼公 Lady Eshinni). Niigata: Niigataken Arai betsuin, 1956.

Fujiwara, Ryōsetsu (藤原凌雪). Nembutsu shisō no kenkyū (念仏思想の研究 A study of the Nembutsu ideology). Kyoto: Nagata bunshodo, 1961.

Fujiwara, Yūsetsu (藤原猶雪). Shinran-shōnin dene no kenkyū (親鸞聖人伝絵の研究 Studies on Shinran's biography). Kyoto: Hozokan, 1954.

_____. Shinshūshi kenkyū (真宗史研究 A study to history of Shinshū). Kyoto: Bukkyo gakkai, 1921.

Fukui, Kōjun (福井康順). "Sangyō-gisho no seiritsu-o utagau" (三経義疏の成立をうたがう Suspicion on the formation of sangyōgisho). Indogaku Bukkyōgaku kenkyū, vol. IV-2. Tokyo: Indogaku Bukkyogakkai, 1961.

Furuta, Takehiko (古田武彦). Shinran (親鸞 Shinran). Tokyo: Shimizushoin, 1970.

Genshin (源信). Kanjin ryakuyōshū (観心略要集 Collection of the essentials of [the Tendai school's] meditation on one's heart). Dainihon bukkyō zensho, vol. 31. Tokyo: Bussho kankokai, 1922.

Groner, Paul. Saichō—The establishment of the Japanese Tendai school.
Berkeley: Berkeley Buddhist studies series, 1984.

Hall, John, Jaffrey Mass et al., eds. Medieval Japan: Essays in Institutional
History. New Haven: Yale University Press, 1974.

Harrison, John A, tr. and ed. "New Light on Early and Medieval Japanese
Historiography" (Two translations and an introduction). University of
Florida Monographs, Social Sciences, 4. Gainesville: University of
Florida Press, 1959.

Hashikawa, Tadashi (橋川 正). Sōgō Nihon bukkyō shi (総合 日本仏教史Synthetic
history of Japanese buddhism). Tokyo: Meguro shoten, 1932.

_____. Gaisetsu Nihon bukkyōshi (概説 日本仏教史 An outline of the history of
Japanese buddhism). Tokyo: Heirakuji shoten, 1929.

Hattori, Shiso (服部之聡). Shinran notes (親鸞ノート (正 続) Shinran notes). Tokyo:
Fukumura shuppansha, 1967, 2 volumes.

Hayashi, Mikiya (林 幹弥). "Kamakura jidai no taishi shinkō" (鎌倉時代の
太子信仰 Honor of Prince Shōtoku in the Kamakura era). Nihon rekishi,
241. Tokyo: Jikkyo shuppan, 1968.

Hazama, Jikō (硲 慈弘). Nihon bukkyō no kaiten to sono kichō (日本仏教
の開展とその基調（上 下）Japanese Buddhism: its development and characteristics). Tokyo: Sanseido, 1948, 2 volumes.

Hirai, Shōkai (平井正戒). Ryūkan-ritsushi no jōdokyō (隆寛律師の浄土教Pure Land
teaching of Ryūkan ritsushi).   Tokyo: Kanazawabunko Jodoshuten
kenkyukai, 1941.

Hiramatsu, Reizō (平松令三). "Takada hōko shinhakken shiryō ni yoru shiron"
(高田宝庫 新発見資料による試論 Essay based on new discoveries by Takada
School's Possession). Takada gakuhō, 46. Mie: Takada gakkai, 1959.

Hirano, Danzō (平野団三).   Echigo to Shinran Eshinni no sokuseki (越後と
親鸞 恵信尼の足跡 Shinran and Eshinni's activities in Echigo).   Niigata:
Kakimura shoten, 1972.

Hori, Ichirō (堀 一郎). Nittō guhō junreiki no kenkyū (入唐求法巡礼記の研究 A study
of Nittō guhō junreiki). Tokyo: Suzuki gakujutsu zaidan, 1964.

_____. "The Phenomenological Development of Pure Land School in Japan."
Religious Studies in Japan. Japanese Association for Religious Studies.
Tokyo: Maruzen, 1959.

Hosokawa, Gyōshin (細川行信). Shinshū seiritsushi no kenkyū (真宗成立史の研究 A
study of the history of the formation of Shinshū). Kyoto: Hozokan, 1977.

Hughes, Stuart H. History as Art and as Science. New York: Harper and Row,
1964.

Hurvitz, Leon. Chih-I (538-597): An Introduction to the Life and Idea of the
Chinese Buddhist Monk. Belge: Melanges Chinois et Buddhiques, vol. I-
XIII, 1963.

_____. Scripture of the Lotus Blossom of the Fine Dharma. New York: Columbia University Press, 1976.

Ienaga, Saburō (家永三郎). Nihon shisōshi ni okeru hitei no ronri no hattatsu (日本思想史における否定の論理の発達 The development of negative logic in the history of Japanese thought). Tokyo: Shinsensha, 1969.

_____ et al., eds. Nihon bukkyōshi (日本仏教史 History of Japanese Buddhism). Kyoto: Hozokan, 1967. 3 vols.

_____. Jōdai bukkyō shisōshi kenkyū (上代仏教思想史研究 Study of the history of Buddhist thought in ancient Japan). Kyoto: Hozokan, 1966.

_____. Chūsei bukkyō shisōshi kenkyū (中世仏教思想史研究 Study of Buddhist thought in Medieval Japan). Kyoto: Hozokan, 1960.

_____, ed. Nihon bukkyō shisōshi no tenkai—Hito to sono shisō (日本仏教思想史の展開 —人とその思想— The development of the history of Buddhist thought in Japan: Man and his thoughts). Kyoto: Heirakuji shoten, 1956.

_____. Jōgū Shōtoku hōō teisetsu no kenkyū, sōronhen (上宮聖徳法王帝説の研究 総論編 The study of a one-fascicle biography of Prince Shōtoku, general research). Tokyo: Sanseido, 1953.

_____. Jōgū Shōtoku hōō teisetsu no kenkyū, kakuronhen (上宮聖徳法王帝説の研究 各論編 The study of a one-fascicle biography of Prince Shōtoku, individual research). Tokyo: Sanseido, 1951.

_____. Nihon shisōshi ni okeru shūkyōteki shizenkan no tenkai (日本思想史における宗教的自然観の展開 The development of the religious outlook on nature in the history of Japanese thought). Tokyo: Sogensha, 1944.

_____. "Asuka hakuhō no bunka" (飛鳥 白鳳の文化 Culture in the Asuka and Hakuhō periods). Iwanami kōza Nihonshi, vol. 2. Tokyo: Iwanami shoten, 1962.

Ikukuwa, Kanmei (生桑完明). Shinran-shōnin senjutsu no kenkyū (親鸞聖人選述の研究 Study of Shinran's own writings). Kyoto: Hozokan, 1970.

Imaeda, Aishin (今枝愛真). Dōgen—Sono kōdō to shisō (道元 —その行動と思想— Dōgen: His movement and thought). Tokyo: Hyoronsha, 1970.

_____. Zenshū no rekishi (禅宗の歴史 A history of the Zen sect). Tokyo: Shibundo, 1962.

Imakōji, Kakuson (今小路覚尊). Zonkaku shōnin sode nikki (存覚上人袖日記 A diary of Zonkaku-shōnin). Kyoto: Kokyo shoin, 1923.

Inaba, Shūken and Issai Funabashi. Jōdo shinshū: An Introduction to the authentic Pure Land teaching. Kyoto: Otani University, 1961.

Ingram, Paul Owens. "Hōnen and Shinran's Justification for their Doctrine of Salvation and Faith through 'Other Power'." Contemporary Religions in Japan, 9, no. 3. Tokyo: International Institute for the Study of Religions, 1970.

_____. "Pure Land Buddhism in Japan: A Study of the Doctrine of Faith in the Teachings of Hōnen and Shinran." Thesis, Claremont Graduate School and University Center, 1968.

Inoue, Kaoru (井上 薫). Narachō bukkyōshi no kenkyū (奈良朝仏教史の研究 A study of the history of Buddhism in the Nara era). Tokyo: Yoshikawa kobunkan, 1966.

Inoue, Mitsusada (井上光貞). Nihon kodai no kokka to bukkyō (日本古代の国家と仏教 Nation and buddhism in ancient Japan). Tokyo: Iwanami shoten, 1971.

_____. Nihon Jōdokyō seiritsushi no kenkyū (日本浄土教成立史の研究 A study of the formative history of Pure Land buddhism in Japan). Tokyo: Yamakawa Shuppansha, 1957.

_____. "Fujiwara jidai no Jōdokyō" (藤原時代の浄土教 Pure Land buddhism in the Fujiwara period). Rekishigaku kenkyū, 131. Tokyo: Rekishigaku Kankyukai, 1948.

Inoue, Toshio (井上鋭夫). Honganji (本願寺 The Honganji temple). Tokyo: Shibundo, 1962.

Inouye, Yansushi (井上 靖). "Kanmuryōjukyō-san" (観無量寿経讃 Admiration of Kanmuryōjukyō), The Honganji shinpō, January 1, 1975. Kyoto: Nishi honganji, 1975.

Ishida, Ichirō (石田一郎). Bunkashigaku—Riron to hōhō (文化史学—理論と方法— Cultural Historiography: Its theory and method). Tokyo: Yoyosha, 1955.

Ishida, Mitsuyuki (石田充之). Kamakura jōdokyō seiritsu no kiso kenkyū (鎌倉浄土教成立の基礎研究 Basic studies to formation of Kamakura Pure Land teaching). Kyoto: Hyakkaen, 1966.

_____. Shinran kyōgi no kisoteki kenkyū (親鸞教義の基礎的研究 Fundamental studies of Shinran's doctrine). Kyoto: Nagata bunshodo, 1971, vol. 1, 1977, vol. 2.

_____. "Tendai elements in the doctrinal systems of Hōnen's disciples." Indogaku Bukkyōgaku kenkyū, 11-2. Tokyo: Nihon Indogaku Bukkyo-gakkai, 1963.

_____. Nihon jōdokyō no kenkyū (日本浄土教の研究 Japanese Pure Land buddhism). Kyoto: Hyakkaen, 1952.

Ishida, Mizumaro (石田瑞麿). Shinran (親鸞 Shinran). Tokyo: Chuokoronsha, 1969.

_____. Jōdokyō no tenkai (浄土教の展開 Development of Pure Land buddhism). Tokyo: Shunjusha, 1965.

_____. "Dōgen—Sono kai to shingi" (道元 —その戒と清規— Dōgen: His precepts and pure regulation). Kanazawabunko kenkyū, 76-81. Tokyo: Kanazawa bunko, 1962-3.

_____. "Hōnen-shōnin no kairitsu-kan" (法然上人の戒律観 Hōnen-shōnin and his view on precepts). Bukkyōshigaku, 2-3, 3-1. Tokyo: Bukkyoshigakkai, 1954.

Ishii, Kyōdō (石井教道). Senjakushū no kenkyū (選択集の研究 A study of Senjakushū). Kyoto: Heirakuji shoten, 1951.

Ishii, Ryōsuke (石井良助). Taika no kaishin to Kamakura bakufu no seiritsu (大化の改新と鎌倉幕府の成立 The Taika reform and the formation of the Kamakura bakufu). Tokyo: Sobunsha, 1958.

Ishimoda, Shō (石母田 正). Kodai makki seijishi josetsu: Kodai makki no seiji katei oyobi seiji keitai 古代末期政治史序説：古代末期の政治過程及び政治形態 全2巻 Introduction to the political history of the late ancient period: Political process and political form at the late ancient period). Tokyo: Miraisha, 1956, 2 vols.

_____. Chūseiteki sekai no keisei (中世的世界の形成 The formation of the mediaeval world). Tokyo: Ito shoten, 1946.

Ishimoda, Shō and Eiichi Matsushima (石母田 正 松島栄一). Nihonshi gaisetsu I (日本史概説 An introduction to Japanese history). Tokyo: Iwanami shoten, 1955.

Jien (慈 円). Gukanshō (愚管鈔 Miscellany of ignorant view). Nihon koten bungaku taikei, vol. 86. Tokyo: Iwanami shoten, 1957.

Jikei daishi den (慈恵大師伝 Biography of great master Jikei [Ryōgen]). Zoku gunsho ruijū, vol. 8. Tokyo: Zoku gunsho ruiju kankokai, 1904.

Jōkei (貞 慶). Kōfukuji sōjō (興福寺奏上 Kōfukuji report to the throne). Nihon shisō taikei, vol. 15. Tokyo: Iwanami shoten, 1967.

Kageyama, Haruki (景山春樹). Hieizan (比叡山 Hieizan). Tokyo: Kadokawa shoten, 1960.

Kakunyo (覚 如). Kuden shō (口伝鈔 Summary of transit by word of mouth). Shinran-shōnin zenshū, vol. 4. Kyoto: Hozokan, 1969.

Kamata, Shigeo and Hisao Tanaka, ed. (鎌田茂雄 田中久夫 編). Kamakura kyū bukkyō (鎌倉舊仏教. Kamakura traditional buddhism). Nihon shisō taikei, vol. 15. Tokyo: Iwanami shoten, 1971.

Kamata, Shigeo (鎌田茂雄). "Nanto kyōgaku no shisōshiteki igi" (南都仏教の思想史的意義 Significance to historical thought of south capital Buddhism). Kamakura kyū bukkyō, Nihon shisō taikei, vol. 15. Tokyo: Iwanami shoten, 1971.

Kaneko, Daiei. "The Meaning of Salvation in the Doctrine of Pure Land Buddhism." Eastern Buddhist, 1, no. 1. Kyoto: Otani University, 1965.

Kaneko, Daiei (金子大栄). Kyōgyōshinshō kōdoku (教行信証講読 Lectures on Kyōgyōshinshō). Kyoto: Zenjinsha, 1952, 3 volumes.

Karaki, Junzō (唐木順三). Mujō (無 常 Impermanence). Tokyo: Chikuma shobo, 1965.

_____. Muyōsha no keifu (無用者の系譜 Genealogy of a recluse). Tokyo: Chikuma shobo, 1965.

Kasahara, Kazuo (笠原一男). Shinran kenkyū notes (親鸞研究ノート Notes for the study of Shinran). Tokyo: Tosho shinbunsha, 1965.

_____. Shinran (親 鸞 Shinran). Tokyo: Chikuma shobo, 1962.

_____. Shinran to tōgoku nōmin (親鸞と東国農民 Shinran and the peasantry in east Japan). Tokyo: Yamakawa shuppansha, 1957.

_____. Kakumei no shūkyō (革命の宗教 Religion of revolution). Tokyo: Jinbutsu oraisha, 1964.

Katō, Shūichi (加藤周一). Shinran—Jūsan seiki shisō no ichimen (親鸞 一十三世紀 思想の一面— Shinran: One of the thoughts in the thirteenth century of Japan). Tokyo: Shinchosha, 1960.

Katsumata, Shunkyo (勝又俊教). "Kamakura jidai ni okeru Hossō kyōgaku no shomondai" (鎌倉時代における法相教学の諸問題 Some of the problems of Hossō [fa-hsiang-tsung] doctrine in the Kamakura period). Indogaku Bukkyōgaku kenkyū, vol. XXVI-2. Tokyo: Indogaku Bukkyo gakkai, 1968.

Kawasaki, Tsuneyuki (川崎庸之). "Iwayuru Kamakura jidai no shūkyō kaikaku ni tsuite" (いわゆる鎌倉時代の宗教改革について Concerning religious reformation in the Kamakura era). Rekishi Hyōron, 15. Tokyo: Minshushugi kagakusha kyokai, 1948.

_____ et al. Shūkyōshi (宗教史 History of religion). Taikei Nihonshi sōsho, vol. 18. Tokyo: Yamakawa shuppan, 1964.

Kawazoe, Shōji (川添昭二). "Chūsei bukkyō seiritsu no rekishiteki haikei" (中世仏教成立の背景 Historical background to formation of mediaeval buddhism). Nihon rekishi. Tokyo: Nihon rekishi gakkai, 1956, vols. 97, 98.

Kazue, Kyōichi (数江教一). Nihon no mappō shisō—Nihon chūsei shisōshi kenkyū (日本の末法思想 —日本中世思想史研究— The degenerate Dharma thought in Japan: Study of the thought of mediaeval Japan). Tokyo: Kobundo, 1961.

Keika bunka kenkyūkai, ed. (慶華文化研究会 編). Kyōgyōshinshō senjutsu no kenkyū (教行信証選述の研究 A study of the compilation of Kyōgyōshinshō). Kyoto: Hyakkaen, 1954.

Kidder, Jonathan Edward. "Japan Before Buddhism." Ancient Peoples and Places, vol. 10. London: Thames and Hudson, 1959.

Kitagawa, J. Mitsuo. Religion in Japanese History. New York: Columbia University Press, 1966.

_____. "Prehistoric Background of Japanese Religion." History of Religions, 2. Chicago: University of Chicago Press, 1963.

Kobayashi, Tomoaki (小林智昭). Chūsei bungaku no shisō (中世文学の思想 Thought in the literature of mediaeval Japan). Tokyo: Shibundo, 1964.

Kōsaka, Kō (高坂 好). "Jiryō shōen no tokushitsu" (寺領 荘園の特質 Characteristics of ecclesiastic shōen). Rekishigaku kenkyū, 7-5. Tokyo: Nihon rekishigaku kenkyukai, 1939.

Kuroda, Toshio, ed. (黒田俊雄). Nihon bunkashi: Hōgen, Heiji, Ōnin (日本文化史 : 平治 応仁History of Japanese culture, Hōgen, Heiji and Ōnin periods). Kōza Nihon bunkashi, vol. 3. Tokyo: Sanichi shobo, 1971.

_____. Nihon chūsei no kokka to shūkyō (日本中世の国家と宗教 Nation and religion of mediaeval Japan). Tokyo: Iwanami shoten, 1975.

Kusaka, Murin (日下無倫). Sōsetsu shinran dene (総説 親鸞伝絵 General study of the biography of Shinran). Tokyo: Shiseki kankokai, 1958.

_____. Shinshūshi no kenkyū (真宗史の研究The study of Shinshū history). Kyoto: Heirakuji shoten, 1931.

Lipset, Seymour Martin, ed. Sociology and History: Methods. New York: Basic Books, 1968.

Lu, David. Source of Japanese History. New York: McGraw-Hill, 1974, 2 volumes.

Mass, Jaffre. Warrior Government in Early Medieval Japan: A Study of Kamakura bakufu, shigo, and jitō. New Haven: Yale University Press, 1974.

Masutani, Fumio (増谷文雄). Shinran, Dōgen, Nichiren (親鸞 道元 日蓮 Shinran, Dōgen and Nichiren). Tokyo: Shibundo, 1961.

_____. A Comparative study of Buddhism and Christianity. Tokyo: CIIB Press, 1957.

Matsubara, Yūzen (松原祐善). Shinran to mappō shisō (親鸞と末法思想 Shinran and degenerate of Dharma thought). Kyoto: Hozokan, 1968.

Matsuno, Junkō (松野純孝). Shinran—Sono kōdō to shisō (親鸞 —その行動と思想— Shinran: His movement and thought). Tokyo: Hyoronsha, 1971.

_____. "Genzeriyaku to Shinran" (現世利益と親鸞 Shinran and his idea of Genzeriyaku). Miyazaki Enjun hakase kanreki kinen kai, ed. Shinshūshi no kenkyū. Kyoto: Nagata bunshodo, 1966.

_____. Shinran—Sono shōgai to shisō no tenkai (親鸞 —その生涯と思想の 展開— Shinran: His life and the developmental process of his thought). Tokyo: Sanseido, 1960.

Mibu, Taishun (壬生台舜). Eizan no shinpū (叡山の新風 Reformer of Hieizan), vol. 3. Tokyo: Chikuma shobo, 1967.

Mills, Wright C. The Sociological Imagination. New York: Oxford University Press, 1959.

Miyagi, Eishō (宮城栄昌). Engishiki no kenkyū: Shiryōhen; Ronjutsuhen (延喜式の研究：史料編 論述編 全 2 巻 Study of the Engishiki: Sources; Discussions). Tokyo: Taishukan shoten, 1957, 2 volumes.

Miyai, Yoshio (宮井義雄). "Ritsuryō bukkyō no henkaku to Shinran, Dōgen no tachiba" (律令仏教の変革と親鸞，道元の立場 The reform of Ritsuryō buddhism and the situation of Shinran and Dōgen). Yamanashi kenritsu joshi tanki daigaku kiyō, 1, 2. Yamanashi: Yamanashi kenritsu joshi daigaku, 1967-1968.

Miyaji, Kakuei (宮地廓慧). Shinran-den no kenkyū (親鸞伝の研究 A study of the biography of Shinran). Kyoto: Hyakkaen, 1968.

Miyamoto, Shōson et al. (宮本正尊 他著). Kōza Bukkyō (講座 仏教 全7巻 Buddhism, lecture series). Tokyo: Daizo shuppan, 1967, 7 volumes.

Miyazaki, Enjun, ed. (宮崎円遵 編). Shōganji-zō Honganji shinran-shōnin dene (照願寺蔵 本願寺親鸞聖人伝絵 全4巻 解説1巻 Shōganji collection, Honganji shinran-shōnin's biography). Tokyo: Daihorin kaku, 1979, 4 volumes, 1 commentary volume.

_____. Shoki shinshū no kenkyū (初期真宗の研究 Studies on the early period of Shinshū). Kyoto: Nakata bunshodo, 1971.

_____. Shinran to sono montei (親鸞とその門弟 Shinran and his disciples). Kyoto: Nagata bunshodo, 1956.

_____. Chūsei bukkyō to shomin seikatsu (中世仏教と庶民生活 Mediaeval buddhism and the life of the common people). Kyoto: Heirakuji shoten, 1951.

_____. Shinshū shoshigaku no kenkyū (真宗書誌学の研究 Bibliographical study of the Shinshū text). Kyoto: Nagata bunshodo, 1950.

_____. "Shinran to sono kyōdan" (親鸞とその教団 Shinran and its institution). Kōza Bukkyō, vol. 5, Daito shuppansha, 1967.

Miyoshi no Tameyasu (三善為康). Shūi ōjōden (拾遺往生伝 Compiled historical account of those born in the Pure Land). Dainihon Bukkyō zensho, vol. 51. Tokyo: Bussho kankokai, 1930.

Mochizuki, Kinkō (望月歓厚). Nichiren kyōgaku no kenkyū (日蓮教学の研究 Studies in the Nichiren doctrines). Kyoto: Heirakuji shoten, 1961.

Mochizuki, Shinkyō (望月信亨).   Hōnen shōnin to sono monka no kyōgi (法然上人とその門下の教義 Doctrines of Hōnen shōnin and his disciples). Kyoto: Mochizuki sensei 13 kaiki kinen shuppankai, 1960.

Morris, Ivan. The World of the Shining Prince: Court Life in Ancient Japan. London: Oxford University Press, 1964.

Murakami, Sokusui (村上速水). Shinran kyōgi no kenkyū (親鸞教義の研究 A study of Shinran's doctrine). Kyoto: Nagata bunshodo, 1968.

_____. Shinran dokuhon (親鸞読本 Lectures on Shinran). Kyoto: Hyakkaen, 1968.

Murdoch, James H. and Isoh Yamagata. A History of Japan. Reprint. London: Routledge & Kegan Paul, 1949, 3 volumes.

Nabata, Takashi (名畑 崇). "Shinran-shōnin no Rokkakudō no ge ni tsuite" (親鸞聖人の六角堂の偈について A study of Shinran and the Rokkakudō verse). Shinshūkenkyū, 8. Kyoto: Shinshu rengo gakkai, 1963.

Naemura, Takatsuna (苗村高綱). "Shikan jisshū to shite no jōgyō zanmai" (止観実修としての常行三昧 Samadhi of constant practice as practical method of Mo-ho shih-kan). Bukkyō kenkyū VII. Tokyo: Bukkyo gakkai, 1956.

Naganuma, Kenkai (長沼賢海). "Shinran-shōnin-ron" (親鸞聖人論 A study of Shinran). Shigaku zasshi, vol. 21, no. 3-12. Tokyo: Tokyo University, 1910.

Nagazumi, Yasuaki (永積安明). Chūsei bungakuron—Kamakura jidai-hen (中世文学論 —鎌倉時代編— Essay on mediaeval literature: Kamakura period). Tokyo: Doshinsha, 1953.

Nakamura, Hajime et al., eds.(中村 元 他編). Asia Bukkyōshi, Nihon Bukkyō II (アジア仏教史：日本仏教 II The Buddhist history of Asia, Japanese Buddhism II). The Buddhist History of Asia, vol. 4. Tokyo: Kosei shuppan, 1972.

Nakamura, Hajime (中村 元). Tōyōjin no shii-hōhō (東洋人の思惟方法 The ways of thinking of eastern peoples). Tokyo: Shunjusha, 1962, 4 volumes.

Nakazawa, Kenmyō (中沢見明). Shinshū genryūshi-ron (真宗源流史論 Origin of Shinshū history). Kyoto: Hozokan, 1951.

_____. Shijō no Shinran (史上の親鸞 Shinran in history). Kyoto: Bunkenshoin, 1923.

Naoki, Kōjirō (直木孝次郎). Kodai kokka no seiritsu (古代国家の成立 Formation of ancient nation). Nihon rekishi, vol. 2. Tokyo: Chuo koron sha, 1962.

Nihon Bukkyō Gakkai, ed. (日本仏教学会 編). Kamakura bukkyō keisei no mondaiten (鎌倉仏教成立の問題点 Some problems of formation to Kamakura buddhism). Kyoto: Heirakuji shoten, 1970.

Nihonshi kenkyūkai shiryōkenkyū bukai, ed. (日本史研究会史料研究部会 編). Chūsei shakai no kihon kōzō (中世社会の基本構造 The basic structure of mediaeval society). Tokyo: Ochanomizu shobo, 1958.

Nihon Shisōshi Kenkyūkai, ed. (日本思想史研究会 編). Nihon ni okeru rekishi shisō-no tenkai (日本における歴史思想の展開 Development of historical thought in Japan). Sendai: Tohoku shuppan kabushiki kaisha, 1962.

Nishi honganji (西本願寺). Honganji shinpō, January 1975 (本願寺新報 The journal of Nishi honganji). Kyoto: Nishi honganji, 1975.

Nogami, Shunsei (野上俊静). Dentō no seija (伝燈の聖者 Patriarchs in the tradition of Pure Land Buddhism). Kyoto: Hyakkaen, 1961.

Ōe, Junjō (大江淳誠). Kyōgyōshinshō to Bukkyō shisō (教行信証と仏教思想 Kyōgyōshinshō and Buddhism), Kyoto: Hyakkaen, 1964.

Ōhara, Shōjitsu (大原性実). Shinshū kyōgakushi kenkyū (真宗教学史研究 全3巻 Study of the history of Shinshū doctrines). Kyoto: Nagata bunshodo, 1956, 3 volumes.

Ōhashi, Shunnō (大橋俊雄). Hōnen—Sono kōdō to shisō (法然 —その行動と思想— Honen: His movement and thought). Tokyo: Hyoronsha, 1970.

_____. Hōnen, Ippen (法 然 一 遍 Hōnen and Ippen). Nihon shisō taikei, vol. 10. Tokyo: Iwanami shoten, 1971.

Ōno, Tatsunosuke (大野達之助). Nihon bukkyō shisōshi (日本仏教思想史 History of Japanese Buddhist thought). Tokyo: Yoshikawa kobunkan, 1961.

Ōsumi, Kazuo (大隅和雄). "Kodai makki ni okeru kachikan no hendō" (古代末期 に於ける価値観の変動 The change of values in the late ancient times). Hokkaidō daigaku bungakubu kiyō, 16-1. Hokkaido: Hokkaido daigaku, 1968.

_____. "Kamakura bukkyō to sono kakushin undō" (鎌倉仏教とその革新運動 Kamakura buddhism and its reformatory movement). Iwanami kōza Nihonshi, vol. 5. Tokyo: Iwanami shoten, 1975.

Ōya, Tokujō (大屋徳成). Nihon bukkyōshi no kenkyū (日本仏教史の研究 A study of the history of Japanese Buddhism). Kyoto: Hozokan, 1953.

_____. Nara Bukkyōshi ron (奈良仏教史論Studies on history of Nara buddhism). Tokyo: Tohobunken kankokai, 1935.

Reischauer, August Karl. A study in Japanese buddhism. New York: AMS, 1970.

Reischauer, Edwin O. "Japanese Feudalism." Coulborn, ed. Feudalism in History. Princeton: Princeton University Press, 1956.

_____. Ennin's Travel in Tang China. New York: Ronald Press, 1955.

_____. Ennin's Diary: The Record of a Pilgrimage to China in Search of the Law. New York: Ronald Press, 1955.

Reischauer, Edwin and John Fairbank. A History of Eastern Asia Civilization: East Asia—The Great Tradition. Boston: Houghton Mifflin, 1960.

Robinson, Richard. The Buddhist Religion. Belmont, California: Dickenson, 1970.

Ryōgen (良 源). Kubon ōjōgi (九品往生義 Essence of the nine levels of quality in Pure Land rebirth). Dainihon Bukkyō zensho, vol. 24. Tokyo: Bussho kankokai, 1922.

Ryūkoku University Translation Center. The Kyōgyōshinshō. Kyoto: Ryukoku University, 1966.

_____. Jōdo wasan. Kyoto: Ryukoku University, 1965.

_____. Tannishō. Kyoto: Ryukoku University, 1962.

_____. Shōshin ge. Kyoto: Ryukoku University, 1961.

Sanjō, Nagakane (三条長兼). Sanchō ki (三長記 Record of three talents). Shiryō taisei, vol. 31. Kyoto: Rinsen shoten, 1965.

Sansom, Sir George B. "A History of Japan to 1334." Civilizations of the East. Stanford series, vol. 1. Stanford: Stanford University Press, 1958.

_____. Japan: A Short Cultural History, 2nd rev. ed. New York: Appleton-Century-Crofts, 1952.

Satō, Shinichi and Yoshisuke Ikeuchi (佐藤進一　池内義資). Chūsei hōsie shiryō shū: Kamakura bakufu-hō, Muromachi, bakufu-hō (中世法制史料集 鎌倉幕府法 室町幕府法 全2巻 A collection of historical materials of mediaeval laws: The Kamakura bakufu laws; Murromachi bakufu laws). Tokyo: Iwanami shoten, 1955, 2 volumes.

Satō, Tetsuei (佐藤哲英). Tendai-daishi no kenkyū (天台大師の研究　Study of Tendai-daishi). Kyoto: Hyakkaen, 1961.

Saunders, Ernest Dake. Buddhism in Japan with an Outline of its Origins in India. Philadelphia: University of Pennsylvania Press, 1964.

Sei shōnagon (清少納言). Makura no sōshi (枕草子 The pillow book [of Sei shōnagon]). Nihon koten bungaku taikei, vol. 19. Tokyo: Iwanami shoten, 1967.

Sekiguchi, Shindai (関口真大). "Tendai shikan no seiritsu to tenkai" (天台止観の成立と展開Formation and development of Tendai Mo-ho shih-kan). Bukkyō no konpon shinri. Tokyo: Shinseido, 1957.

_____. Tendai shikan no kenkyū (天台止観の研究 Studies on Tendai Mo-ho shih-kan). Tokyo: Iwanami shoten, 1969.

Shigematsu, Akihisa (重松明久). Nihon Jōdokyō seiritsu katei no kenkyū (日本浄土教成立過程の研究 A study of the formation of Japanese Pure Land teaching). Kyoto: Heirakuji shoten, 1964.

_____. Kakunyo (覚　如 Kakunyo). Tokyo: Yoshikawa kobunkan, 1962.

_____. "Sengo ni okeru Jōdoshūshi no kenkyū" (戦後における浄土宗史の研究The studies in the history of Jōdo sect in post-World War II). Shinshūshi kenkyūkai, ed. Hōken shakai ni okeru Shinshū kyōdan no tenkai. Kyoto: Heirakuji shoten, 1957.

Shimaji, Daitō (島地大等). Nihon Bukkyō kyōgakushi (日本仏教 教学史 The history of Japanese Buddhist doctrine). Tokyo: Meiji shoin, 1933.

Shinoda, Minoru. "The Founding of the Kamakura Shōgunate, 1180-1185" with selected translations from the Azuma Kagami. Records of Civilization, Sources and Studies, vol. 57. New York: Columbia University Press, 1960.

Shinshūshi Kenkyūkai, ed. (真宗史研究会 編). Hōken shakai ni okeru Shinshū kyōdan no tenkai (封建社会における真宗教団の展開 The development of the organization of the Shinshū in feudal society). Tokyo: Sankibo busshorin, 1957.

Shioda, Gison (塩田義遜). Nichiren kyōgakushi no kenkyū (日蓮教学史の研究 Studies in the history of Nichiren's doctrine). Kyoto: Heirakuji shoten, 1959.

Stuart, Gilbert, tr. The Stranger. New York: Alfred A. Knopf, 1946.

Suzuki, Daisetsu Teitarō. Shin Buddhism. New York: Harper and Row, 1970.

Tachibana no Narihira (橘 成平). Kokon chomon shū (古今著聞集 Collection of occurrences, old and present). Nihon koten bungaku taikei, vol. 84. Tokyo: Iwanami shoten, 1957.

Takachiho, Tetsujō (高千穂徹乗). Hōnen kyōgaku no tokushitsu to dōkō (法然教学の特質と動向 Characteristics of Hōnen's doctrine and his movement). Kyoto: Nagata bunshodo, 1954.

Takahatake, Takamichi (高畑崇導). Bukkyō kyōten josetsu (仏教経典叙説 Introduction to Buddhist sūtra). Tokyo: Ryubunkan, 1980.

_____, tr. The sūtra of the Buddha Amitābha, Amida-kyō. Montreal: Monchanin Centre, 1979.

Takakusu, Junjirō. The Essentials of Buddhist Philosophy. Honolulu: Office Supply Company, 1956.

Takeuchi, Michio (竹内道雄). Dōgen (道 元 Dōgen). Tokyo: Yoshikawa kobunkan, 1962.

Takeuchi, Yoshinori (武内義範). Kyōgyōshinshō no tetsugaku (教行信証の哲学 Philisophy of Kyōgyōshinshō). Tokyo: Kobundo, 1941.

Tamaki, Kōshirō (玉城康四郎). Nihon bukkyō shisōron (日本仏教思想論 A study of Japanese buddhist thought). Kyoto: Heirakuji shoten, 1974.

Tamamuro, Taijō (圭室諦成). Nihon bukkyōshi gaisetsu (日本仏教史概説 An outline of Japanese buddhist history). Tokyo: Risosha, 1940.

Tamura, Enchō (田村円澄). Shōtoku taishi (聖徳太子 Prince Shōtoku). Tokyo: Chuokoronsha, 1964.

_____. Hōnen (法 然 Hōnen). Tokyo: Yoshikawa kobunkan, 1959.

_____. Hōnen to sono kyōdan (法然とその教団 Hōnen and his organization). Kyoto: Hozokan, 1958.

_____. Hōnen-shōnin den no kenkyū (法然上人伝の研究 Studies in the biography of Hōnen). Kyoto: Hozokan, 1956.

_____. Jōdo shisō no tenkai (浄土思想の展開 The development of the Pure Land thought). Kyoto: Nagata bunshodo, 1948.

Tamura, Yoshirō (田村芳郎). Nihon bukkyōshi nyūmon (日本仏教史入門 Introduction to history of Japanese buddhism). Tokyo: Kadokawa shoten, 1969.

_____. Kamakura shin bukkyō shisō no kenkyū (鎌倉新仏教思想の研究 Study of Kamakura new buddhism). Kyoto: Heirakuji shoten, 1967.

Tanishita, Ichimu (谷下一夢). "Kazoku no mondai" (家族の問題 Some problems of family [of Shinran]). Shinran-shōnin no kyōgaku to denki. Kyoto: Hyakkaen, 1963.

Terasaki, Shūichi (寺崎秀一). "Mappō shisō no shiteki kōsatsu" (末法思想の史的考察 A historical study of degenerate Dharma thought). Bunka, vol. I, 4. Tokyo: Iwanami shoten, 1934.

Tillich, Paul. Morality Beyond. New York: Harper and Row, 1963.

Toda, Yoshimi (戸田芳美). "Chūsei bunka keisei no zentei" (中世文化の前提 A premise of the formation of medieval culture). Kōza Nihon bunka shi, vol. 2. Tokyo: Sanichi shobo, 1971.

Tokoro, Shigemoto (戸頃重基). Nichiren no shisō to Kamakura bukkyō (日蓮の思想と鎌倉仏教 Nichiren's thought and Kamakura Buddhism). Tokyo: Toyama shobo, 1967.

_____, ed. Nichiren (日 蓮 Nichiren). Nihon shisō taikei, vol. 14. Tokyo: Iwanami shoten, 1970.

Thomas, Edward. The History of Buddhist Thought. London: Routledge and Kegan Paul, 1956.

Tsuchihashi, Shūkō (土橋秀高). "Shinran-shōnin to Nehangyō" (親鸞聖人と涅槃経 Shinran-shōnin and Nehangyō [Mahāparinirvāna sūtra]). Ryūkoku daigaku ronshū, vols. 355-356. Kyoto: Ryukoku daigaku, 1961.

Tsuji, Zennosuke (辻 善之助). Shinran-shōnin hisseki no kenkyū (親鸞聖人筆跡の研究 The study of Shinran's penmanship). Tokyo: Kinkodo, 1920.

_____. Nihon bukkyōshi (日本仏教史 全10巻 Japanese Buddhist history). Tokyo: Iwanami shoten, 1947-1951, 10 volumes.

Tsunoda, Ryūsaku et al., eds. Sources of Japanese Tradition. New York: Columbia University Press, 1958, 2 volumes.

Tsutsumi, Genryū (堤 玄立). Shin to shō—Shinran kyōgaku josetsu (信と証 —親鸞教学序説— Faith and attainment: An introduction to Shinran's doctrine). Kyoto: Hozokan, 1980.

Umehara, Ryushō (梅原隆章). Shinran-den no sho-mondai (親鸞伝の諸問題 Various problems on the biography of Shinran). Kyoto: Kenshin gakuen, 1951.

Umehara, Shinryū (梅原真隆). Eshinni monjo no kōkyū (恵信尼文書の考究 A study of Eshinni's letters). Toyama: Senchoji bunsho dendobu, 1956.

Washio, Kyōdō (鷲尾教導). Eshinni monjo no kenkyō (恵信尼文書の研究 A study of Eshinni's letters). Kyoto: Chugai shuppan, 1955.

Watanabe, Shōkō. "Japanese Buddhism: A Critical Appraisal." Japanese Life and Culture, 8. Tokyo: Kokusai Bunka Shinkokai, 1964.

Wolfenstein, E. Victor. The Revolutionary Personality: Lenin, Trotsky, Gandhi. New Jersey: Princeton University Press, 1967.

Wright, Mills. The Sociological Imagination. New York: Oxford University Press, 1959.

Yamabe, Shūgaku and Chizen Akanuma (山辺習学 赤沼智善). Kyōgyōshinshō kōgi (教行信証講義 Lectures on Kyōgyōshinshō). Kyoto: Hozokan, 1951, 2 volumes.

Yamada, Bunshō (山田文昭). Shinran to sono kyōdan (親鸞とその教団 Shinran and his group). Kyoto: Hozokan, 1948.

_____. Shinshūshi kō (真宗史稿 Notes on Shinshū history). Nagoya: Hajinkaku, 1934.

Yamaguchi, Kōen (山口光円). Tendai Jōdokyō shi (天台浄土教史 History of Pure Land teaching in Tendai sect). Kyoto: Hozokan, 1967.

Yamaguchi, Kōsaku. "Some Problems of the Feudal Institutions and the Infeudation in the Kamakura Period." Economic Review, vols. 3, 4. Osaka: St. Andrew's University, 1962.

Yamamoto, Kōshō. An Introduction to Shin Buddhism. Ube: Karinbunko, 1963.

_____, tr. Kyōgyōshinshō. Tokyo: Karinbunko, 1958.

_____, tr. The private letters of Shinran-shōnin. Tokyo: Karinbunko, 1956.

_____, tr. The Shinshū seiten. Honolulu: Honpa Honganji Mission, 1955.

_____, tr. The words of Saint Rennyo. Yamaguchi: Karinbunko, 1968.

Yasui, Kōdo (安井広度). Hōnen-shōnin monka no kyōgaku (法然上人門下の教学 The teachings of Hōnen's disciples). Kyoto: Hozokan, 1938.

_____. "Kaisetsu Kangyō amidakyō shūchū" (解説 観経 阿弥陀経集註 Commentary to annotations of Kangyō and amidakyō). Shinran-shōnin zenshū, vol. 7. Kyoto: Hozokan, 1969.

Appendix

An Annotated Chronological Table of Shinran's Life

Contents

Western calendar; Japanese era & year	Shinran's age	Events in Shinran's Life	Verification for dating*	Verification material volume & page number**
1173 (Shōan 3) 承安		May 21: Shinran is born.	Based on his <u>Jōdo-wasan</u>, etc.	II:75
1181 (Yōwa 1) 養和	9	He enters Tendai monastic life on Mt. Hiei, beginning his practice as an 'ordinary temple monk' (dōsō).	<u>Shinran-shōnin dene</u> (Chapter 1); <u>Eshinni monjo</u> (letter 3)	IV:3 III:186
1182 (Juei 1) 寿永	10	Shinran's future wife Eshinni is born.	<u>Eshinni monjo</u> (letters 8 & 9)	III:200
1201 (Kennin 1) 建仁	29	Shinran has spent 20 years studying the Tendai school's encyclopedic organization of prevalent Buddhist doctrine and practice while living as a monastic on Mt. Hiei. In the process he begins to turn toward the Pure Land movement as the major avenue for the salvation of sentient existence. Eventually this conviction strengthens to the degree that he decides to find the Pure Land master Hōnen and become his disciple.		
		Shinran visits the Rokkakudō (said to have been built by Shōtoku-taishi) to pray and meditate for the courage to clearly make his final decision.	<u>Eshinni monjo</u> (letter 3)	III:81

* For Japanese equivalents for these titles, see Glossary and Bibliography.
** The Roman and Arabic numerals refer to the volume and page numbers of <u>Shinran shōnin zenshū</u>. See Bibliography p. 165.

Western calendar; Japanese era & year	Shinran's age	Events in Shinran's Life	Verification for dating	Verification material volume & page number
		He remains in retreat for 100 days.		
		At dawn on the 95th day, Shōtoku-taishi appears to him in a dream—this convinces Shinran to join Hōnen.	Eshinni monjo (letter 3)	III:81
		Shinran leaves Mt. Hiei.	Kyōgyōshinshō (volume 6)	I:381
1203 (Kennin 3)	31	April 5: A bodhisattva appears to Shinran during a dream. Based on the revelation from this dream he decides to marry.	Shinran muki; Shinran-shōnin dene (chapter 3)	IV:201 IV:6
1204 (Genkyū 1) 元久	32	November 7: Due to mounting criticism by Mt. Hiei religious authorities over the Pure Land teachings and practices of Hōnen's movement, his disciple Seikaku composes an apology and Shinkū writes a defense entitled the 'Seven-article pledge' for Hōnen, inviting major disciples to sign it.	Saihō shinan-shō	V:171
		November 8: Shinran signs the Seven-article pledge (not as 'Shinran' but with 'Shakkū', which was his self-styled name at the time).		
1205 (Genkyū 2)	33	April 14: With Hōnen's permission, Shinran has copied Hōnen's Pure Land masterpiece, the Senjaku-hongan nembutsu-shū; Hōnen inscribes the copy with 'Namu amida butsu—the basis for the act of rebirth is the Nembutsu'.	Kyōgyōshinshō (volume 6)	I:381

Western calendar; Japanese era & year	Shinran's age	Events in Shinran's Life	Verification for dating	Verification material volume & page number
		July 29: Shinran borrows and copies Hōnen's portrait. Hōnen inscribes it with a modified quotation from Shan-tao's Wang-sheng li-tsan-chieh.		
		In October, the major Nara Buddhist monastic institution, Kōfukuji, requests an imperial ban on the Nembutsu movement, as the Hossō School monk-scholar Jōkei presents a nine article petition entitled 'Kōfukuji Report to the Throne' (Kōfukuji-sōjō) accusing Hōnen and his followers of heresy. (Some modern scholars claim that Shinran may have later written his Kyōgyōshinshō to refute Jōkei's petition.)	Kōfukuji Sōjō	Nihon shisō taikei* XV:32
1207 (Shōgen 1) 承元	35	In early February, the imperial court government orders the Nembutsu movement banned. Hōnen is banished to Tosa and his major disciples are either exiled or executed. Shinran is exiled to Kokufu in the Echigo district. He is deprived of this monastic status and given the lay name 'Yoshizane Fujii'— however, he calls himself 'Toku' ('the bald') during exile.	Kyōgyōshinshō (volume 6)	I:381
1211 (Kenryaku 1) 建暦	39	In March, his son Shinrembō Myōshin is born.	Eshinni monjo (letter 5)	III:197
		November 17: Hōnen, Shinran and others are recalled from exile.	Kyōgyōshinshō (volume 6)	I:381

* See Bibliography p. 173.

Western calendar; Japanese era & year	Shinran's age	Events in Shinran's Life	Verification for dating	Verification material volume & page number
1212 (Kenryaku 2)	40	January 25: Hōnen dies at the age of eighty.	Kyōgyōshinshō (volume 6)	I:381
1214 (Kempō 2) 建保	42	In the spring, Shinran leaves Echigo to go to the Kantō area (eastern Japan). On his journey, especially during a few day's stay at Sanuki in Kōzukenokuni, he understands the true misery of the ordinary Japanese people, so he immediately plans to recite the three Pure Land sūtras (Jōdo sanbu-kyō) 1000 times to create karmic merit for this poverty-stricken people. He realizes, however, that this practice cannot be true to a total commitment to the saving Other-power of the Buddha Amida's compassion, so he stops this 'Self-effort' after a few days.	Eshinni monjo (letter 5)	III:194
1217 (Kempō 5)	45	At some time before this year, Shinran completes his Kangyō-amidakyō-shūchū (Annotated Amitāyur-dhyāna sūtra and Shukhāvati-vyūha sūtra).	Kanmuryōjukyō- shūchū; Amidakyō- shūchū	VII:3
1224 (Gennin 1) 元仁	52	Shinran's daughter Kakushinni is born.	Eshinni monjo (letter 4)	III:193
		During this year, Shinran probably completed the first draft of the overall structure of his Kyōgyō shinshō. (This is based on the present tense language found in volume 6 and the year itself, identified by Shinran as 1224.)	Kyōgyōshinshō	I:314

Western calendar; Japanese era & year	Shinran's age	Events in Shinran's Life	Verification for dating	Verification material volume & page number
		Shinran writes that the year 1224 is the 683rd year of the decay of the Dharma. He is angry at the ban on Nembutsu ordered in August by the government, because it is his belief that the Nembutsu is the only teaching for salvation in the age of the decay of the Dharma.	Kyōgyōshinshō (volume 6)	I:314
1230 (Kanki 2) 寛喜	58	May 25: Shinran copies Seikaku's Yuishin-shō (Summary of 'Only-faith'). Both were Hōnen's disciples and close friends. (Shinran copied the Yuishin-shō more than any text during his lifetime—six times.)	Senjuji collection	VI:19
1231 (Kanki 3)	59	April 4 – April 8: During an illness and the subsequent recovery, he confides to his wife what has burdened him for 17 years. He confesses that he has practised chanting the three Pure Land sūtras 1000 times to save sentiency, even when this belief was contrary to a thorough faith in the Buddha Amida's total compassionate 'Other-power'.	Eshinni monjo (letter 5)	III:194
1233 (Tempuku 1) 天福	61	At this time Shinran's family leaves the Kantō area and moves to Kyoto. (This occurred because of growing antagonism to Nembutsu practice in eastern Japan. On July 24, 1235 Nembutsu practice would be prohibited and disciples banished from Kamakura by the military bakufu government.)	Kamakura bakufu hō	Chūsei hōsei shiryō-shū* I:101

* See Bibliography p. 179.

Western calendar; Japanese era & year	Shinran's age	Events in Shinran's Life	Verification for dating	Verification material volume & page number
1235 (Katei 1) 嘉禎	63	June 19: Shinran copies the <u>Yuishin-shō</u> for the second time (this time in the Japanese hiragana syllabary).	Senjuji collection	VI:39
		Shinran's grandson Nyoshin is born, the son of Zenran.	Written on the back of a portrait of Nyoshin.	Nishi honganji collection
1241 (Ninji 2) 仁治	69	October 14: Shinran copies Seikaku's <u>Yuishin-shō</u> for the third time.	Shinsūji collection	VI:39
		October 19: Shinran copies the <u>Yuishin-shō</u> for the fourth time.	Senseiji collection	VI:39
1242 (Ninji 3)	70	September 21: Shinran's portrait is painted by Jōzen.	<u>Shinran-shōnin dene</u> (Chaper 7)	IV:118
1243 (Kangen 1) 寛元	71	December 21: Shinran signs a document witnessing the transfer of the servant girl Iya-onna from Shōamidabutsu to Higashi-no-nyōbō. (The relationship of Iya-onna to Shinran is unclear.) It is possible that Iya-onna had formerly served Shinran, as is seen in his reply to his daughter Kakushinni when she inquires about Iya-onna.	<u>Iya-onna yuzuri jō</u> <u>Shinran shinseki shokan</u> (letter 7)	IV:177 III:27
1246 (Kangen 4)	74	March 14: Shinran copies Seikaku's <u>Yuishin-shō</u> for the fifth time.	Senjuji collection	VI:83

Western calendar; Japanese era & year	Shinran's age	Events in Shinran's Life	Verification for dating	Verification material volume & page number
1247 (Hōji 1) 宝治	75	March 15: Shinran copies the <u>Jiriki tariki no koto</u> by Ryūkan, a close friend.	Ōtani Daigaku collection	VI:83
		February 5: Shinran's disciple Sonren copies the <u>Kyōgyōshinshō</u> (which would suggest that the text was completed before this time, since copying was only permitted with finished texts).	Ōtani Daigaku collection (Described by Ekū in his copy as written by Shinran at this time.	I:3
1248 (Hōji 2)	76	January 21: Shinran completes the first drafts of his <u>Jōdo-wasan</u> and <u>Kōsō-wasan</u>.	Senjuji collection	II:4
1250 (Kenchō 2) 建長	78	October 16: Shinran writes the <u>Yuishin-shō mon-i</u>, a commentary on Seikaku's <u>Yuishin-shō</u> and the scripture cited in it.	Honseiji collection	III:155
1251 (Kenchō 3)	79	September 20: Shinran writes a letter to disciples (names unknown) in Hitachi, admonishing them for discussing the conditions for Pure Land rebirth (such distinctions were contrary to the total absolute Other-power of the Buddha Amida).	<u>Mattō-shō</u> (letter 1)	III:51

Western calendar; Japanese era & year	Shinran's age	Events in Shinran's Life	Verification for dating	Verification material volume & page number
1252 (Kenchō 4)	80	February 24: Shinran writes a letter to a disciple (name unknown), expressing his gratitude for financial assistance. He also denies a heresy attributed to Shinken, claiming that one could intentionally commit evil misdeeds and still be saved because the Buddha Amida had such strong compassion for evil persons.	Mattō-shō (letter 20)	III:113
		March 4: Shinran writes the Jōdo-monruijushō, setting forth essentials drawn from his Kyōgyōshinshō.	Senjuji collection	II:129
1254 (Kenchō 6)	82	February (date unknown): Shinran copies the Yuishin-shō for the sixth time.	Ōtani Daigaku collection (Ekū's copy)	VI:39
		September 16: Shinran copies the Gose monogatari-kiki-gaki (author unknown, but possibly Ryūkan).	Shōganji collection	VI:93
		(Before) September 27: Shinran's oldest son Zenran returns to Kantō from Kyoto.	Shinran-shōnin goshōsoku-shū (letter 6)	III:144
		November 18: Shinran copies an extract from Shan-tao's Kuan-wu-liang-shou-ching-shu (entitled 'Ni-ga byakudō hiyu' in Japanese) and sends it to Kantō area disciples.	Shōganji collection	VIII:187

Western calendar; Japanese era & year	Shinran's age	Events in Shinran's Life	Verification for dating	Verification material volume & page number
1255 (Kenchō 7)	83	April 23: Shinran copies Ryūkan's Ichinen tanen funbetsu no koto for the second time.	Ōtani Daigaku collection (Ekū's copy)	VI:75
		April 23: Shinran also copies Ryūkan's Jiriki tariki no koto.	Ōtani Daigaku collection (Ekū's copy)	VI:83
		April 24: Shinran polishes his own Jōdo-wasan and Kōsō-wasan.	Senjuji collection	II:4 & II:76
		May 23: Shinran copies a letter that Hōnen had previously written to his disciple Ōko Tarō.	Senjuji collection	V:231
		June 2: Shinran writes the Songō-shinzō meimon.	Hōunji collection	III:73
		June 3: Shinran copies the Hongan sō-ō-shū.	Anyōji collection	
		June 22: Senshin copies Shinran's Kyōgyōshinshō.	Senjuji collection	I:3
		July 14: Shinran copies his Jōdo-monrui jushō for the second time.	Higashi honganji collection	II:129

Western calendar; Japanese era & year	Shinran's age	Events in Shinran's Life	Verification for dating	Verification material volume & page number
		August 6: Shinran writes the <u>Jōdo-sangyō ōjō-monrui</u>, exploring the subject of Pure Land rebirth by denoting such differences in the three major Pure Land sūtras.	Nishi honganji collection	III:21
		August 27: Shinran writes the <u>Gutokushō</u> (2 Volumes), on the essentials of Pure Land teaching.	Senjuji collection (Zonkaku's copy)	II:3
		October 3: Shinran writes a letter to his disciple Shōshin in Kantō, in reply to questions by Kasama district disciples in the Kantō area.	<u>Mattō-shō</u> (letter 2)	II:63
		November 9: Shinran writes a letter to his oldest son Zenran, concerning a rumour that Zenran has expressed heretical statements.	<u>Shinran-shōnin goshōsoku</u>	II:229
		November 30: Shinran writes the <u>Kōtaishi-shōtoku hōsan</u> as seventeen poems which are hymns in praise to Shōtoku-taishi.	Senjuji collection	II:229
		December 10: A fire burns Shinran's residence.	<u>Shinseki-shokan</u> (letter 3)	III:10

Western calendar; Japanese era & year	Shinran's age	Events in Shinran's Life	Verification for dating	Verification material volume & page number
		December 15: Shinran writes a letter to his disciple Shimbutsu, requesting that he intercede on behalf of another disciple, Embutsu, who had visited Shinran in Kyoto without Embutsu's employer's permisssion.	Shinseki-shokan (letter 3)	III:10
		During this year, Chōen draws Shinran's portrait, naming it 'Anjō no goei' (Portrait of Relief).	Zonkaku-shōnin sode nikki	Zonkaku-shōnin* sode nikki 132
1256 (Kōgen 1) 康元	84	January 9: Shinran writes a letter to his disciple Shinjō, advising him not to fight the gradual prohibition against Nembutsu teaching and practice in the Kantō area (with the aid of a prominent government official). Shinran also warns his disciples to stand firm in their beliefs in spite of Zenran's heretical pronouncements. Shinran is concerned because Nyūshin is questioned by government officials.	Shinran-shōnin goshōsoku (letter 2)	III:147
		March 23: Shinran writes the Nyūshitsunimon-ge about Pure Land practice.	Hōunji collection	II:109
		March 24: Shinran copies his own Yuishin-shō mon-i.	Kōtokuji collection	III:187

* See Bibliography p. 171.

Western calendar; Japanese era & year	Shinran's age	Events in Shinran's Life	Verification for dating	Verification material volume & page number
		April 13: Shinran writes the Shijūhachidaigan, a personal memorandum about the Buddha Amida's 48 vows.	Senjuji collection	II:161
		April 13: Shinran also copies his own October 3, 1255 letter to Kantō disciples on questions of Pure Land teaching. (This letter is further copied by Kantō disciples and circulated among area followers.)	Senjuji collection (identical to Mattō-shō: letter 2)	II:63
		May 26: Shinran receives a letter with money from his disciple Kakushin in Kantō. The letter contains questions about his Pure Land teachings.	Shinseki-shokan (letter 2)	III:8
		May 26: Shinran replies to Kakushin's letter, requesting that Kakushin come to Kyoto if possible.	Shinseki-shokan (letter 2)	III:8
		May 29: Shinran writes to his oldest son Zenran, disowning him because Zenran's most recent letter to Nembutsu follower in Kantō area clearly express views strongly heretical to Shinran's Pure Land teachings.	Kosha shokan (letter 3)	III:40
		May 29: Shinran writes a letter to his disciple Shōshin, notifying him of his disowning of Zenran. Shinran here states that as his father he assumes all responsibility for Zenran's errors.	Shinran-shōnin kechimyaku-monjū (letter 2)	III:167

Western calendar; Japanese era & year	Shinran's age	Events in Shinran's Life	Verification for dating	Verification material volume & page number
		June 27: Zenran receives the letter of disownment from Shinran.	Senjuji collection (identical to Kosha-shokan: letter 3)	III:40
		July 9: Shinran writes a letter to his disciple Shōshin, expressing his pleasure about Kamakura bakufu officials' inquiries into the Nembutsu movement (in which Shōshin had acted as intermediary).	Shinran-shōnin goshōsoku (letter 2)	III:127
		July 25: Shinran writes a reading commentary to T'an-luan's Wang-sheng-lun-chu-chieh.	Nishi honganji collection	VIII:8
		In late July or early August, Shinran writes a letter to his disciple Shōshin mentioning that Shinran will meet with Minamoto Tōshirō (a person from Shōshin's home town). Shinran is pleased that Kamakura area Nembutsu practice has created no new problems with the military bakufu government and that freedom to practice has thus been granted to the Kantō area Nembutsu movement.	Shinran-shōnin goshōsoku (letter 8)	III:152

Western calendar; Japanese era & year	Shinran's age	Events in Shinran's Life	Verification for dating	Verification material volume & page number
		September 7: Shinran writes a letter to his disciple Shōshin indicating his approval of Shōshin's conversion of two new Nembutsu followers.	Shinran-shōnin kechimyaku-monjū (letter 4)	III:173
		October 13: Shinran copies the Saihō shinan-shō (volume 1).	Senjuji collection	V:3
		October 14: Shinran copies the Saihō shinan-shō (volume 2).	Senjuji collection	V:113
		October 25: Shinran copies the Hachiji-myōgō and Jūji-myōgō.	Senjuji collection	
		October 28: Shinran copies the Jūji-myōgō.	Myōgenji collection	
		October 28: Shinran also copies the Rokuji-myōgō.	Nishi honganji collection	
		November 8: Shinran copies the Saihō shinan-shō (volume 3).	Senjuji collection	V:221
		November 29: Shinran copies the Saihō shinan-shō (volume 3).	Senjuji collection	V:221

Western calendar; Japanese era & year	Shinran's age	Events in Shinran's Life	Verification for dating	Verification material volume & page number
		November 29: Shinran writes the Ōsō-ekō gensō-ekō monrui, explaining the Buddha Amida's 17th, 18th, 11th, and 22nd vows, citing a Chinese translation of Vasubandhu's Sukhāvatī-vyuhopadeśa.	Jōgūji collection	
1257 (Shōka 1) 正嘉	85	January 1: Shinran has his Saihōshinan-shō copy (volume 1) proofread.	Senjuji collection	V:3
		January 2: Shinran copies volume 1 of the Saihō shinan-shō and then it is proofread.	Senjuji collection	V:113
		January 11: Shinran copies his own Yuishin-shō mon-i for the second time and presents it to his disciple Kenchi.	Senjuji collection	III:155
		January 17: Shinran copies his Yuishin-shō mon-i for the third time, presenting it to his disciple Shinshō.	Senjuji collection	III:155
		February 5: Shinran copies volume 3 of the Saihō shinan-shō.	Senjuji collection	V:221
		February 9: Shinran dreams of a hymn to Shōtoku-taishi (which he writes at a later date).	Shō-zō-matsu wasan	II:157
		February 17: Shinran writes the Ichinen tanen mon-i, a bibliographical introduction to citations in Ryūkan's Ichinen tanen fumbetsu no koto.	Higashi honganji collection	II:157

Western calendar; Japanese era & year	Shinran's age	Events in Shinran's Life	Verification for dating	Verification material volume & page number
		February 30: Shinran writes the Dai-nihonkoku zokusan–ō Shōtoku-taishi hōsan.	Kakunyo's copy	II:157
		March 1: Shinran writes a hymn which originated as a dream (on February 9), adding it to his Shō-zō matsu wasan.	Shō-zō-matsu wasan	II:157
		March 2: Shinran copies his own Jōdo-sangyō ōjō monrui.	Kōshōji collection	III:21
		March 3: Shinran writes a letter (address unknown), mentioning that his memory and eyesight have become rather weak.	Mattō-shō (letter 8)	III:80
		March 21: Shinran writes his Nyorai nishu-ekō mon-i, a commentary on some of the Pure Land scriptural explanations of 'Osō ekō' (transfer of the Buddha Amida's merit toward Pure Land rebirth) and 'Gensō ekō' (transfer of the Buddha Amida's merit in return (to this world) as response to sentiency).	Senjuji collection	III:21
		May 11: Shinran edits the Jōgū-taishi gyoki, a brief history of Shōtoku-taishi's life.	Nishi honganji collection	V:371
		June 4: Shinran copies his own Jōdo-monrujiushō.	Ōtani Daigaku collection	II:129

Western calendar; Japanese era & year	Shinran's age	Events in Shinran's Life	Verification for dating	Verification material volume & page number
		August 19 Shinran copies his Ichinen tanen mon-i.	Higashi honganji collection	III:123
		August 19: Shinran also copies his Yuishin-shō mon-i for the fourth time.	Myōganji collection	III:155
		October 10: Shinran writes respectful letters to his disciples Shōshin and Shimbutsu, encouraging them to believe that a person of true faith can be equal to the Tathāgata (the Buddha).	Mattō-shō (letter 3 and 4)	III:68 & 71
1258 (Shōka 2)	86	June 28: Shinran adds four verses of praise to his Songō shinzō meimon.	Senjuji collection	III:73
		August 18: Shinran copies Hōnen's Sanbu-kyō tai-i, presenting it to his disciple Keishin.	Senjuji collection	VI:3
		September 24: Shinran re-examines his Shō-zō-matsu wasan.	Senjuji collection	II:157
		October 29: Shinran's letter is sent to Keishin by Renni, referring to his teaching that a person of true faith can be considered equal to the Tathāgata.	Senjuji collection (letter of Renni)	
		(About this time Shinran is afflicted with a throat problem.)	Senjuji collection (letter)	

Western calendar; Japanese era & year	Shinran's age	Events in Shinran's Life	Verification for dating	Verification material volume & page number
		December 14: Shinran preaches to his disciple Kenchi about 'jinen hō-ni' (his final teaching of the 'natural inevitability of the Dharma as it is'), while Kenchi directly records his words.	Mattō-shō (letter 5)	III:72
1259 (Shōgen 1) 正 元	87	September 10: Shinran completes his copying of Hōnen's Senjaku-hogan nembutsu-shū (which he had begun copying on September 1st of this same year).	Senjuji collection	VI:1
		October 29: Shinran writes a letter to his disciple Takada-no-Nyūdō, lamenting the death of Kakunen (another disciple). Shinran also indicates that he has received financial support from disciples.	Shinseki-shokan (letter 5)	III:22
1260 (Bunnō 1) 文 応	88	November 3: Shinran copies his Jōdo sangyō ōjō monrui.	Bukkōji collection	III:21
		November 13: Shinran writes a letter to his disciple Kōshin, in sorrow over the death of so many Japanese by epidemic and starvation.	Mattō-shō (letter 6)	III:75
		December 2: Shinran writes the Midanyorai myōgō-toku expounding on the twelve virtues of the Buddha Amida.	Shōgyōji collection	III:225
1261 (Kōchō 1) 弘 長	89	During November, Shinran's wife Eshinni is taken ill (Shinran and his wife have been living apart since 1233 for reasons unknown) in Echigo.	Eshinni monjo (letter 4)	III:192

Western calendar; Japanese era & year	Shinran's age	Events in Shinran's Life	Verification for dating	Verification material volume & page number
1262 (Kōchō 2)	90	In May, Eshinni recovers from her illness.	Eshinni monjo (letter 4)	III:192
		Towards the end of November, Shinran becomes ill.	Shinran-shōnin dene (volume 6)	IV:93
		November 28: Shinran dies.	Shinran-shōnin dene (volume 6)	IV:94
		November 29: Shinran's body is cremated.	Shinran-shōnin dene (volume 6)	IV:94
		November 30: Shinran's ashes are laid to rest.	Shinran-shōnin dene (volume 6)	IV:94
		December 1: Shinran's daughter Kakushinni notifies her mother Eshinni of Shinran's death.	Eshinni monjo (letter 3)	III:187
		December 20: Eshinni receives her daughter's letter about Shinran's death.	Eshinni monjo (letter 3)	III:187

1. Shinran's Major Writings and Their Probable Dates of Appearance

		Age	A.D.	S S Z vol.*
1)	Ken jōdo shinjitsu kyō gyō shō monrui 6 volumes 顯浄土真実教行証文類 "The collection of passages expounding the true teaching, practice, faith, and realization of the Pure Land." Also known as Kyōgyōshinshō. "Teaching, practice, faith and realization." It is in this book that Shinran lays down and systematizes all doctrines of Jōdo shinshū. Shinran's fervent faith and profound philosophical insight are fully found in it.		52	1224 (Kennin 1) 建 仁	I:4
2)	Jōdo-wasan 1 volume 浄土和讃 "Hymns on the Pure Land." 116 Stanzas in the style of popular Japanese verse praising the virtues of the Buddha Amida and the glory of the Pure Land. The doctrine of Jōdo shinshū taught through the Three sūtras of Pure Land.		76	1248 (Hōji 2) 宝 治	II:4
3)	Kōsō-wasan 1 volume 高僧和讃 "Hymns on the high priests." 117 Stanzas praising the historical and doctrinal contributions of seven Pure Land teaching patriarchs throughout India, China, and Japan. The historical and doctrinal essence of Jōdo shinshū in Buddhism are taught.		76	1248 (Hōji 2)	II:75

* The Roman and Arabic numerals refer to the volume and page numbers of Shinran shōnin zenshū. See Bibliography p. 165.

	Age	A.D.	S S Z vol.
4) Jōdo monruijushō 1 volume 浄土文類聚鈔 "Collection of passages expounding the Pure Land teaching." This is a setting forth of essentials drawn from <u>Kyōgyōshinshō</u>, particularly a concise account of "Faith".	83	1255 (Kenchō 7) 建 長	II:129
5) <u>Gutoku-shō</u> 2 volumes 愚禿鈔 "An abstract—the writing of a baldheaded ignoramus." The essence of the teaching of Jōdo shinshū is explained. The position of Jōdo shinshū doctrine in Buddhism is shown. Gutoku is the name which Shinran adopted himself. <u>Shō</u> literally means collection or an abstract.	83	1255 (Kenchō 7)	II:3
6) Kōtaishi-shōtoku hōsan 1 volume 皇太子聖徳奉讃 "Hymns on Prince Shōtoku." 17 Stanzas which are hymns of praise of Prince Shōtoku. Prince Shōtoku is called the 'Father of Japanese Buddhism' by Japanese Buddhists.	83	1255 (Kenchō 7)	II:229
7) Jōdo-sangyō ōjōmonrui 1 volume 浄土三経往生文類 "A collection of passages on rebirth expounded in the Three sūtras of Pure Land teaching." This explores the subject of Pure Land rebirth, denoting differences in the three major Pure Land sūtras.	83	1255 (Kenchō 7)	III:3

	Age	A.D.	S S Z vol.
8) Songō shinzō meimon 1 volume 尊号真像銘文 "Eulogies inscribed on the scrolls of the holy name and portraits." This is a collection of commentaries on sacred Pure Land objects.	83	1255 (Kenchō 7) 建 長	III:41
9) Nyūshitsu nimon ge 1 volume 入出二門偈 "Gatha on the two gates, entering and outing." 74 Stanzas appreciating the compassion necessary for our rebirth to (entering) and return from (outing) the Pure Land to help others practise the way for rebirth to the Pure Land.	d84	d1256 (Kenchō 8)*	II:109
10) Ōsō-ekō gensō-ekō monrui 1 volume 往相廻向還相廻向文類 "A collection of passages on entering and returning of merit-transference." Also known as Nyorai nishu-ekō-mon. 如来二種廻向文 "Two kinds of passages on merit-transference of Tathāgata Amida." This collection explains the Buddha Amida's 17th, 18th, and 22nd vows, citing a Chinese translation of Vasbandhu's Sukhāvati-vyūhopadesa.	84	1256 (Kōgen 1)* 康 元	III:217

---

* At age 84, the Emperor reigning at the time died and was succeeded by the next Emperor, thus explaining the year Kenchō 8 and Kōgen 1 to be the same year.

		Age	A.D.	S S Z vol.
11)	Shō zō matsu wasan 1 volume 正像末和讃 "Hymns on righteousness, imitative, degenerate." 113 Stanzas of Shinran's appreciation of the Buddha Amida's opening the path to enlightenment for men of the three periods after Buddha's demise. The doctrine of Jōdo shinshū and its applicability in the degenerate age of the Dharma.	85	1257 (Kōgen 2) 康 元	II:143
12)	Yuishin-shō mon-i 1 volume 唯信鈔文意 "Commentary of Yuishinshō (Summary of the only faith)." A commentary of Seikaku's book, Yuishin-shō which is a detailed explanation of the Pure Land teaching in simple Japanese language. Seikaku was a respected friend of Shinran.	85	1257 (Kōgen 2)	III:155
13)	Ichinen tanen mon-i 1 volume 一念多念文意 "Commentary of Ichinen tanen (single invocation and many invocations)." This commentary is a bibliographical introduction to the citation in Ryūkan's book, Ichinen tanen funbetsu no koto which, translated into English, is Matters of Distingushing between Single Invocation and Many Invocations. Ryūkan was also a respected friend of Shinran and leader of Tanengi (many invocations).	85	1257 (Kōgen 2)	III:123

2. Shinran's Letters

There are four volumes of Shinran's letters:

			S S Z vol.
1)	Goshōsoku shū 御消息集	"Collection of private letters." Edited by Zenshō, one of Shinran's disciples. This volume is comprised of eight letters.	III:161
2)	Shinran-shōnin Kechimyaku monjū 親鸞聖人血脈文集	"Collection of letters of blood pledge." Editor unknown. Comprised of 5 letters.	III:184
3)	Mattō-shō 末灯鈔	"Collection on light of later days." Edited by Jūkaku. Comprised of 23 letters.	III:57
4)	Goshōsoku shūi 御消息拾遺	"Collection of private letters." Editor unknown. Comprised of 18 letters.	III:125

The sum of the letters in the above four volumes is fifty-three. However, many of the letters are duplicated in these volumes and when this is taken into account, there are actually thirty-six letters. Also, there are five more letters which are not compiled into any of the above four volumes, which are those that have been copied by the disciple Kenchi. Therefore, the total of Shinran's letters is forty-two.

3. Shinran's Citations of the Seven Pure Land Patriarchs

Name of patriarch with its Japanese equivalents	Native place	Title of text and its Japanese equivalents	S G Z vol.*
Nāgārjuna (ca. 2nd-3rd c. A.D.) Ryūju 龍 樹	India	Daśabhūmika-vibhāsā-śāstra 17 vols. Jūjū bibasha ron 十住毘婆沙論 (vol. 5, chapter 9) Igyō hon 易行品	I:253
Vasubandhu (ca. 4th c. A.D.) Seshin, or Tenjin 世親／天親	India	Sukhāvatī-vyūhopadeśa 1 vol. Jōdo ron 浄土論	I:269
T'an-luan (476-542) Donran 曇 鸞	China	Ching-t'u lun chu 2 vols. Jōdoron chū 浄土論註	I:279
		Tsan A-mi-t'o-fo chieh 1 vol. San Amidabutsu ge 讃阿弥陀仏偈	I:350
Tao-ch'o (562-645) Dōshaku 道 綽	China	An-lo chi 2 vols. Anraku shū 安楽集	I:377

* The Roman and Arabic numerals refer to the volume and page number of Shinshū shōgyō zensho. See Bibliography p. 165.

Name of patriarch with its Japanese equivalents	Native place	Title of text and its Japanese equivalents	S G Z vol.
Shan-tao (613–681) Zendō 善導	China	Kuan-wu-liang-shou ching ssu-t'ieh su　4 vols. 観無量寿経四帖疏 Kan muryōju-kyō shijō sho	I:441
		Fa-shih tsan　2 vols. 法事讃 Hōjisan	I:561
		Kuan-nien fa-men　1 vol. 観念法門 Kannen bōmon	I:618
		Wang-sheng-li tsan　1 vol. 往生礼讃 Ōjō raisan	I:648
		Pan-chou tsan　1 vol. 般舟讃 Hanju san	I:685
Genshin (942–1017) 源信	Japan	Ōjō yōshū　3 vols. 往生要集	I:729
Hōnen (1133–1212) 法然	Japan	Senjaku hongan nembutsu shū　2 vols. 選択本願念仏集	I:929

4. Hōnen's Major Disciples

1100	1150	1200	1250	1300

Shinkū　信 空　1146-1228
Leader, Shirakawa-monto　白川門徒

Ryūkan　隆 寛　1148-1227
Leader, Tanengi　多念義

Benchō　弁 長　1162-1238
Founder, Chinzei-ha　鎮西派

Kōsai　幸 西　1163-1247
(Leader, Ichinengi)　一念義

Seikaku　聖 覚　1167-1235
Author, Yuishinshō　唯信鈔

Shinran　親 鸞　1173-1262
Founder, Jōdo Shinshū　浄土真宗

Shōkū　証 空　1177-1247
Founder, Seizan-ha　西山派

Genchi　源 智　1183-1238
Leader, Murasakino-mont.　柴野門徒

Chōsai　長 西　1184-d. 1261
Shogyō hongangi　諸行本願義

Gyōkū　行 空　? - ?
Leader, Ichinengi　一念義

5. Hōnen's Major Disciples: Their Writing

Name	Writings	Jōdo shū zensho vol.**	Page No.
Shinkū 信空	Writes Hichikajō kishōmon 七ヶ条起請文 for Hōnen Seven-Article Pledge*	IX	446-449
Ryūkan 隆寛	Ichinen-tanen funbetsu no koto 1 vol. 一念多念分別事 Matters of Distinguishing between Single Invocation and Many Invocations*	continued vol. IX	27-29
	Jiriki-tariki no koto 1 vol. 自力他力事 Matters of Distinguishing between Self-Power and Other-Power*	continued vol. IX	31-33
Benchō 弁長	Tetsu Senjaku shū 2 vols. 徹選択集 Admiration of "Passages on the Nembutsu of the Chosen Vow"*	VII	83-111
	Jōdoshū Yōshū 6 vols. 浄土宗要集 Collection of the Essence of Pure Land School*	X	124-242
Kōsai 幸西	Gengibun shō 1 vol. 玄義分鈔 Summary of "On the Sūtra's Essential"*	*** Yasui's "Hōnen shōnin monka no Kyōgaku"	41-88
Seikaku 聖覚	Yuishinshō 1 vol. 唯信鈔 Summary of Only-Faith*	continued vol. IX	65-76
Shinran 親鸞	refer to Shinran's Major Writings		

* English translation.   ** See Bibliography p. 165.   *** See Bibliography p. 182.

Name	Writings	Jōdo shū zensho vol.**	Page No.
Shōkū 証空	Kangyōsho shiki 1 vol. 観経疏私記 Notes on "On the Meditation Sūtra in Four Books"*	1-412	
Tankū 耽空	Honchō soshi denki eshi 4 vols. 本朝祖師伝記絵詞 Biography of Japanese Great Master (Hōnen)*	XVII	53-83
Genchi 源智	Senjaku yōketsu 1 vol. 選択要決 A key to "Passages on the Nembutu of the Chosen Vow"*	VII	176-185
Chōsai 長西	Jōdo ehyō kyō ron shaku shō sho mokuroku 1 vol. 浄土依憑経論釈章疏目録 Catalogue of Pure Land Teaching: Sūtra, Upadeśa, Interpretations Commentary and Chapter References*	XX	501

* English translation.　　** See Bibliography p. 165.

6. Shinran and Contemporary Masters of Other Buddhist Schools

Timeline (years 1100 – 1350):

Zōshun 蔵 俊 1104–1180

Hōnen 法 然 1133–1212

Eisai 栄 西 1141–1215

Jōkei 貞 慶 1155–1213

Shunjō 俊 芿 1166–1227

Myōe 明 恵 1173–1232

Shinran 親 鸞 **1173–1262**

Ryōhen 良 遍 1194–1252

Shōjō 証 定 1194– ? ....

Kakujō 覚 盛 1194–1249

Dōgen 道 元 1200–1253

Eizon 叡 尊 1201–1290

Shūshō (宗 性 1202–1277

En'ni Ben'en 円爾弁円 1202–1280

Rankei Dōryū (蘭渓道隆 1213–1278

Ninshō 忍 性 1217–1303

Enshō 円 照 1220–1277

Nichiren 日 蓮 1222–1282

Ippen 一 遍 1239–1289

Gyōnen 凝 然 1240–1321

7. Shinran and Contemporary Masters: Their Buddhist Schools and Temples

Name	Buddhist School	Temple	Location
Zōshun 蔵俊	Hossō 法相	Kōfukuji 興福寺	Nara 奈良
Hōnen 法然	Founder, Jōdo school 浄土宗		
Eisai 栄西	Founder, Rinzai school 臨済宗		
Jōkei 貞慶	Hossō 法相	Kōfukuji 興福寺	Nara 奈良
Shunjō 俊芿	Ritsu 律	Senyūji 泉涌寺	Kyoto 京都
Myōe 明恵	Kegon 華厳	Kōzanji 高山寺	Kyoto 京都
Shinran 親鸞	Founder, Jōdo shinshū 浄土真宗		
Ryōhen 良遍	Ritsu 律	Chikurinji 竹林寺	Nara 奈良
Shōjō 証定	Kegon 華厳	Kōzanji 高山寺	Kyoto 京都
Kakujō 覚盛	Ritsu 律	Tōshōdairitsuji 唐招提律寺	Nara 奈良
Dōgen 道元	Founder, Sōtō school 曹洞宗		
Eizon 叡尊	Shingon Ritsu 真言律	Saidaiji 西大寺	Nara 奈良
Shūshō 宗性	Kegon 華厳	Tōdaiji 東大寺	Nara 奈良
En'ni Ben'en 円爾弁円	Rinzai 臨済	Tōfukuji 東福寺	Kyoto 京都
Rankei Dōryū 蘭渓道隆	Rinzai 臨済	Kenchōji 建長寺	Kamakura 鎌倉
Ninshō 忍性	Ritsu 律	Saidaiji 西大寺	Nara 奈良
Enshō 円照	Ritsu 律	Yamato Kaidanin 大和戒壇院	Nara 奈良
Nichiren 日蓮	Founder, Nichiren school 日蓮宗		
Ippen 一遍	Founder, Ji school 時宗		
Gyōnen 凝然	Kegon 華厳	Tōdaiji 東大寺	Nara 奈良

8. The Lineage of the Imperial Family during Shinran's Era

(Ruler indicated by number)

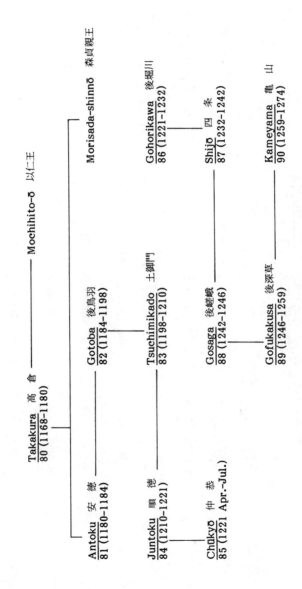

Takakura 高倉
80 (1168–1180)

Antoku 安徳
81 (1180–1184)

Mochihito-ō 以仁王

Morisada-shinnō 森貞親王

Gotoba 後鳥羽
82 (1184–1198)

Juntoku 順徳
84 (1210–1221)

Chūkyō 仲恭
85 (1221 Apr.–Jul.)

Tsuchimikado 土御門
83 (1198–1210)

Gohorikawa 後堀川
86 (1221–1232)

Shijō 四条
87 (1232–1242)

Gosaga 後嵯峨
88 (1242–1246)

Gofukakusa 後深草
89 (1246–1259)

Kameyama 亀山
90 (1259–1274)

9. Japanese Buddhist Schools, Their Founders and Years of Institution

School's name	Founder's name	Year of institution
Hossō 法相	Dōshō 道昭 (629 – 700)	660 (Saimei 斉明 6)
Kegon 華厳	*Shinjō 審祥 (? – 742)	740 (Tenpyō 天平 2)
Ritsu 律	**Chien-chen 鑑真 (688 –763)	759 (Tenpyō hōji 天平宝字 3)
Tendai 天台	Saichō 最澄 (767 – 822)	806 (Daidō 大同 1)
Shingon, 真言, 古義 kogi	Kūkai 空海 (774 – 835)	816 (Kōnin 弘仁 7)
Yūzū nembutsu 融通念仏	Ryōnin 良忍 (1072 – 1132)	1117 (Eikyū 永久 5)
Shingon, 真言, 新義 shingi	Kakuban 覚鑁 (1095 –1143)	1140 (Hōen 保延 6)
Jōdo 浄土	Hōnen 法然 (1133 – 1212)	1175 (Angen 安元 1)

*Shinjō, Korean origin and naturalized person.

**Chien-chen, Chinese monk. He is known as Ganjin.

School's name	Founder's name	Year of institution
Zen, 禅, 臨済 Rinzai	Eisai 栄 西 (1141 – 1215)	1202 (Kennin 建 仁 2)
Jōdoshū-Seizan 浄土宗西山宗	Shōkū 証 空 (1177 – 1247)	1213 (Kenpō 建 保 1)
Jōdo shinshū 浄土真宗	**Shinran** 親 鸞 (1173 – 1262)	1224 (Gennin 元 仁 1)
Zen, 禅, 曹洞 Sōtō	Dōgen 道 元 (1200 –1253)	1227 (Antei 安 貞 1)
Shingon-ritsu 真言律	Eizon 叡 尊 (1201 – 1290)	1236 (Katei 嘉 禎 2)
Nichiren 日 蓮	Nichiren 日 蓮 (1222 – 1282)	1253 (Kenchō 建 長 5)
Ji 時	Ippen 一 遍 (1239 –1289)	1276 (Kenji 建 治 1)
Zen, 禅, 黄檗 Ōbaku	*Yin-yuan 隠 元 (1592 –1673)	1654 (Shōō 承 応 3)

*Yin-yuan, Chinese monk. He is known as Ingen.

10. Important Locations for Shinran's Activities

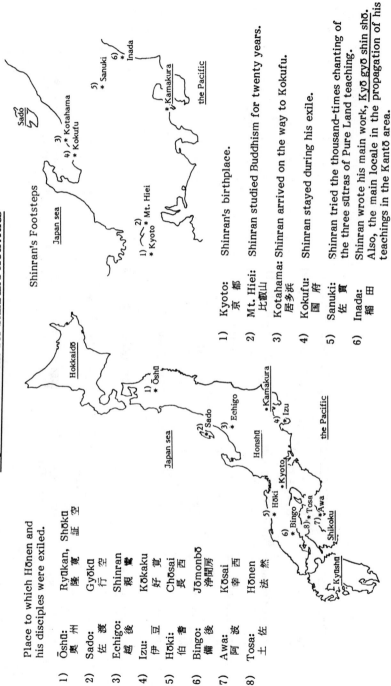

Place to which Hōnen and his disciples were exiled.

1) Ōshū: 奥州　Ryūkan, Shōkū 隆寛　証空
2) Sado: 佐渡　Gyōkū 行空
3) Echigo: 越後　Shinran 親鸞
4) Izu: 伊豆　Kōkaku 好覚
5) Hōki: 伯耆　Chōsai 長西
6) Bingo: 備後　Jōmonbō 浄聞房
7) Awa: 阿波　Kōsai 幸西
8) Tosa: 土佐　Hōnen 法然

Shinran's Footsteps

1) Kyoto: 京都　Shinran's birthplace.
2) Mt. Hiei: 比叡山　Shinran studied Buddhism for twenty years.
3) Kotahama: 居多浜　Shinran arrived on the way to Kokufu.
4) Kokufu: 国府　Shinran stayed during his exile.
5) Sanuki: 佐貫　Shinran tried the thousand-times chanting of the three sūtras of Pure Land teaching.
6) Inada: 稲田　Shinran wrote his main work, Kyō gyō shin shō. Also, the main locale in the propagation of his teachings in the Kantō area.

Glossary

Japanese Equivalents for References used in Verification for Dating

A)

Amidakyō shūchū 阿弥陀経集註

Anyōji 安養寺

B)

Bukkōji 仏光寺

E)

Ekū 恵空

Eshinni monjo 恵信尼文書

H)

Higashi honganji 東本願寺

Honseiji 本誓寺

Hōunji 法雲寺

I)

Iyaonna yuzurijō いや女讓状

J)

Jōdo wasan 浄土和讃

Jōgūji 上宮寺

K)

Kakunyo 覚如

Kamakura bakufuhō 鎌倉幕府法

Kammuryōjukyō shūchū 観無量寿経集註

Kōfukuji sōjō 興福寺奏状

Kosha shokan 古写書簡

Kōshōji 興正寺

Kōtokuji 光德寺

Kyō gyō shin shō 教行信証

M)

Mattō shō 末灯鈔

Myōganji 妙嚴寺

N)

Nishi honganji 西本願寺

Nyoshin 如信

O)

Ōtani daigaku 大谷大学

S)

Saihōshinanshō 西方指南鈔

Senjuji 專修寺

Shinran muki 親鸞夢記

Shinran-shōnin dene 親鸞聖人伝絵

Shinran-shōnin goshōsoku 親鸞聖人ご消息

Shinran-shōnin keechimyakumonjo 親鸞聖人血脈文書

Shinseki shokan 真蹟書簡

Shinshūji 真宗寺

Shōganji 照願寺

Shōgyōji 正行寺

Shozōmatsu wasan 正像末和讃

Z)

Zonkaku 存覚

Zonkaku shōnin sode nikki 存覚上人袖日記

Index

SR SUPPLEMENTS

EDITIONS SR

STUDIES IN CHRISTIANITY AND JUDAISM / ETUDES SUR LE CHRISTIANISME ET LE JUDAISME

THE STUDY OF RELIGION IN CANADA / SCIENCES RELIGIEUSES AU CANADA

COMPARATIVE ETHICS SERIES/ COLLECTION D'ETHIQUE COMPAREE

Also published / Avons aussi publié

Available from / en vente chez:

Wilfrid Laurier University Press

Wilfrid Laurier University
Waterloo, Ontario, Canada   N2L 3C5

Published for the Canadian Corporation for Studies in Religion/ Corporation Canadienne des Sciences Religieuses by Wilfrid Laurier University Press